# BRITAIN'S
# BLACK
# REGIMENTS

Also by Barry Renfrew

*Agincourt 1415: Field of Blood*
*Wings of Empire: The Forgotten Wars of the Royal Air Force, 1919–1939*
*Forgotten Regiments: Regular and Volunteer Units of the British Far East*
*British Colonial Badges Vols. 1 and 2 (with Margaret Renfrew and Bill Cranston)*
*Chechnya: Crimes of War*

# BRITAIN'S BLACK REGIMENTS

## FIGHTING FOR EMPIRE AND EQUALITY

### BARRY RENFREW

The
History
Press

First published 2020

The History Press
97 St George's Place, Cheltenham,
Gloucestershire, GL50 3QB
www.thehistorypress.co.uk

British Library Cataloguing in Publication Data.
A catalogue record for this book is available from the British Library.

ISBN 978 0 7509 9496 5

Typesetting and origination by The History Press
Printed and bound in Great Britain by TJ International Ltd.

For Margaret

# CONTENTS

# THE STRANGEST CARGO

The arrival in Jamaica of a slave ship sometime in 1797 was unlikely to have attracted much attention from the merchants, clerks and labourers thronging the docks. Such vessels with their human cargoes from Africa for the island's plantations were a humdrum part of life in the thriving British colony. And yet this vessel had caused a political storm at the highest levels of power because it carried the first recruits for an army of slave soldiers. Clad in the red tunics of the British infantry, these captives would be formed into black regiments of the regular army to fight the king's enemies and guard his far-flung colonies. It was the start of one of the most remarkable and unlikely chapters in the long history of the British Empire.

In three global conflicts and countless campaigns between 1795 and 1945, tens of thousands of black West Indians fought and died for Britain and its empire. Their story is unique in that, unlike the Indian Army and other colonial forces, these formations were part of the British Army. For almost a century and a half, the West India Regiment, which began as a slave formation, was a regular regiment composed of West Indian and African troops. The British West Indies Regiment, which served in Europe, the Middle East and Africa during the First World War, and the 1st Caribbean Infantry, which served in Italy and the Middle East during the Second World War, were also part of the British Army rather than colonial formations. All were stepchild units, unloved and unwanted, an embarrassment to an army that was loath to number blacks in its ranks, and yet unable to do without them: their courage, endurance and loyalty were all too often repaid with prejudice, mistreatment and imperial ingratitude. Denied their due recognition in their lifetimes, the story of Britain's black soldiers is all but forgotten.

For many years, the West Indies rather than India was the heart of the British Empire. Control of the Caribbean and its riches dominated British colonial policy in the seventeenth and eighteenth centuries. Britain fought a long series of wars against France and other European powers for mastery of the West Indies: islands encompassing a few square miles became some of the most fought over real estate in history.

Entire British armies were annihilated in these conflicts, not by enemy bullets and blades, but by disease and the climate. The military's losses were often far greater than anything it endured on the battlefields of Europe, earning the West Indies a morbid reputation as 'the graveyard of the British Army'. Despairing British generals concluded that the only way to avoid defeat was by raising regiments of black slaves who could withstand the local conditions far better than white troops.

Slave troops under white officers would help save British fortunes in the Napoleonic Wars, and later serve against the young United States in the War of 1812. After the abolition of slavery, the West India Regiment would serve in Africa and Latin America, battling slave raiders, Islamic war lords and even the French Army. West Indian soldiers were often the only regular British troops in the most remote and pestilential imperial outposts, places deemed lethal for white men. They were also the first black soldiers to win the Victoria Cross and other awards for exceptional bravery. And all the time, these men faced mounting discrimination and disdain as the British military immersed itself in pseudo-scientific notions of white supremacy. Many of their own officers despised and mistreated the West Indians, and yet they showed unswerving loyalty.

Patriotic fervour swept the British West Indies on the outbreak of the First World War in 1914. Thousands of young black West Indians, proud to be citizens of the British Empire, clamoured to fight alongside volunteers from Australia, Canada and other colonies. Government and military officials were horrified at the prospect of thousands of black men descending on Britain to fight in a 'white man's war' and rejected the offers of the West Indies to raise troops for the war effort.

A few black men who were determined to fight stowed away on ships bound for Britain with the idea of enlisting in the army, only to be arrested, mocked and jailed as criminals. At the same time, white West Indians, many of them the sons of wealthy planters and businessmen, were welcomed by the British Army with open arms.

It took the direct intervention of King George V to overcome the military's opposition to enlisting his black West Indian subjects. While the High Command had to bow to royal pressure, the generals waged a rearguard action to use the West Indians as labourers. Men who had volunteered and trained to fight were instead used to carry artillery shells up to the front line or build roads, despite the army's dire need for infantry to replace its vast losses. West Indian troops suffered shocking mistreatment, with some forced to use unheated accommodation in winter or denied adequate medical care; their white officers complained that German prisoners were treated better.

Throughout the conflict, these men who had left their homes and families and travelled thousands of miles to serve the empire, endured official discrimination from the generals and insults and violence from some white troops. Resentment at the unfairness and humiliation finally exploded in 1919 in a mutiny that shook the British Army.

Even harsher treatment was meted out in the Second World War when West Indians once again volunteered in their droves to fight for Britain. The British Army did not want black troops in its ranks, especially West Indians, who saw themselves as British and expected to be treated the same as white troops. Not even Winston Churchill could shake the generals' implacable resistance. The High Command found time during some of the darkest days of the war to wage a bureaucratic campaign against accepting black West Indian troops despite the army's chronic manpower shortage. It was only towards the end of the war that a single, token West Indian regiment arrived in Italy to be almost immediately sent packing. British commanders snorted at the idea of such men fighting in a war proclaimed as a crusade for democracy.

While this book is intended as the first narrative history of the British Army's black regiments, the 300-year story of the local West Indian defence forces during the colonial era is also touched on. These ranged from skilled fighting units to comic opera outfits with almost as many generals and officers as privates. Their history, which is wound up with that of the regular units, has been even more neglected.

In recent years, the non-white soldiers of the British Empire have started to receive at least a modicum of the attention they merit. The British Army, namely white troops from Great Britain and Ireland, was a small force that never remotely met the demands of a worldwide empire. Asian, African and West Indian soldiers were more numerous and indispensable to the conquest and garrisoning of the empire from its earliest beginnings to its last days; they made up one of the most remarkable armies the world has seen.

Much of the modern academic and popular interest in colonial troops focuses on the Indian Army, the largest and most powerful of the British imperial legions, followed by African forces. West Indian soldiers, by contrast, have received very little attention, despite their long and unique history. Perhaps this is because, at least in part, the history of European colonialism in the West Indies is especially uncomfortable for modern consciences. While slavery in the United States has received enormous attention, Britain's role is all but ignored, and yet for every slave sent to North America, fifteen slaves were transported to the British West Indies where they laboured and died, often under unspeakable conditions.[1]

Well-intentioned efforts to correct the historical neglect of colonial soldiers tend to portray them either as unsung heroes or oppressed unfortunates: both approaches fall far short of the full story. The factors that motivated black West Indians to fight for Britain over the decades ranged from the mundane to the complex, some of them common to all armies, others unique to the West Indies. Some West Indians simply wanted a better or more bearable life, and being a soldier was far better than the back-breaking existence of a slave or landless peasant; some wanted excitement and adventure or to escape personal difficulties; some saw themselves as proud citizens of a global empire; some preferred to serve the colonial oppressor rather than be oppressed, and relished the power it gave them over other black people; others saw fighting for the empire as a way to earn greater freedoms and rights for themselves and their kin.

Recounting the story of the West Indian soldier presents particular challenges because of modern controversies over race and colonialism. Some readers will find it inexplicable that black soldiers fought and died for an empire that condemned millions of black men, women and children to slavery and subsequent oppression following abolition; they will be particularly uncomfortable with the fact that most black West Indian soldiers believed in the British Empire as a great and largely benevolent force and

---

1   James Walvin, *Black Ivory: A History of British Slavery*, p.318.

were proud to serve it. Other readers may dismiss such qualms as political correctness and insist that it holds no place in the study of military history.

The aim of this work is to neither champion nor castigate, but rather to give some sense of these men, their circumstances and motivations, and how these shaped their actions and outlooks on and off the battlefield. It is a challenging, not always comfortable story, and yet it is the only way we can begin to understand why they acted as they did. If black West Indian soldiers are to be judged, their story should at least be told as fully as possible, just as an abhorrence of racism and prejudice should not prevent or distort the telling of a remarkable saga.

The West Indies are the most neglected facet of the military history of the British Empire, given their importance. With a few notable exceptions, such as the pioneering work of Norman Buckley, Brian Dyde and Glenford Howe, little has been written about the military forces of the region.

This book is based, as far as possible, on original records and accounts. Regrettably, all too little evidence survives for many of these formations, especially in the early decades: few records were kept, and the ravages of time and climate have destroyed much of what was compiled. Most frustrating is the lack of accounts from the ranks that give voice to the experiences, thoughts and feelings of the ordinary soldiers.

# ACKNOWLEDGEMENTS

Many helped, knowingly and otherwise, in the creation of this book. Much of the research was done at the National Archives, the Imperial War Museum and the National Army Museum and I am greatly indebted to their knowledgeable and helpful staffs.

I drew insight from the work of three eminent historians, Roger Buckley, Brian Dyde and Glenford Howe, especially on the earlier decades.

Numerous friends provided help and encouragement, including Mark Shields, Geoff and Moira Newman, Wendell Hollis, Rob Taggart and Jim Donna. Bill Cranston, who devoted much of his life to the study of British colonial forces, unfortunately did not live to see its final completion. I am also indebted to Field Marshal Sir John Chapple who has selflessly given of his time and wisdom whenever asked.

My thanks to The History Press and Amy Rigg for taking on the book at a particularly difficult time, and to Alex Waite and her colleagues for their skilled and sympathetic editing which saved me from far too many slips. Evgenia North provided her usual brilliant and unflappable assistance with images. Sarah Renfrew did valuable research and rescued a befuddled father from the mysteries of computers and their programs. I am also indebted to Jo and her colleagues at our local Waterstones who tracked down innumerable obscure titles with cheerful skill.

My wife Margaret inspired and aided me throughout; whatever is good in these pages is largely due to her. We hope the book will bring some small measure of honour and homage to that forgotten army of West Indian and African men who endured so much only to be repaid with scorn and cruelty by those they fought for.

PART I

# THE WARS OF EMPIRE

# 1

# THE GRAVEYARD OF THE BRITISH ARMY

Almost nothing is known about the little band of settlers who founded England's first permanent colony in the West Indies on the tear-shaped island of St Christopher around 1624; records do not even agree on their number, putting it at somewhere between thirteen and nineteen.[1] This seemingly insignificant event was the start of an extraordinary era of power, wealth and conflict that would ensnare millions of people from Europe, Africa and the Americas over the coming centuries.

Most of the men, women and children who sailed to the West Indies from the British Isles in the seventeenth century were lured by hopes of a better life. Most found only gruelling hardship and early deaths in the seemingly idyllic green islands ringed by sparkling blue seas. Malaria, yellow fever and other diseases killed countless numbers, often within weeks or months of stepping ashore: two-thirds of the first 12,000 settlers in Jamaica were dead within six years.[2] The climate was a torment; heat and humidity made life unbearable and terrifying hurricanes flattened homes, devastated fields and hurled the unwary to their deaths. And then there were the human threats: fierce local tribes called Caribs decimated some of the English settlements, carrying off the hapless survivors. Conflicts with rival French, Spanish and

---

1    J.H. Parry & J.M. Sherlock, *A Short History of the West Indies*, p.48.
2    Richard Dunn, *Sugar & Slaves*, p.153.

other European settlers claimed more lives and pirates murdered and pillaged indiscriminately.

Those who survived rarely found the riches or easy lives that the settlers had imagined would be theirs for the taking. When Captain Ketteridge, one of the leading men in Barbados, died in 1635, his earthly possessions comprised a chest, six hammocks, a broken kettle, a sieve, a few pewter dishes, three napkins and three books.

The first descriptions of the West Indies as an earthly paradise soon gave way to accounts of a living inferno: 'As Sickly as an Hospital, as Dangerous as the Plague, as Hot as Hell, and as Wicked as the Devil,' wrote one traveller.[3] The islands became a dumping ground for criminals, rebels, paupers and the rest of England's human waste. Henry Whistler, a visitor to Barbados, complained in 1655, 'This Illand is the Dunghill warone England doth cast its rbidg: Rodgs and hors and such like people are those were generally Broght here [this island is the dunghill where on England doth cast its rubbish: rogues and whores and such like people are those who were generally brought here].'[4]

And then it was discovered that one of the world's most precious commodities flourished in the West Indian soil and climate. Sugar had been a prized luxury for centuries in Europe, only available in minute quantities and enjoyed by the wealthiest. Soon the English, French and other islands were flooding Europe with the sweet delight: sugar mania swept the continent as people gorged on sweet beverages, puddings and other sickly treats. Almost overnight the islands became the most valuable acreage on the planet as the sugar boom created enormous wealth. Britain now gloried in its West Indian empire. Pineapples, a symbol of the islands and their exotic wealth, were etched on the swords of army officers alongside the traditional figures of Britannia and the royal coat of arms.

Sugar transformed the physical and human geography of the West Indies. Every possible scrap of land was given over to sugar production. Cane cultivation required vast amounts of intensive labour, and the white settlers were too few and generally disinclined to do the necessary back-breaking work. Black slaves purchased on the west coast of Africa solved the planters' dilemma. The populations of the British and other European sugar islands

---

3    Quoted in Julian Hoppit, *A Land of Liberty?* p.266.
4    Quoted in Frank Pitman, *The Development of the British West Indies 1700–1763*, p.6.

rocketed with the influx of slaves. Census records show Jamaica in 1673 had a population of 7,700 whites and 9,500 blacks, the latter nearly all slaves; fifty years later, the number of whites was virtually unchanged while the black population had soared to 74,000, again, mostly slaves.[5]

A debauched and garish society sprang up with a tiny and fabulously wealthy planter caste ruling over legions of brutalised slaves: the West had seen nothing like it since the days of the Roman Empire. The humble cottages, patched hammocks and wooden dishes of the early settlers were replaced by planters' mansions, regiments of liveried slave servants, gleaming gold and silver tableware, the finest fashions, and endless dinners and entertainments. Planters were obsessed with getting rich fast, living well and escaping to Europe before the climate or disease claimed them.

Slavery also brought new dangers as the islands were transformed into the equivalent of vast labour camps where tens of thousands of black captives were brutalised and worked to death. Such harsh treatment stoked defiance that led to periodic slave revolts. The tiny white minority lived in dread of being slaughtered by their own field hands and servants.

Hundreds of slaves rebelled in 1673 in Jamaica in one of the first revolts, killing dozens of whites. Subsequent rebellions grew in both size and the degree of carnage and cruelty. Governor James Kendall of Barbados wrote at the end of the seventeenth century, 'Our most dangerous enemies [are] our black slaves.'[6]

Risings were suppressed with murderous ferocity. Six slaves were burned alive and eleven beheaded in Barbados in 1675 just for planning an uprising. A 1692 plot on the island provoked even more horrific reprisals. Dozens of slaves were hanged, burned or starved to death in cages, and a slave woman was paid to castrate forty-two men.

The wealth of the West Indies, and the desire to monopolise it, became a major factor in the protracted European wars of the eighteenth century. Vast armies and fleets battled for tiny Caribbean islands that were deemed more valuable than entire provinces or great cities in Europe. British soldiers who fought for the sugar islands knew no deadlier place, except that it was disease which wiped out regiment after regiment rather than battles and sieges. Doctors had little or no idea what caused the pestilences that scythed down

---

5    Walvin, *Black Ivory*, p.69.
6    Quoted in Matthew Parker, *The Sugar Barons*, p.160.

the troops. Men frequently perished within hours of being stricken, often dying in agony as they choked on black bile or were convulsed by fever. 'If you sup with a man at night and enquire for him the next day he is ill or dead,' lamented Major Frederick Johnson.[7]

Almost every aspect of army life made the soldiers more vulnerable to sickness, not that anyone realised it at the time. Most men were recruited from the poorest depths of society, where they had known only hunger and deprivation, and were often weak, emaciated and chronically ill when they arrived in the West Indies. Many barracks were built in low-lying areas or near swamps where land was cheapest, and where mosquitoes, responsible for the deadliest diseases, thrived. The men's quarters were filthy, and they rarely washed despite the heat; their thick woollen uniforms, intended for European climates, bred pests, inflicted sun stroke and drained their strength; and staple rations of salted meat and rotting biscuit, utterly unsuited for a tropical climate, further weakened them. Officers and soldiers sought protection or solace from these afflictions in copious amounts of alcohol, but the crude local rum, a cheap by-product of the sugar industry, was laced with deadly lead and fusel oil which inflicted lingering and painful deaths. It was hardly surprising that the West Indies became known as the graveyard of the British Army.

British campaigns in the Caribbean frequently ended in disaster. The concentration of thousands of troops in camps and siege works bred deadly epidemics that wiped out armies, and there were always shortages of food, medicine and other necessities. It did not help that in an age when the army had more than its share of miscreants and outcasts, it was often the worst men who were sent to the West Indies. Governor Valentine Morris of St Vincent complained in 1777 that newly arrived troops had the look of men reprieved from the gallows:

> [They] are in general the very scum of the Earth. The Streets of London must have been swept of their refuse, the Gaols emptied ... I should say the very Gibbets had been robbed to furnish such Recruits, literally most of them fit only ... to fill a pit with.[8]

---

7   Quoted in O'Shaughnessy, *Redcoats*, p.110.
8   Quoted in L.J. Ragatz, *The Fall of the Planter Class in the British Caribbean 1700–1763*, p.31.

Morris was not far wrong; the *London Magazine* reported in 1762 that eight criminals sentenced to hang were spared the noose after agreeing to enlist in a regiment bound for the West Indies.

Despite their vast wealth, the defences of the British settlements were frequently inadequate or virtually non-existent. Government penny-pinching routinely stinted the regular garrisons of money and supplies, except in war time. William Stapleton, the Governor of Nevis, pleaded with London in 1675 to send back pay for the island's two companies of starving, ragged infantry. 'They live in a most miserable condition … it is a disparagement rather than an honour to the nation to have soldiers naked and starving,' he wrote.[9] Bermuda's[10] garrison complained in 1739 that it had not received any supplies since 1696.[11]

Officials in London tried to shrug off the woeful state of the West Indian defences, arguing it was the duty of the colonists to protect their wealthy settlements. Each island had its own militia, and service was compulsory for most white men, but they were not always willing to fight. Some settlers put up fierce resistance when attacked, while others allowed French or Spanish invaders to wade ashore unopposed so as to avoid the destruction of their homes and businesses. When a French fleet raided Nevis in 1783, the council opted not to resist, and the enemy commander allowed the islanders to pose as neutrals to save their property.

Many of the poor whites who made up the bulk of the militias saw little point in dying to protect the property of the rich planters who looked down on them. When Spanish ships raided Nevis, most of the defenders tossed away their arms and deserted to the enemy, shouting, 'Liberty, joyful Liberty!'[12] In 1734 Governor William Mathew of the Leeward Islands conceded such men had little reason to fight while still damning them as human vermin:

Such unwilling, Worthless, Idle Vagabonds, as from whom but Little Service can be hop'd for on Military Emergencies. Most of these Serve for a Term of Years, without wages, poorly Cladd, hard fedd … Are these

---

9 Quoted in Brian Dyde, *The Empty Sleeve*, p.68.
10 While Bermuda is not geographically part of the West Indies it was regarded as part of the region under the British Empire, and the two retain close ties to this day.
11 J.W. Fortescue, *A History of the British Army*, Vol. 2, p.44.
12 Dunn, *Sugar and Slaves*, p.120.

the Men that are to Die in Our Defence? My Lords we must have a recruit of a better Sort or better none at all.[13]

Not that the white elite was much better. Many of the militias' shortcomings reflected the nature of white West Indian society, particularly its maniacal obsession with wealth and status. Every white man with more than a few pounds expected to be an officer in the militia and wealthy planters and businessmen insisted on being colonels and generals in units barely big enough to warrant a single subaltern. Militias were absurdly top heavy with officers and NCOs: some Jamaican regiments had fifty officers, fifty NCOs and 300 privates.

Contemporary observers never tired of parodying the West Indian militias and their shortcomings. Among the most perceptive was Lady Maria Nugent, wife of the general in command of British troops in Jamaica around 1800. Lady Nugent, who accompanied her husband when he reviewed the local militia, wrote of seeing sweating, portly planters trailed by slave boys carrying their masters' muskets, the 6ft weapons towering over the young bearers, and geriatric generals and colonels too doddery to leave their carriages.

'The whole review, in fact,' she wrote after one inspection:

> … was most funny. Not one of the officers, nor their men, knew at all what they were about, and each had displayed his own taste, in the ornamental part of his dress. They were indeed a motley crew, and the Colonel whispered me – 'Ah, ma'am, if the General did not know half the trouble I have had to draw up the men as you see them, he would not ask me to change their position; for what they will do next I don't know. You see I have drawn a line with my cane for them to stand by, and it is a pity to remove them from it.' Poor man! I did pity him, for at the first word of command they stared, and then moved in every direction, and such a sense of confusion at any review I believe was never beheld.[14]

Free black and mixed-race men were obligated to serve in many of the militias: in fact, they became increasingly indispensable as plantations took

---

13  Quoted in Pitman, p.57.
14  Lady Maria Nugent, *Lady Nugent's Journal*, p.78.

over much of the arable land, forcing poorer whites to emigrate because they could no longer make a living. In 1764, Jamaica's militia had some 4,000 whites and 830 black and mixed-race men: by 1817 the ratio was much altered with 5,644 whites and 3,265 black and mixed-race men under arms. Not that service in the militia and risking death on the battlefield conferred equal rights. Non-whites were banned from being officers and had to serve in segregated units, which were often based on racial gradations: the Kingston Militia Regiment in Jamaica had separate companies of whites, blacks, 'mulattos' (half black) and 'quadroons' (one-quarter black).

The long struggle of the European powers for control of the West Indies peaked with the French Revolution and the ensuing Revolutionary and Napoleonic Wars. Some of the largest armies ever to leave Britain's shores set out for the Caribbean in the 1790s with orders to turn it into a British lake. Initially, all went well, with the capture of several French islands: the defenders were outnumbered, Paris could send little aid, and civil war raged between local royalists and revolutionaries.

While news of the successes was welcomed in Britain, the army endured some of the highest losses in its history. Sir John Fortescue, the epic historian of the British Army, estimated that it suffered 100,000 casualties in the West Indies between 1793 and 1799, half of them fatalities and nearly all from disease.[15] Soldiers saw a posting to the West Indies as a death sentence. Typical was the experience of the 31st Regiment: leaving England with 986 officers and men in 1794, it suffered 719 deaths over the next two years, of which just fifty-five were on the battlefield. Britain was soon facing calamity in the Caribbean, her forces decimated by sickness, and the French rebounding from their early defeats.

Despairing British generals said the army must do the seemingly unthinkable and raise an army of slave soldiers to fight for the country and the plantation system that oppressed them and their families. Only the vast slave population could provide the replacements the army desperately needed, and the slaves were far less vulnerable to disease and the climate than whites, especially the troops fresh from Britain. Lieutenant General Sir John Vaughan, the senior army commander in the Caribbean, told his superiors in London that without slave troops Britain could lose its West Indian empire. 'I cannot hesitate to declare that unless His Majesty will be

---

15 Fortescue, *A History of the British Army*, various references.

graciously pleased to sanction and promote the measure of forming Negroe men into Regiments commanded by British officers', the sugar islands would be lost, he wrote.[16] If not, he warned, the British Army would be destroyed unless the ruinous cycle of dispatching white regiments to perish in the fever-ridden islands was not broken.

Nor did Vaughan see slave troops as just a temporary, wartime measure. He said slave regiments must be a permanent part of the regular army, imbued with its high professional standards, and no different from its white regiments. The slave regiments would be paid, armed and clothed like the rest of the army, and housed in the same barracks as white troops; in short, they would be treated in virtually the same way as white regulars except for the fact the men would not be free. Once the French were defeated, slave soldiers would garrison the West Indies, permitting sharp cuts in the number of white troops stationed in the region. Otherwise, Vaughan said, 'the whole army of Great Britain would not suffice to defend the Windward Islands', let alone the entire West Indies.[17] Thousands of slaves must be enlisted at once, he insisted, with every colony providing a quota of their fittest and strongest bondmen.

Vaughan's plan was not the lunacy it might have seemed at first glance. Slaves had fought and died for their white owners since the early days of European settlement. Nor was it a secret that black West Indians made fine soldiers: they were generally fitter and stronger than whites and their expert knowledge of the terrain meant they excelled at the bush fighting that typified local warfare. Some British commanders said experience had shown that one black soldier was worth three white soldiers in the West Indies.

The regular army had sometimes used slaves and free blacks in the West Indies as labour troops and artisans: called the 'King's Negroes', they built roads and forts and did other work regarded as too gruelling for white soldiers. Some of the West Indian militias had slave units, which occasionally served as fighting troops, but more often acted as pioneers and labourers.

The St Kitts Corps of Embodied Slaves was outfitted with uniforms, pikes and cutlasses, and trained weekly. Barbados appears to have raised the first slave unit when threatened by a Dutch invasion in 1666; the governor ordered that every white soldier be backed by 'two able-Negro-men, well

---

16  TNA/PRO WO 1/82.
17  Quoted in Fortescue, Vol. 3, p.425.

armed'.[18] Slaves who served in the militias often received better treatment and sometimes pay, although their owners might pocket up to two-thirds of the money. Barbados rewarded slaves who did military service with an annual gift of a coat and a hat from official funds, and their owners were expected to give them the same amount of food as white servants.

Slaves sometimes put up the fiercest resistance when settlements were attacked because they faced the greatest danger. A key aim in West Indian warfare was to destroy an enemy colony's sugar industry, thereby reducing competition. Invading troops burned cane fields, refineries and, above all, abducted the slaves on whose labour the plantation system depended. Slaves were shipped off to be sold in some strange new place with the loss of homes, families, friends and whatever little they might possess. Free black and mixed-race people were also rounded up and sold into slavery.

After a French fleet invaded Nevis in 1706, the white militia surrendered immediately while some of their slaves fought to the bitter end. Eventually the French rounded up 3,000 slaves to ship to their islands, and the British settlers turned over another 1,400 slaves as part of a deal to end hostilities. William Dickson, a government official in Barbados, wrote that the French might capture the island, but they would never be able to hold it, 'and one reason always assigned was the Negroes would cut their garrisons to pieces, which I verily believe would be the case'.[19]

Not that the whites necessarily returned such loyalty. Some slaves who fought for Britain in the 1790s were sent back to the hard labour of the plantations despite loyal and excellent service.

Any attempt to explain why slaves would loyally serve in the British Army is likely to be both complex and imperfect. The earlier use of slaves for military service in the West Indies was always on a small scale and tightly controlled to ensure they did not become a threat to white power. And yet Vaughan wanted to raise a fighting force that would be more formidable and numerous than anything the white colonists were likely to field. Nor was he suggesting that only slaves willing to serve should be enlisted or that they would be granted their freedom. It was made clear from the start that slave soldiers would never be liberated and would have no more say over their fate than the slaves who laboured in the sugar fields.

---

18  Jerome Handler, *Freedmen and Slaves in the Barbados Militia*, p.8.
19  Quoted in Handler, p.16.

Slaves were not a vast homogenous group. Individuals had differing, often conflicting, circumstances and attitudes. Some slaves had key roles in the plantation system as overseers and servants, and others wanted to join their ranks in the hope of an easier life and other privileges. Military service was a way to escape from the harsh existence endured by most slaves as slave soldiers were paid and received much the same treatment and rations as white regulars. And there was always the hope that military service could earn a slave freedom no matter what the rules for the new regiments stipulated; a 1707 Barbados Act liberated any slave who killed an enemy soldier. Moreover, the methods the army used to control white troops would prove remarkably adept at turning slaves into loyal soldiers.

The mere idea of raising regiments of slave soldiers for the regular army provoked consternation and fury. Astonished government officials in Britain rejected the scheme as unworkable. West Indian colonists denounced the notion as monstrous, insisting the slave soldiers would run amok at the first opportunity, slaughtering every white man, woman and child.

However, mounting problems soon forced the government to reconsider. The military situation in Europe and elsewhere was worsening, the West Indian whites would never be able or willing to play a major role in their own defence, and the generals had strengthened the case for slave troops by showing they would be cheaper than white regulars. Above all, no one could see any other way to stem the losses in the West Indies that were bleeding the British Army dry at a time when troops were desperately needed in other theatres.

In April 1795, London gave approval to raise the first slave regiments. The British Army was about to become the largest owner of slaves in the West Indies, and possibly the world.

# 2

# AN ARMY OF SLAVES

Sir John Vaughan never saw the creation of the first slave regiments. He died in the Caribbean in June 1795, two months after London consented to the scheme, cut down by the pestilential climate that had killed so many of his white troops.

Vaughan had proposed starting with two slave regiments, each with 1,100 men in ten companies under white officers and NCOs. It seemed a sensible beginning since the army would be faced with training and controlling soldiers of a type it had never known before. Only now London insisted on a dramatic expansion in the number of regiments because of the desperate need for fresh troops everywhere. Four additional regiments were authorised in May 1795 and a further two in September. A total of twelve regiments would be raised by 1798 – a breakneck pace for what even its advocates acknowledged was a daunting experiment. The first two formations were named Whyte's Regiment of Foot and Myers' Regiment of Foot in honour of their colonels. It was decided to rename them the 1st and 2nd West India Regiments (WIR) in 1796 with the subsequent regiments numbered by seniority.

Every West Indian colony was asked to donate a quota of their strongest, most able male slaves to fill the ranks of the new formations. Free black and mixed-race volunteers would also be enlisted. If these measures did not raise enough recruits, slaves would be purchased on the open market – not that the military thought this would be necessary. Army commanders were expressly told not to promise the slaves freedom under any circumstances: the government did not want to alienate the white settlers by doing anything that might suggest slavery would ever end. It was assumed the colonists would eagerly support the scheme and not expect payment for their slaves, after all, the new regiments would be defending their power and prosperity. Such expectations proved to be utterly deluded.

Far from being welcomed, the slave regiments triggered a political crisis in the West Indian settlements. Whites denounced the scheme as a threat to their lives and everything they stood for. Planters and other owners refused to give slaves to the army. Colonial legislatures did everything they could to undermine the plan. Lawmakers in Barbados predicted that the black troops would sack the island if they were ever permitted to step foot on it, while Jamaica's assembly denounced the scheme as an assault on the white population's rights and liberties as free-born Britons. Meetings were held across the Caribbean at which speakers thundered that arming slaves was utter madness that would lead to the end of white domination. Hellish pictures were conjured up of the slave troops overrunning the settlements and unleashing an orgy of carnage, destruction and looting.

Even more unexpected was the opposition of anti-slavery groups in Britain, which denounced the plan almost as sharply as the West Indian slave owners who normally were their most bitter foes. William Wilberforce and other leading abolitionists admitted the life of a soldier in the regular army might not be as bad as that of a slave on a sugar plantation but argued that it was still wrong and the need for thousands of recruits would boost the slave trade, causing greater misery and destruction in Africa.

Recruiting was a fiasco. A despairing officer predicted that the regiments would never be raised, 'not a Man having been given by any one of the Islands towards completing them'.[1] By 1797, the first four regiments had just 186 black and mixed-race soldiers between them, mostly men from irregular black formations raised earlier in the war: the 3rd WIR had just two drummers. The nominal strength of each regiment was cut to 600 rank and file, and a plan for companies of dragoons was dropped. It made no difference; the military could not find enough slaves to fill a single regiment.

Things went no better when the army tried to recruit volunteers from the free black and mixed-race population. Despite being mostly poor, these

---

1   Quoted in Roger Buckley, *Slaves in Red Coats*, p.37.

men were no keener than impoverished whites in Britain to exchange their liberty for the harsh existence of the regular army.

The army refused to abandon the plan despite opposition from the unholy alliance of slave owners and abolitionists. Black infantry, the generals insisted, must form a third of the regular forces in the Caribbean. Government ministers, exasperated with the colonists' intransigence, agreed in October 1796 to purchase as many slaves as needed to bring the twelve regiments up to full strength. Major General Ralph Abercromby, commander-in-chief in the West Indies and a strong proponent of black troops, wanted to buy Creole or West Indian slaves rather than new captives from Africa. It was thought that West Indian slaves would be easier to train because they were acclimatised, understood at least some English, and knew local conditions. He envisaged a ratio of two Creoles for each African.

The colonists were almost as unwilling to sell slaves to the army as they had been to donate them; the few who were willing generally offered only the most truculent slaves or old and sickly men who could no longer work. It soon became clear that the only way to man the new regiments was to buy captives straight out of the slave ships as they arrived from Africa. Orders were placed through dealers, with the military expressing a preference for men from the most warlike tribes on the assumption they would make the best soldiers. It was further stipulated that the slaves be at least 16 years old, 5ft 3in tall, and unmarried. Such standards had to be frequently skirted because of the need to find thousands of men as quickly as possible. Skittish officials in London, nervous about criticism from colonists and abolitionists, shrouded the transactions in secrecy. Despite many difficulties, the army would buy some 13,000 slaves over the next decade.

Nothing in its long experience had seemingly prepared the British Army for the challenge of turning slaves into soldiers. Men, violently torn from their homes and all they knew, had to be moulded to fight for the people who had enslaved them, people of whose language, customs and values they knew little or nothing.

History is not without examples of slave troops. The Ottoman Empire had a long tradition of elite slave soldiers, albeit they were subjected from a very young age to intense religious and cultural indoctrination as well as military training. British soldiers were supposed to be proud, free-born volunteers and patriots. In reality, most recruits came from the very bottom of society – drunks, rogues, idiots, criminals, paupers, absconding husbands and the merely unfortunate. Long experience of controlling such men and turning them into some of the finest troops in the world meant the army was not entirely unprepared for the challenge of slave soldiers.

Slaves purchased by the army would have had little or no idea what faced them. They had been captured in wars or abducted in raids, marched to the coast in shackles, and held in slave pens. They then endured the arduous ocean crossing in the packed holds of slave ships, arriving in the West Indies in a state of shock, grief and fear. They faced further bewildering indignities as they were examined and prodded like livestock by army inspectors. Those who were accepted by the military were herded to the barracks by shouting NCOs and armed soldiers. Accustomed to the light, minimal dress of West Africa, the captives were forced into stifling, prickly and constricting uniforms – wool tunics, trousers, tight belts, leather neck stocks and headgear – all totally unsuited for the West Indian heat and humidity. Then came months of gruelling training and harsh discipline: of being forced to stand rigidly in ranks for hours; marching endlessly around a parade ground as NCOs bellowed and struck at them; being confined at night in dank and airless barracks; being herded to church services to worship a god they likely did not comprehend; and all with little or no idea of why.

Every slave was given an English name as part of the process of breaking the men and remoulding them. English names were also easier for white officers and NCOs to remember and pronounce. Names taken from a list or made up on the spot were written on a board hung around each new recruit's neck. Common names like Tom, Dick or Harry were soon exhausted so the officers used the same method as they employed to christen their horses and pet dogs, naming the slaves after famous generals and statesmen, British cities and rivers, gods and heroes of the ancient world, and celebrated race horses and prize fighters of the day. A newly arrived officer found himself commanding a company that included the Duke of Wellington, Julius Caesar, Thunderbolt, Scipio Africanus, Mars, Congo Jack and Lively, among others. Such tricks exhausted most officers' limited imaginations or patience after a time, so names were recycled by adding numerals: thus, a company might have London 1, London 2, etc. Many officers thought it was hilarious to give exalted or fancy names to men they saw as savages.

Next came teaching the slaves English so that they could understand and obey orders. Some regiments worked hard to ensure the troops were proficient in their new tongue, while in others the men acquired only a smattering of pidgin. A new commanding officer of the 2nd WIR was shocked to find men with years of service who could not pronounce their own names. He instructed the officers and NCOs to make every effort to correct the problem, insisting they show 'patience and perseverance'[2] to achieve the best results. As a first step, at every roll call and parade each man had to pronounce his name until perfect. They then went through the same process naming their weapons and clothing. Men were forbidden to speak their 'country language' until they had mastered English. Those who made good progress and passed tests in English were given cash prizes.

There was never any doubt that the slave regiments would use English. Not only was it the language of the army, in which all commands and instructions were given, but the slaves spoke numerous African dialects and often could not understand each other. Some of the men had to be taught to read and write English because regiments provided their own clerks to handle a unit's administrative tasks and keep records. A number of slave regiments had schools to teach basic literacy, numeracy and other skills to the men, although it was difficult to find white teachers because of the poor pay and the ignominy of tutoring black men.

New recruits were converted to Christianity, or at least classified on paper as Christians. The army presented this as the commendable act of civilising benighted savages – it also fended off criticism for not tending to the troops' souls. One officer recalled how recruits on their first Sunday in the army were 'marched into church as a matter of course along with their Christian comrades'.[3] Far from being pleased, some churchmen were appalled at what they saw as the army's flippant attitude, saying it made a mockery of true faith. Charles Kingsley, the eminent Victorian cleric and writer, wrote, 'It may be asked, if they had any will in the matter, how could they understand the duties to be imposed on them.'[4] Kingsley seemed most outraged by what he regarded as the besmirching of the gospels by men he regarded as cannibals.

New men were kept in line with harsh discipline; slaps, kicks and worse were often as much a part of the recruits' lives as eating and sleeping. George Pinckard, an army surgeon, left an account of what life could be like:

---

2   2nd WIR Order Book.
3   A.B. Ellis, *The History of the First West India Regiment*, p.129.
4   Quoted in Ellis, p.130.

Often when stepping to the words 'left, right, left, right,' a stout black serjeant suddenly seizes the leg of some one who does not put it forth to his
mind, and jerks it with a force that endangers the dislocation of his hip:
when the poor fellow, forgetting that his body must maintain the military
square, whatever becomes of his limbs, looks down to see that he steps out
better next time; but another serjeant instantly lodges his coarse fist under
his chin, and throws back his head with such violence as almost to break
his neck ... Then, by some mistake, the right leg advances instead of the
left, or the left instead of the right, the remedy for which is a hard kick, or
a rough blow on the shin ... thus the poor black is beset on all quarters
and at all points, and whether standing or moving, feels the weight of the
cane, the fist or some other weapon, upon either his head or his shoulders,
his back, knees, shins, or naked toes.[5]

Soldiers in white regiments could be treated in much the same way.

Some senior officers believed the slaves would make better soldiers if
treated with kindness and patience. The NCOs of the 2nd WIR were told
to treat the men 'with more gentleness',[6] while the regiment's officers were
expected to ensure that the men understood their duties, 'delivering their
instructions with patience and in a clear and concise manner will have a
much better effect than perpetual repetition without explanation'.[7]

And while the British Army was notorious for its use of flogging to
enforce discipline, the WIR could employ more subtle methods of control. Slave soldiers were kept in line with the implicit threat that men who
refused to submit would be sold to the plantations. There is no evidence that
the army ever did this, and yet the mere possibility of being worked to death
in the sugar fields must have been highly effective. 'Compared to slavery
the restrictions of military discipline are as exquisite freedom,' one officer
wrily wrote.[8] Some regiments punished delinquents by treating them like
common slaves: men were stripped of their weapons and uniforms, forced
to do menial labour and endure the mockery of their comrades.

Most commanding officers stressed the importance of giving the men
plentiful and nourishing food to maintain their fitness and morale. Ration

---

5   Quoted in Dyde, *The Empty Sleeve*, p.38.
6   2nd WIR Order Book.
7   2nd WIR Order Book.
8   Quoted in Buckley, p. 34.

tables were set for each unit, and officers had to inspect the food to ensure quality and quantity. Black troops received two meals a day, as did white regulars. Typical fare in the West India regiments included:

Breakfast (served at 7 AM) – A pint of coffee, 1 ounce of sugar, ½ pound of bread.
Dinner (served at 1 PM)
Monday & Thursday – 1 pound fresh beef, 3 ounces rice, herbs, ½ pound of bread.
Wednesday & Friday – 1 pound salt beef, ½ pound yams or plantains, ½ pound bread.
Sunday, Tuesday & Saturday – 11¾ ounces salt pork, ½ pound pease or 3 ounces rice, ½ pound bread.

Black soldiers supplemented their rations with fresh vegetables, herbs and spices purchased with their pay in the local markets, something white regulars don't appear to have emulated, perhaps because of ignorance about local foodstuffs or aversion to such fare. Rum was issued daily to soldiers in both black and white regiments. Standing orders that the rum must be mixed with water were sometimes ignored, leading to drunkenness. However, the 2nd WIR avoided such problems by having it diluted in a bath tub – one part rum to three parts water – under the gaze of the duty officer.

Occasional bonuses allowed the slave troops to add some extra cheer to their lives and diets. Christmas was celebrated in the 2nd WIR in 1802 with a parade, prayers and the award of half a dollar to each man 'to be laid out in buttering his dinner and in adding to his happiness', along with an admonition that 'the commanding officer warns them against intoxication and noise in honour of the day'.[9]

In an age that did not always value cleanliness, great stress was placed on hygiene in the black regiments. Set times were reserved each week for washing clothes, and NCOs had to ensure their men were 'perfectly clean'.[10] New recruits were taught basic hygiene by the regimental doctor. When the 2nd WIR shared barrack quarters with the white 85th Regiment, the slave soldiers complained of 'very bad smells' coming from

---

9   Quoted in Buckley, p. 34.
10  Quoted in Buckley, p. 34.

the white troops' quarters.[11] Every slave regiment had a doctor, medical attendants and infirmaries, and the sick were given wine or porter as extra nourishment twice a day.

What the slave troops felt and thought about their new life is virtually unknown. And yet it is clear that virtually all of the men accepted their situation and were good soldiers. The regiment became the slave troops' home, providing shelter, security and camaraderie; desertion was much rarer than in the rest of the army. A key part of the WIR's training was instilling the men with the belief that they were superior to other slaves. Another major aid to assimilation was the *esprit de corps*, or unit identity, that all effective military formations require. In addition to generating unit pride and comradeship, it helped to set all soldiers apart from civilians. Slave troops saw themselves as a privileged elite who were allowed to carry guns, with much the same status as white regulars.

Life was fairly easy for the slave troops once training was complete. Their peacetime routine consisted mainly of drills, chores and guard duty. The men were frequently allowed out of barracks when off duty and could socialise with the local black community. Soldiers in their resplendent red uniforms, with their superior social status and regular pay, must have found little difficulty in finding female companionship and other diversions among the vast slave population. Some men were allowed to marry, with their wives living in the barracks. After the shock of being torn from everything they knew and forced into slavery, life in the WIR may have seemed like some form of deliverance.

All of these factors helped to ensure that the WIR soon earned a reputation as excellent, well-disciplined soldiers. An official inspection of the 4th WIR in 1810 commented:

> ... the Non-commissioned Officers and Privates are in general extremely sober, quiet and docile and as tractable as it is possible for men to be, who have so slight a knowledge of the language of their Officers, being most of them Africans by birth, and purchased by Government out of Guinea ships.[12]

---

11  Quoted in Buckley, p. 34.
12  Quoted in Buckley, p.113.

The true proof of the WIR's success was that the army never had to impose special controls on the regiment despite the potential threat posed by thousands of heavily armed and trained slave troops who could rebel at any time. There were only two significant revolts by slave troops, and there were special factors in both cases.

Even in an age rife with corruption, Colonel Andrew Johnstone, the commander of the 8th WIR, was notorious for enriching himself from army funds. When the regiment was based in Dominica in 1802, he illicitly used the troops to work on his own land and diverted much of their pay into his pocket. Local plantation slaves taunted the soldiers, claiming they were being made to do manual labour because the army planned to sell them as field hands. Fearing the worst, the men mutinied and took over the fort where they were based, killing several officers and taking others hostage.

Johnstone, who had been absent when the trouble broke out, assembled a force of white troops and artillery and rushed to the fort. Some accounts suggest the mutineers had decided to surrender after concluding that their situation was hopeless. Whatever the truth, Johnstone stormed into the fort to find the regiment neatly drawn up on the parade ground with three of the officers who had been hostages now restored to their posts. The enraged colonel began to berate the troops as criminals and scum. Some of the men protested, calling out that they were loyal soldiers of the king. Seeing he was losing control of the situation Johnstone brusquely ordered the 8th to lay their muskets on the ground. Just a few of the men obeyed, the rest continuing to loudly insist on their loyalty. At which point the white troops opened fire, killing or wounding around seventy of the black soldiers. Some of them fired back, inflicting a few casualties on the white troops. Most of the black soldiers then fled; more than 200 men hurled themselves from a nearby cliff into the sea as they tried to escape.

At least fifty of the mutineers were dead by the time order was restored. Seven of the ringleaders were court-martialled and executed by firing squads. A subsequent inquiry into the incident did not go well for their colonel. Evidence revealed that Johnstone and some of his officers had stolen army funds and property and the men had not been paid for months. Despite surviving a subsequent court martial, Johnstone was pointedly not offered any further posts. He left the army and went on to a spectacular career of fraud and embezzlement. The troops were posted to other WIR regiments after the 8th was disbanded, an unusual show of clemency indicating the army recognised that the men had been treated badly.

A mutiny of a different kind erupted in 1808 in the 2nd WIR when it was stationed at Fort Augusta near Kingston in Jamaica. Some thirty new men who were being drilled in the fort by two NCOs tried to escape. Lacking ammunition for their muskets, the men used bayonets to force their way through the main gate although not before guards killed several of them.

The rest of the regiment was being drilled on a field outside the fort. Major Darley, the senior officer, and the regimental adjutant, Lieutenant Ellis, hearing the sound of fighting at the gate, rode over to investigate. Both men were pulled from their saddles and bayoneted to death by the mutineers. Seeing this, the entire regiment broke ranks and mobbed the killers. Ten of the mutineers were beaten to death by the enraged soldiers despite the efforts of some of the officers to intervene. Sixteen of the mutineers escaped into the bush, only to be quickly caught by loyal troops. Six of the mutineers were subsequently condemned by court martial and shot. The other ten survivors were pardoned and allowed to remain in the ranks in a remarkable act of mercy by the standards of the time. All of them did well in the regiment, with several becoming NCOs in later years.

The 2nd WIR had proved its overwhelming loyalty, and yet the military authorities feared the incident would inflame local white colonists who were already deeply unhappy about the presence of a slave regiment. The island's commanding general had the 2nd mount a guard at his house to demonstrate his trust in the regiment. A regimental history said of the incident, 'Far from being a stain on the military reputation of the Regiment … [it proved] its loyalty and devoted … attachment of the men to their officers.'[13]

★★★

Slave regiments presented the army with unique legal and moral as well as military challenges. While the army treated slave troops much the same as white regulars, the black soldiers faced a very different situation outside their bases. Some colonial legislatures made the WIR subject to the so-called 'slave laws', which strictly curtailed every aspect of a slave's existence.

---

13  J.E. Caulfield, *100 Years' History of the 2nd West Indian Regiment 1795 to 1898*, p.28.

For example, a black soldier faced whipping, mutilation or the death sentence for merely approaching a white person.

Army protests about its troops being subject to such measures were undermined when government lawyers ruled that the colonial authorities were in the right. It also meant that soldiers who were discharged because of injury or sickness risked being treated as runaway slaves by the civil authorities. Abercromby tried to resolve the problem by granting freedom to discharged men. Colonial legislatures refused to recognise that the men were free and the government's lawyers, as unhelpful as ever, said they were still slaves unless the local authorities ruled otherwise.

Turning slaves into soldiers called for leaders of more than average ability. Most British officers regarded black men as little more than animals and savages, and leading them was not a fit occupation for gentlemen. The stigma of commanding black troops meant that throughout its history the WIR would endure both a chronic shortage of officers and more than its share of indifferent and dishonest ones. It also attracted many men from humble or poor backgrounds who had to live on their pay in an army where officers were expected to have private incomes and live in style: life in the WIR was cheap, if nothing else.

Poor officers did not necessarily make bad officers, but they were drawn to the WIR because of empty bank accounts rather than any enthusiasm for the regiment. All too often, they shared the general disdain for black troops and bolted at the first chance. And yet, the regiment also attracted a hardcore of talented and dedicated officers who devoted their careers, and often their lives, to making the WIR a first-class fighting formation. Some saw black soldiers as men like any others; some regarded leading them as a worthy challenge; others craved action and the hard life of the colonial frontier rather than enduring the dull routine of British garrison towns.

The first WIR officers were seconded from regular white regiments in the Caribbean in the 1790s, although these could spare only a few from their disease-ravaged ranks. The army sought to make up the shortage by selling commissions in the WIR, the usual practice in an age when officers purchased their posts. While the commissions sold quickly, the great majority were bought as a way to get into the army and then transfer straight to white regiments. Only a few of the new officers ever joined the slave regiments. At the end of 1795, the 1st WIR had just eleven officers despite an official strength of fifty-nine officers, and those who took up their posts spent much of their time and energy seeking transfers.

It had been intended that the slave regiments would have white NCOs who were drawn from regular units. The initial establishment of the 1st WIR provided for twenty-two sergeants and eleven corporals – all of them white. Finding white NCOs for the regiments proved to be just as difficult as obtaining officers. Whites from the lower ranks were as racist as white officers, and very few wanted to leave their regiments to serve in a black unit, especially if it meant staying in the West Indies with all of its deadly risks. The army soon accepted that black NCOs were the only solution. While black soldiers would never be allowed to be officers, thousands served as NCOs over the coming decades, providing the vital framework needed to hold any military unit together and make it effective.

The first of the slave regiments were just a few months old when they were tested on the battlefield for the first time.

# 3

# THE EQUAL OF ANY SOLDIERS IN THE WORLD

By 1795 the war in the West Indies was going badly for Britain. French forces, reinforced and infused with revolutionary zeal, went on the offensive, winning a series of victories. British commanders faced an unfolding nightmare as their disease-ravaged regiments were pushed back; a general committed suicide after one defeat too many. The first of the new slave regiments, untrained and short of everything from men to muskets, were hurled piecemeal into the desperate efforts to staunch the enemy onslaught.

Among the threats facing the beleaguered British were uprisings on several former French islands. The most serious was on St Vincent, where British colonists had appropriated much of the best land and generally thrown their weight about. French settlers, the Carib tribes and runaway slaves shelved their mutual animosity to form an alliance to drive the British into the sea. French forces in the region aided the insurgents when fighting erupted in March 1795. The local militia, the only British troops in the colony, were routed, and fled to the capital of Kingstown at the southern end of the island. Insurgent forces pounded the besieged town with artillery and set fire to surrounding sugar plantations as the encircled British glumly watched. It was the start of what the British dubbed the 'Brigands' War' in a clumsy attempt to vilify their opponents as criminals.

The newly formed 2nd West India Regiment was part of the meagre reinforcements dispatched to St Vincent. While on paper the 2nd WIR fielded 1,100 infantry, it consisted of little more than a handful of officers,

NCOs and drummer boys when it landed on the island. Lieutenant Colonel Samuel Graham, the commanding officer, faced the seemingly impossible task of creating a regiment on the battlefield. Little is known of Graham: a regular officer, he had taken command just four months before the 2nd WIR arrived in St Vincent. He proved to be an outstanding fighting commander who believed in the skill and courage of his black soldiers. Graham hastily assembled a force of some 400 loyal slaves and free black soldiers.

Graham's men saw action for the first time in January 1796. A white British unit holding a heavily fortified position on a ridge was surprised one night when enemy forces attacked on several sides. Pandemonium ensued as the bewildered defenders blundered into each other in the dark. The garrison soon broke and fled, abandoning several cannon and large quantities of supplies. Graham, with 200 of his men, was about a mile away when he heard the sounds of the fighting. A raw unit like the 2nd WIR might have frozen or fled. Instead, it hastened toward the clash, and soon ran into the white troops fleeing from the pursuing enemy.

Graham's virtually untrained soldiers carried out one of the most difficult of battlefield tasks – covering a retreat by beaten troops against a much larger force scenting victory. His men formed ranks and held off the enemy with steady volleys as they slowly gave ground. It was enough to stop the retreat turning into a rout. The 2nd WIR paid a high price with 152 killed and wounded while the white British troops who fled suffered fewer than fifty casualties.

Substantial British reinforcements finally arrived on St Vincent in June and defeated the main insurgent force. It did not end the fighting, however, which turned into a cruel and protracted conflict against Carib and slave bands in the island's rugged interior. Slaves fought slaves as the 2nd WIR helped hunt down the insurgents. It was a task the WIR would perform with unflinching discipline and considerable skill in the years ahead. Little mercy was shown by either side, with the insurgents knowing they faced execution, enslavement or exile if defeated.

The British forces knew virtually nothing about the island's interior, where dense vegetation blanketed steep, rocky hills. Patrols had to force their way through what seemed like an endless wall of bushes, vines and creepers broken only by sheer precipices. Paths had to be laboriously hacked through the undergrowth as mosquitoes, wasps and other insects bedevilled the troops. Clad in wool uniforms, the white soldiers suffered agonies in the suffocating heat and humidity. What was unknown and dangerous territory to the British was home for the insurgents, who seemed to know every tree and rock. Enemy marksmen lurked unseen in the bush just inches from British patrols that repeatedly blundered into ambushes. Guerrillas hidden in the tree tops riddled the confused and helpless troops below with musket fire.

British commanders soon realised the WIR was far better suited to this kind of warfare than white units. Black troops knew how to move silently and quickly through the bush and did not get lost. They were also far less susceptible to the heat, humidity and insects – or at least endured them more stoically than white soldiers. And they were healthier and fitter, eating mainly vegetables and fruit, and imbibing far less alcohol than the rum-sodden whites.

Graham and his men were instrumental in hunting down the main guerrilla bands. He was leading a patrol when it stumbled across a large Carib fort in the mountains. Hoping the Caribs would surrender, Graham went forward under a white flag with a small party after the defenders signalled that they were willing to talk. He was just a few feet from the stockade when the Caribs fired a volley. Graham was hit by a musket ball that tore through a lung and out of his back, while a second ball shattered his hand. Graham's men dashed forward, braving the Carib fire to carry him to safety. Troops of the 2nd WIR and the 34th Regiment then stormed the stockade, taking some 700 Caribs prisoner. Graham was forced to give up command of the regiment because of his wounds.

After months of bitter fighting, the British finally broke the last resistance. Thousands of Carib men, women and children were deported to desolate, fever-ridden islands in the Gulf of Honduras where many perished. Very few of the 2nd WIR survived the St Vincent campaign; there were just 100 or so men in its ranks when it was withdrawn, many of them sick or injured. For its bravery and endurance, the regiment received the praise of the white British colonists, the first such accolade for the slave troops. A vote of thanks was passed by the assembly and expensive gifts presented to the officers. Nothing beyond words went to the men, however, and yet it was a kind of equality since the rank and file in white regiments traditionally were treated in the same way.

The 1st WIR also took part in a protracted and bitter guerrilla campaign after a revolt on the former French island of Grenada in 1795 was put down. White troops were sent to track down the guerrillas in the interior while the 1st WIR was used to garrison the coastal settlements. It was the same story as at St Vincent: the white soldiers were disoriented by the terrain, heat and humidity and units became lost as they tried to slash their way through the dense undergrowth. Patrols were attacked by unseen marksmen who vanished before the British could respond.

This continued until the 1st WIR and local black troops were deployed in the interior. They soon tracked down the enemy hideouts and routed the main insurgent bands. The ground in many areas was so rugged that the black troops frequently had to half-lead, half-carry their exhausted white officers. Many of the insurgents fought to the death, and it was not until 1800 that the 2nd WIR, which had taken the place of its sister regiment, crushed the last of the resistance.

Army commanders in the West Indies had no doubts about the worth of the WIR after the regiment's achievements in St Vincent and Grenada. Brigadier General John Moore, one of the leading British generals of the day, was convinced that black troops could be the equal of any troops in the world. 'They possess, I think, many excellent qualities as Soldiers, and may with proper attention become equal to any thing. Even at present as they are, for the W. Indies they are invaluable,' he wrote.[1]

A display of heroic devotion by the 2nd WIR in 1800 further enhanced the reputation of the slave regiments. A ship carrying the 2nd WIR to Trinidad was swept onto rocks as it neared the colony. There was only room in the handful of lifeboats for the women and children, and the soldiers and sailors were forced to swim to the rocks. Many of the white officers were saved from drowning by their men, who pulled and carried them through the pounding surf. Most of the regiment's supplies went down with the ship, but the men risked drowning by clinging to their muskets. No one was lost in the wreck, largely because of the bravery of the slave troops. Boats from Trinidad rescued the survivors the next day.

★★★

Despite their services, the slave regiments were still feared and loathed by many of the white colonists for whom they were fighting and dying. While British settlers on St Vincent and Grenada praised their black saviours, other

---

1    Quoted in Buckley, *Slaves in Red Coats*, p.90.

settlements would not even allow the WIR on their soil. Jamaica agreed in 1794 to pay for white regulars rather than accept slave troops. When the 2nd WIR was moved to the island because of a French invasion threat in 1802, the enraged legislature passed a resolution branding the soldiers as 'enemies in disguise'.[2]

Peace descended briefly on the Caribbean after the 1802 Treaty of Amiens. But the resumption of hostilities the following year would see the slave regiments shoulder an ever greater share of the war effort in the West Indies. White units continued to wither away from disease and the climate, and London could spare few reinforcements because of pressing needs elsewhere. Slave troops also had to do much of the army's heavy labour – building fortifications, moving supplies and repairing roads – because most white troops were too weak and run down. It was a thankless task that the WIR shared with the white sailors of the Royal Navy. Slave soldiers also worked as orderlies in army hospitals, caring for both white and black troops who used the same facilities on a largely equal basis.

The WIR remained well below strength because of losses and the time needed to purchase and train thousands of slaves to fill the ranks. The twelve regiments were reduced to eight because of the shortage of men: the 9th, 10th and 12th were merged into the 7th, and the 11th was renumbered as the 8th in place of the unit that had mutinied in Dominica that year. This restructuring and an influx of new troops enabled the eight remaining regiments to be increased from 600 men to 1,000 men apiece as the WIR readied for its next major test.

When the war resumed in 1803, a British force of some 3,000 troops, including the 1st WIR, captured St Lucia, with the French defenders capitulating after a single day. Paris had not abandoned its hopes of victory in the West Indies and dispatched a fleet with 5,000 troops to the region in early 1805. It attacked Dominica, which was defended by a small force comprising four companies of the 1st WIR, three companies of the white 46th Regiment and the local militia. The French fleet flew British flags, and it was not until the ships began disgorging troops near the town of Roseau that the garrison realised the island was under attack. Three companies from the 1st WIR, the 46th and the militia pinned the French on the beach until cannon fire from the enemy warships forced them to retreat.

---

2   Caulfield, *110 Years' History of the 2nd West India Regiment 1795 to 1898*, p.25.

Falling back, the outnumbered British took position in ruined buildings, which the pursuing French could only approach on a path between the sea and the overlooking cliffs. British reinforcements arrived with artillery to bolster the defenders, and Major Nunn of the 1st WIR took command. French infantry attacked the position four times, suffering some 300 casualties in six hours of intense fighting. Nunn was mortally wounded during the battle, and command passed to Captain O'Connell of the 1st WIR. Unable to break through, the French troops returned to their ships. A French force landed north of Roseau, which was protected by a redoubt held by just five men each of the 1st WIR and the 46th with a few militiamen. The men held out until all of the white and black regulars were killed or badly injured.

O'Connell and the remnants of his command set off to join the rest of the British garrison at the town of Prince Rupert. Even though the force only had to cover some 25 miles, it took four exhausting days to force their way through the densely forested interior, carrying the wounded and whatever supplies they had salvaged. Survivors of the march who had campaigned in other parts of the world said the terrain was more difficult than anything they had ever encountered. It now seemed as if the French were on the cusp of a victory that would shake the entire British position in the Caribbean. Dissension or doubt bedevilled the French commanders, however, and they sailed away after being paid a paltry £5,500 by the colonists to save their homes and property from destruction.

Dominica was a skirmish compared to the battles being fought in Europe, and yet the heroism of the island's garrison heartened Britain at a time when France seemed invincible. Grateful colonists passed resolutions extolling the 1st WIR, the troops once again getting only words while their officers received rich gifts. Far more heartening was the award of the regiment's first battle honour, allowing them to inscribe Dominica on their standard. Such distinctions were among the highest honours afforded British regiments, and proof that the army now saw the WIR as the equal of its regular white regiments.

It was not until 1809 that British forces finally vanquished the French in the Caribbean. A British army of some 10,000 men invaded the key French island of Martinique that year. Four of the West India regiments – the 1st, 3rd, 4th and part of the 8th – comprised a quarter of the force, underlining how essential and trusted the slave regiments had become. French troops fell back as the British landed on the east and south coasts and advanced inland. It was not an easy pursuit. Constant, heavy rain turned the dirt tracks that passed for roads into ribbons of mud, which gripped the feet of the men and the hooves of the horses pulling cannon and wagons. There was little or no shelter for the exhausted troops as they struggled across the all too familiar landscape of dense vegetation and rocky hills.

Two days passed before the British ran into the main French force dug in on a line of hills fronted by a river; it was an immensely strong position bristling with batteries. An assault force made up of elite light infantry and grenadier companies, including some from the WIR, launched a frontal attack. French cannon balls scythed the attackers down, severing heads and shattering torsos, as the infantry struggled up the slopes. Hunching their heads and shoulders as if they were being buffeted by rain rather than showers of lead, the white and black infantry reached the crest and swept away the defenders with a bayonet charge. An attempt by the French to hold a hilltop position a few miles away was unsuccessful.

Most of the French troops escaped to Fort Bourbon, an even stronger position. British commanders, overconfident after their initial successes, decided to storm it. Once again, the grenadier companies of the various white and black regiments led the attack, only to be mangled as they advanced into a wall of cannon fire. Some 350 British soldiers were killed or wounded before the assault was abandoned. All the attack did was to waste British lives and invigorate the defenders' morale. The French commander refused to surrender, confident that disease would break out in the British ranks and destroy the invading force. Instead, the British brought up artillery and began a massive bombardment. Much of the heavy work of hauling cannon and shot fell to the black soldiers. Slave troops also helped man the siege lines around the fort. A detachment of the 1st WIR was nearly burned to death when French cannon fire ignited the brush around their post. After six days of bombardment, the French capitulated with the surrender of 2,700 men and dozens of cannons. For its role in the victory, the WIR was awarded a second battle honour, adding Martinique to its flag.

Guadeloupe was now the last significant French bastion in the West Indies. This time, the British could only scratch together 6,700 troops of which the 1st, 3rd, 4th, 6th and 8th WIRs made up 40 per cent – the starkest testimony yet of how important the slave units had become to British military fortunes. There were only scattered clashes as the British landed, with the French retiring to a series of redoubts lodged atop 2,000ft hills.

British troops had to endure searing heat and humidity, heavy rain and murderous artillery and musket fire as they assailed the positions. Eventually, the French gave up after suffering 600 dead and wounded, twice the British losses. Guadeloupe became the WIR's third battle honour.

Britain had finally triumphed in the long wars for the West Indies, albeit at a horrendous cost to the lives and health of her soldiers. If the story of the West Indian campaign was largely one of terrible carnage for modest gains, it was a triumph for the WIR, which more than lived up to the predictions of Vaughan and other generals that black men – free or slaves – could make first-rate soldiers.

★★★

The undeniable bravery and loyalty of the slave soldiers finally helped end their bondage. Army commanders had been increasingly unhappy about the legal status of the WIR, not least because the men were subject to the harsh West Indian slave laws whenever they left their barracks. The quandary was resolved with the abolition of the slave trade in the British Empire in 1807. Parliament inserted a clause liberating the WIR troops in the annual army act. With the stroke of a pen, some 10,000 black soldiers were released from slavery, although it was stipulated that they had to spend the rest of their lives in the army.

Nearly two decades of conflict expanded Britain's West Indian empire. Territories seized from France and other opponents had to be garrisoned, and it invariably fell to the WIR to guard the most remote, disease-ridden outposts, often in small detachments of a few dozen men. Regimental commanders complained it was a waste of excellent fighting troops and impeded training because their units were rarely together in one place. Life for the men was often unpleasant and monotonous: they were frequently housed in squalid barracks and went short of food, clothing and other essentials. Some detachments lived in flimsy cane huts that provided little shelter against rain or sun, and the troops found it almost impossible to keep themselves and their clothes and equipment clean. Most of the men possessed only a single uniform that soon wore out.

Army inspectors who reviewed the 1st WIR in 1806 found the men dressed in rags, and a detachment of the 6th WIR was said to have no uniforms at all. As an economy measure, WIR troops sometimes were given cast-offs from white regiments rather than new uniforms. Worn-out muskets that had been discarded by white units were also issued to the WIR even though they tended to be inaccurate and liable to malfunction.

★★★

The WIR served outside the Caribbean for the first time in 1812, when Britain and the United States stumbled into war. A detachment of the 2nd WIR was with a Royal Navy squadron that raided the coast of Georgia in 1814. It helped rout a larger force of American militia, chasing the fleeing whites for several miles and briefly occupying a town and the nearby fort. A much larger British force of 8,000 troops, including the 1st and 5th WIRs, sailed from the West Indies in late 1814 to attack New Orleans.

Gleeful British commanders saw the inclusion of the regiments as a masterstroke of psychological warfare. It would completely unnerve the Americans to see their homes and lands being occupied by black troops and might incite the local slaves to rebel. A number of American officials had been worrying about just such a possibility. Benjamin Hawkins had warned Washington in 1813 of the danger of 'an invasion of British and West Indian Blacks, several regiments of which are actually concentrated at Jamaica'.[3]

Naval commanders ruled out a frontal assault on New Orleans because of the strong defences at the mouth of the Mississippi River. Instead, the British troops had to cross 60 miles of desolate swamps on foot and in small boats to approach the city from the east. It was December, and the troops endured heavy frosts, winds and torrential rains. There was little shelter in the swamps, and the exhausted men were often short of food. The West Indian units suffered the most: they had never experienced such cold; they had not been issued with overcoats or warm clothing, and had just handful of blankets for more than 1,000 men. An unknown number of black soldiers died from exposure as the army blundered through the morass.

White officers and soldiers reacted to the suffering of the black troops with a mix of sympathy and scorn. Colonel Alexander Dickson wrote:

> It is difficult to express how much the black troops suffered from the excessive cold which they are so little accustomed to, and so improvided

---

3   Jeremy Black, *The War of 1812 in the Age of Napoleon*, p.193.

[*sic*] with warm clothing to protect them. Several have died from mere cold and the whole appear quite torpid and unequal to any exertion; I am quite convinced that little or no benefit will be derived from these troops while exposed to such cold.[4]

It was the start of a cast-iron belief in the British Army that black West Indian troops could only serve in tropical zones and were thus less rugged and useful than white soldiers. No matter how well West Indian troops performed in the coming decades in Europe and elsewhere, especially when given suitable clothing and equipment, they never escaped the slur first hurled at them in the frigid swamps of Louisiana. Fortescue, the Victorian historian, said in his account of the New Orleans campaign that the black soldiers 'were so much numbed with cold that they were absolutely useless even for fatigue duties'[5] – an assertion disproved by his own and others' accounts of the battle.

General Andrew Jackson, the American commander and future president, meanwhile, was overseeing the construction of a defensive wall to protect New Orleans. It was an imposing structure, up to 5ft high and 20ft deep, and studded with cannon emplacements.

The British attacked on 8 January 1815. The assault force was divided into two brigades with a West India regiment in each. Withering cannon and musket fire cut down the white and black troops impartially as they crossed the thousand yards of open ground in front of the American defences. A British NCO left a haunting account of the West Indians dying alongside the white troops:

A few yards behind sat a black man, with all the lower part of his face shot away; his eyes were gone and the bones of his brow all jagged and dripping blood. Near him, in a ditch, lay one of the 43rd (Regiment) trying to hold in his bowels.[6]

About 2,000 British troops were killed and injured before the attack collapsed. American losses were a mere sixty dead and injured. A detachment

4   Quoted in Jon Latimer, *1812 War With America*, p.379.
5   Fortescue, *A History of the British Army*, Vol. X, p.162.
6   Quoted in Latimer, p.386.

of the 1st WIR attempted to circle behind the left flank of the American line. Some accounts suggest the West Indians were surrounded by a unit of Native Americans and surrendered. Among the American forces were several militia units of free black soldiers under black officers, and a slave unit that Jackson had raised a few weeks before. There is no record that the black troops on either side faced each other in the battle. Jackson praised the courage of his black soldiers, only to be accused later of reneging on a promise to free the slaves if they fought well.

British commanders ordered a retreat to the coast. A terrible trek lasting two weeks ensued as the survivors, burdened with hundreds of wounded, struggled through the swamps. The 1st and 5th WIRs returned home with less than half their normal strength fit for duty.

Napoleon's final defeat in 1815 was greeted by the British Government with the rapid demobilisation of the armies and fleets that had won the long struggle. Thousands of soldiers and sailors were thrown on to the streets, many to face poverty and misery. Army commanders insisted that the WIR was needed to hold those colonial outposts considered too unhealthy for white troops, although its numbers were sharply reduced. Between 1817 and 1825, six WIR regiments were disbanded: just the 1st and 2nd were spared after being reduced from 1,000 men to 650 men apiece.

The 4th WIR earned a temporary reprieve after its rank and file pleaded to remain in the army. It was moved to Gibraltar in 1817 to form part of the garrison. Ironically, as part of a formation that owed its origins to its immunity to disease, the 4th was decimated by sickness, suffering a death rate four times higher than that of the white regiments in the garrison – the black soldiers were not invulnerable to European diseases. It was shipped to Africa in 1819 and disbanded. The strength of the WIR would fluctuate over the next century with regiments being revived and disbanded as the army's needs dictated.

★★★

If discharged white soldiers endured hard times in Britain, the West Indian veterans faced even greater upheaval. Most of the black troops did not want to leave the army and several of the regiments petitioned the military authorities not to be broken up. If they could not stay in the ranks, the men wanted to settle in the West Indies, even though most of them were from Africa. The prospect of thousands of black soldiers being settled on the British islands, where tiny white minorities still ruled over vast slave populations, caused predictable panic and outrage. Colonists insisted that the black veterans would seize power and liberate the slaves, and most of the settlements adamantly refused to allow the men to remain. Only Trinidad and British Honduras, both sparsely populated and desperate for labour, accepted a few hundred men each.

Unable to exert its authority in ostensibly British colonies, the government settled most of the discharged troops in Sierra Leone in West Africa, despite the men's unwillingness. Soldiers' families were uprooted from the West Indies and sent to Africa with their menfolk. Veterans were allotted tracts of jungle to clear for homes and farms, and those with sufficient service or war-related disabilities received small pensions. It probably gave the men a better standard of living than some discharged white veterans found in the slums of Britain, and yet it was not what they had served and fought for. Villages founded by the WIR veterans were given names such as Waterloo, Gibraltar and Wellington to mark their service for a country that had no further use for them.

# 4

# RETURN TO AFRICA

Hundreds of black soldiers crowded the decks of two decrepit sailing ships that arrived off the west coast of Africa on 24 May 1819. The *John* and the *Alfred*, both well past their best days, had set out from Jamaica two months earlier with half of the 2nd West India Regiment crammed in their holds. It was a homecoming for some of the troops peering at the shore that day; the slave trade had only been abolished a decade earlier, and there were still men in the WIR's ranks who had been born and enslaved in Africa.

The detachment's arrival was the start of a new role for the army's only black regiment. For the next century, the WIR would guard British interests on the continent, enduring horrendous hardships in countless campaigns.

Delighted colonial officials in the British territory of Sierra Leone welcomed the troops. They also warned London that the detachment was far too small, given Britain's precarious position in West Africa. The 353 officers and other ranks who stepped ashore were soon scattered across hundreds of miles of coast and jungle to garrison a handful of outposts that eked out an impoverished existence trading cloth and trinkets with the local people.

Any sense of new beginnings or exotic mystery that the soldiers felt soon vanished. The squalid settlements and filthy barracks that were their new homes were as bad as anything they had endured in the Caribbean.

West Africa was the British Empire's most desolate backwater. Very few Europeans survived its sweltering climate and deadly diseases for long.

White troops who were sent to the region perished even more rapidly than in the Caribbean.

In a desperate attempt to find troops to garrison the West African outposts, a white regiment with the grand title of the Royal African Corps was formed in 1800. In truth, it was a penal unit made up of white soldiers convicted of serious crimes who were given the choice of Africa or flogging and execution. Enlistment in the formation was a virtual death sentence. A parliamentary report found that half of the men died within three months of reaching Africa and the remainder after fifteen months.[1] Ferocious discipline was needed to control the hardened criminals and troublemakers in the ranks – twelve men were flogged to death in a single year – although the troops were said to have little or no fear because they knew they would be dead in a few weeks or months at the most.

Using the WIR in West Africa was first suggested in 1802 because of the troops' greater resistance to tropical weather and disease. Sierra Leone's administration beseeched London that year for one of the new slave units to protect the settlement. Other tropical colonies also expressed interest in securing the WIR's services as word of its early successes spread. Ceylon raised the possibility in 1803 of using the WIR as part of its garrison, and there was even talk of deploying West Indian troops in India. The most persistent pleas came from West Africa, but London did not accede to them until 1817 when it was clear that France no longer posed any threat to the West Indies. Thereafter, the West Indian regiments would be rotated between the Caribbean and West Africa on a regular basis. Some army officers joked about sending savages to police other savages.

Between 1820 and 1914, the WIR fought a series of now long-forgotten wars in West Africa, the story of which could fill a dozen or more histories. Some were minor police actions against slave raiders or petty chiefs, others were major campaigns against powerful states with large and effective armies. WIR columns that were sent deep into the wilderness never numbered more than a few hundred men and had to operate with little or no support. And yet the West Indians invariably triumphed against far larger forces, helping to bring ever greater swathes of territory, and the people who inhabited them, under British rule.

---

1   J.J. Crooks, *Historical Records of the Royal African Corps*, p.119.

The West African terrain and climate could be a more brutal and unforgiving adversary than the warlike tribes that dominated the interior. Thick forests and jungle blanketed the region, broken only by swamps, fast-flowing rivers and rocky hills. There were no roads beyond the coastal settlements, just the occasional jungle track. Columns often had to hack their way through the dark, tangled undergrowth, taking hours to cover a mile or two. A report by a WIR detachment in Sierra Leone in the 1860s spoke of operating in a:

> … dense and swampy locality (with nowhere to camp) … the roads being nothing more than dried watercourses, through dense jungle, high grass, and swamp in some places so deep that logs had to be laid down before the troops could pass over, the men having to march the whole way in Indian file.[2]

Sweltering heat and humidity alternated with deluging rain that made it impossible to light fires or cook food, coated equipment in thick mould and rusted the troops' weapons. Soldiers lived in the same sodden, rotting uniforms for weeks at a time, and frequently went hungry and thirsty.

A WIR punitive expedition in Gambia in 1849 experienced temperatures of 54°C (130°F). The commander noted that the heat was made worse by the searing flames of the villages that were burned by his men. Legions of snakes, scorpions and flies added to the dangers and discomfort and clouds of insects feasted on the soldiers' sweat-drenched bodies, inflicting maddening bites that bred infection and fever. Thorns and razor grass shredded clothing and flesh impartially. Germs flourished in the airless jungle and reeking swamps, with malaria and other diseases claiming many more lives than any military action. Weeks and months of marching and fighting in the dense bush, where it was often impossible to see more than a few feet, had a deadening psychological impact: some men experienced a choking sense of claustrophobia or their nerves were shattered by the constant fear of ambush. Sleep was difficult or impossible in such conditions, adding to the strain and exhaustion of interminable marches and having to always be on guard against sudden attack.

---

2   Quoted in Caulfield, *100 Years' History of the 2nd West India Regiment 1795 to 1898*, p.129.

Supplies were a constant nightmare for columns operating in the bush. Pack animals quickly died from disease so nearly everything had to be transported by African porters bearing loads of up to 80lb each. Porters generally were supplied by local tribes, sometimes for pay and sometimes at bayonet point. Even a modest expedition might require hundreds of porters, who had to be guarded by the troops to prevent ambushes or stop the bearers deserting. Wounded and sick soldiers were carried in litters with every bounce and bump causing agony on journeys that might take weeks before reaching a hospital. Even the dead had to be borne away after a battle to prevent their corpses being mutilated.

African fighters were masters of bush warfare, their skills often reducing or nullifying the WIR's superior weapons and organisation. Warriors could move unseen through the jungle, approaching within inches of West Indian columns to fire a deadly volley and vanish before the survivors could react. Many Africans were armed with muskets called Dane guns, often made in Birmingham and sold by British merchants on the coast. Primitive and inaccurate, the weapons were still deadly when packed with scrap metal and discharged at an adversary just a few feet away from the muzzle. One officer wrote:

> This class of bush-fighting becomes wearisome to all concerned. Almost every hour a gun goes off at someone or other in the column – sometimes in front, then again in the middle of the column, or perhaps in the rear, even at night the enemy creep up to the camp and fire their guns, which are usually loaded up to the muzzle with all sorts of bits of iron, or pot legs as we call them.[3]

War was a way of life for many of the African peoples; warriors had been trained to fight from boyhood. The most powerful tribes and kingdoms fielded armies with thousands of men. Soldiers who served in West Africa had little patience for the prevailing British view that Africans were cowardly and stupid savages. C. Braithwaite Wallis, a veteran of the region, wrote:

> Savages they might be, but even in their way of fighting they betrayed such admirable qualities as are not always found in the troops of civilised

---

3   Quoted in Hernon, *Britain's Forgotten Wars*, p.721.

nations ... they understand bush fighting as well as you and I do our very alphabet.[4]

Trained to use tactics designed for Western battlefields, the West Indians had to devise new ways of manoeuvring and fighting in the African bush. They learned to advance through the jungle in single file; to fight back to back when columns were ambushed; and to read the ground and foliage for signs of danger.

Maintaining a unit's cohesion in action was essential. Hard experience taught the WIR that an officer could effectively control and direct ten men at most in the bush rather than the usual thirty or fifty in the open. Heavy machine guns, called 'piss guns' by the Africans because of their rapid fire, were sometimes used in later years to lay down withering barrages as a column moved through the jungle to flush out any lurking attackers.

Once they had mastered the bush, the WIR soon learned that their opponents were not invincible. African fighters tended to be poor marksmen, often firing wildly from the hip rather than aiming, and they frequently lacked cohesion or co-ordination on the battlefield. Superior training, discipline and marksmanship told in the end, enabling small British detachments to defeat far larger forces.

Lieutenant Colonel Alfred Ellis, who commanded the 1st WIR, boasted that in the bush his men could march two to three times further than white troops on half as much food. Many in the army tried to belittle the West Indians' prowess, saying they only did well because they were no different from primitive Africans. As time passed, however, more and more of the West Indian soldiers sent to Africa were town youths or peasants from Jamaica or Barbados, and little different in stamina and outlook from the English factory hands or Scottish farm workers who filled the ranks of white regiments.

Africa was as challenging and frightening to the West Indians as it was to white troops. Indeed, the WIR saw little or no difference between itself and the rest of the army. A West Indian soldier thought himself 'in every respect an Englishman,' Ellis said.[5] Conversely, the regiment's African role made it even more difficult to attract white officers. In addition to the enduring

---

4   *Ibid.*, p.712.
5   Ellis, *The History of the First West India Regiment*, p.15.

stigma of commanding black troops, they faced spending years in Africa, with the high risk of death from disease, endless gruelling campaigns, and the acute discomfort and boredom of life in the primitive settlements.

★★★

The WIR's first taste of African warfare was the so-called Rio Pongo War of 1820 against slave traders. The West Indians were often involved in operations against slavery, which continued long after the trade had been outlawed. A Royal Navy midshipman and several sailors had been killed or captured pursuing a large band of slavers led by a white renegade known only as Curtis.

Three companies of the recently arrived 2nd WIR were dispatched in four gunboats to apprehend the slavers, who were holed up in a fort on the banks of the Pongo River in the interior. Curtis had the support of local tribes, which supplied him with slaves. Flying a white flag, the boats slowly approached the fort to give Curtis a chance to surrender. As the soldiers began to land, the slavers suddenly opened fire with cannons and muskets. Deploying, the infantry attacked and overran the fort and a nearby settlement as the slavers fled. Thick plumes of smoke billowed into the sky as the troops burned the pens where slaves were held, destroyed the fort and removed its cannon.

Curtis' tribal allies backed down after the WIR commanders threatened to destroy their towns and villages. It was enough to win the release of the captured sailors, who emerged from the bush a short time later, although Curtis was never apprehended.

In another anti-slavery operation in 1826, the 2nd WIR overran a large slavers' base at Sherbro in Sierra Leone, destroying fortifications, slave stockades and freeing hundreds of captives who were found shackled and waiting to be shipped out of the country.

West African warfare sometimes involved sieges of fortified towns rather than battles on open ground. The WIR became expert at attacking settlements that were protected by wooden walls up to 20ft high, skilfully strengthened with buttresses and rocks and fronted by deep ditches. The largest towns were encircled by two or more concentric walls with open ground between that could be swept by the defenders with musket fire, spears, arrows and rocks. The small field guns used by British forces often had little effect against such walls. British forces sometimes used rockets, which were lighter and easier to transport through the road-less bush than cannons; fired from metal troughs, the crude projectiles packed with gun powder set fire to buildings when they exploded and spread panic among the inhabitants. Nonetheless, infantry assaults were usually the only way to breech a town's fortifications.

A detachment of 130 men of the 2nd WIR was detailed in 1861 to storm a settlement called Madonkia that was ringed by two walls. A subsequent report described the imposing defences:

> Outside the stockade and about six feet from it was a war fence, which had to be got through before the stockade was reached; this fence was made of poles, about four inches in diameter, and about 16 or 18 feet high, let in to the ground about three feet, and bound together with country rope in three different places. The stockade was made of strong beams of wood, and trees about one foot in diameter, crossed obliquely with the same and loopholed. There was also a small tower built in the front on the stockade, about 20 feet high, big enough for two or three men to sit in.[6]

A solitary British howitzer and a rocket detachment bombarded the settlement, killing and injuring some of the defenders, but failed to breech the walls. Troops with axes had to hack at the walls as gunmen peppered them through loopholes. The defenders fled when the troops finally forced an opening and poured through, after which the West Indians burned the settlement to the ground. British losses were remarkably light on this occasion with just one man dead and seven wounded: however, nearly all the casualties were officers and NCOs, illustrating how the WIR's commanders invariably led their men from the front.

Victory was not always on the British side, and the WIR suffered more than one bloody defeat. Captain R. D'Oyley Fletcher was ordered to take and burn the town of Maalgeah in 1855 after its ruler repeatedly defied British authority. He urged local officials to let him wait for reinforcements, pointing out that Maalgeah was a major power and would not be easily subdued.

Fletcher was mortified when civilian officials suggested he was afraid. He promptly took a force of 150 men from the 1st and 3rd WIRs to Maalgeah

---

6    Quoted in Caulfeld, p.133.

on a gunboat, HMS *Teazer*. When British demands to surrender were rejected, the gunboat bombarded the town, after which the infantry went ashore and set fire to the ruler's palace and the other principal buildings. The fires spread and soon most of the town was burning. Buffeted by the flames consuming the wood and thatch buildings, the troops returned to the ship.

A short time later, as the conflagration died down, Fletcher saw that large parts of the town were still standing. It was decided the troops would land again the next day to complete the destruction. When they landed in the morning, the West Indians were ambushed by thousands of African warriors. Little groups of officers and soldiers were cut off and hacked to pieces as the force tried to pull back to the river. Sailors on the *Teazer*, who had exhausted the ship's cannon ammunition the day before, could do nothing to help. Some of the troops got to a rowing boat on the riverbank but were trapped in deep mud as they tried to push the vessel into the water and drowned. About thirty soldiers made a final stand on a sandbank, where half of them were shot down in minutes. A handful then managed to swim to the ship, the rest being butchered in the water. Fletcher, the last man to leave the riverbank, had to swim more than half a mile to reach the ship.

Stunned survivors watched helplessly from the *Teazer* as thousands of jubilant warriors lining the river bank screamed victory cries and brandished a grisly forest of severed white and black heads on raised spears. Of the 145 soldiers who went ashore, eighty-seven were killed and fourteen wounded. It was one of the worst defeats suffered by British forces in West Africa.

★★★

As Britain pushed ever deeper into the West African hinterland during the nineteenth century, it fell to the WIR to do much of the fighting to subdue and hold vast new tracts of territory. The most determined resistance increasingly came from powerful Muslim states that proved to be far more formidable than other African adversaries the regiment had faced.

One of the first encounters was in 1853 when a WIR column was dispatched to subdue Sabbajee in Gambia. The town was more than a mile in circumference, strongly fortified and contained the largest mosque in the region. An unusually large force of 450 men from the 1st, 2nd and

3rd WIRs was assembled for the expedition, along with 150 African militia-men and a battery of four cannon.

Green flags inscribed with Arabic script were flying over the town and some 3,000 fighting men lined the walls when the British column arrived. Lieutenant Colonel Luke Smyth O'Connor, the column commander, ordered the battery to open fire 400 yards from the walls. The shelling soon set fire to many of the buildings inside the town, causing panic among the thousands of residents.

Seeing the confusion, the West Indians stormed the walls, bayonetting many of the defenders, and forced their way into the town. Some of the fighters retreated into the mosque as the rest of the garrison fled into the bush. Imams implored the fighters in the mosque not to surrender and the men kept up their spirits by beating drums and chanting.

O'Connor, fearing his force would suffer many casualties if the mosque was stormed, ordered a rocket detachment to bombard the building, and soon it was burning. Trapped and unable to extinguish the flames, dozens of the holdouts killed themselves or burned to death rather than surrender. Those who tried to escape were shot down by the West Indian infantry surrounding the building. O'Connor ordered the mosque razed to demonstrate British power. It took his men a day and a half to demolish the structure's massive central hall, dome and 3ft thick walls of baked mud that were as hard as rock. Eventually, a large part of the column's gunpowder stocks had to be used to bring the structure crashing down.

A large WIR force came close to defeat in 1860 in a confrontation on the frontiers of Gambia with another Muslim power, the Baddiboo people. British officials imposed a blockade on the state after accusing its ruler of attacking British traders. It failed to break the Baddiboo, and eight companies of the 1st and 2nd WIRs, some 600 men in all, were brought in from Sierra Leone to punish the Africans' defiance.

Transported by gunboats up the Swarra Cunda Creek to a large town with the same name, the West Indians found thousands of warriors manning extensive fortifications on the riverbank. For three hours the boats' cannon, including massive 68-pounders, bombarded the defences. Astonished soldiers and sailors watched as some of the warriors stood in the open despite the deadly cannon fire, taunting them to leave the safety of the gunboats and fight.

A large WIR detachment was attacked as soon as it landed later in the day. West Indians and Africans grappled and lashed at each other in vicious hand-to-hand fighting at the water's edge. Eventually the troops forced the Baddiboo back with their bayonets and were sensing victory when 300 cavalry in armour and flowing robes appeared. Amazed, the West Indians formed squares, something the regiment had not done since the Napoleonic Wars.

The horsemen charged up to the lines of black infantry, leaning down to spear men or slash at them with scimitars. Five soldiers were caught in the open by the cavalry before they could get to the safety of a square. Standing back to back, the five fought to the death; a circle of slain horsemen was later found ringing their bodies.

Eventually, the Baddiboo were driven off, and the West Indians spent an uneasy night on the shoreline, expecting to be attacked at any moment. British reinforcements arrived the next day. The troops burned two large towns, and yet the Baddiboo refused to capitulate. A second battle was fought at Sabba, where thousands of fighters had built a stockade with double walls. British artillery blasted the fortification as the infantry fought off attacks by cavalry and hordes of warriors on foot. Eventually the British forced their way into the stockade, breaking the will of the defenders, who surrendered and accepted a peace agreement.

★★★

At a time when tales of valiant British soldiers on the empire's distant frontiers were a staple of the British popular press, the exploits of the WIR in West Africa were ignored. Ellis, the WIR colonel and historian, said his men never appeared in the pages of British newspapers and magazines because they were black. He gloomily acknowledged that editors were simply recognising the commercial reality that stories of black soldiers did not sell publications. The 1st WIR's heroic defence of an isolated West African outpost in 1874 was only mentioned in the press because six white soldiers were part of the garrison – and they received all the credit despite playing a very minor role. It didn't help that the reading public usually only wanted to hear of African campaigns if they involved set-piece battles and dashing opponents like the Zulus in South Africa or the Dervishes of the Sudan. There is no way of knowing how the West Indian troops regarded the indifference of the people they were fighting and dying for or if they were even aware of it.

If the British public was blind to the exploits of their black West Indian troops, the British Army occasionally showed a modicum of gratitude. Two WIR men were the first black soldiers to win the Victoria Cross, the nation's highest gallantry medal. Samuel Hodge, a 26-year-old soldier from the British Virgin Islands, earned the coveted award in Gambia in 1866 during an attack on yet another well-fortified town. He and fourteen other men volunteered to cut a breach with axes in the settlement's main wall after the artillery failed to clear an opening. George Abbas Koolie D'Arcy, a former WIR officer who saw no reason to miss a fight despite having become the civilian governor of the territory, led the assault.

Nearly all of the men were killed and wounded as they hacked at the wall. Only Hodge, a private named Boswell and D'Arcy managed to force their way through. Boswell was killed and Hodge badly injured as they opened the main gate to admit the rest of the force and secure victory. Hodge was awarded the VC, only to die four months later from the horrific wounds he had suffered in the attack. Boswell went unrecognised because the VC could not be awarded posthumously at the time.

Lance Corporal William Gordon of Jamaica was the second West Indian soldier to win a VC when a small WIR detachment on the trail of a fugitive in 1891 stormed a fortified village where the man was being sheltered. When the party came under fire, Gordon saved Major George Madden from certain death by throwing himself in front of the officer, suffering a serious chest wound. His subsequent story was happier – he served in the 1st WIR for many years and was celebrated as a hero in his native Jamaica.

By the 1820s, the army was struggling to find soldiers for the WIR regiments. A steady flow of recruits were needed to replace battlefield losses and men worn out by illness or old age. Plans to enlist hundreds of American ex-slaves who had served with British forces during the War of 1812 or to find black recruits in Canada had to be abandoned for a lack of volunteers.

Slavery once again played a crucial role in the regiment's fortunes, even though the slave trade had been abolished in the British Empire in 1807. Following the ban, Royal Navy warships patrolled the African coast, intercepting slave ships and rescuing their human cargoes. It was decided to give the armed forces the pick of the freed males, with many going to the WIR to serve in Africa and the Caribbean. The inductees do not seem to have been given a choice.

Officials justified the practice as humane, saying the men would be 'civilised' and given a better life. Protests by church men and anti-slavery campaigners were ignored, even though army officers admitted that at least some of the men were unwilling recruits. Even if the British Government had wanted to return the captives to their homes, it would perhaps have been difficult because there often was no way of reaching the remote regions many of them came from. Simply freeing the captives likely would have exposed them to privation, attack and re-enslavement.

While most of the liberated slaves adapted to their new lives in the WIR, a few were determined to find their way back to Africa and their homes. In 1836, a batch of 300 ex-slaves rebelled in Trinidad after being inducted into the 1st WIR. The only other troops in the barracks at the time were the regimental band and a few orderlies. The revolt was led by Daaga, who had been named Donald Stewart by the regiment, which was still giving new men English names.

Daaga, a giant of a man and reputedly the son of an African ruler, had been selling captives to Portuguese slavers in Africa. The slavers double-crossed him and his men and sold them as slaves. He was rescued by the Royal Navy and pressed into the WIR. Charles Kingsley, the Victorian novelist and cleric, later wrote indignantly that Daaga was a 'cannibal' who had been 'made to swear allegiance to our sovereign on the Holy Evangelists and then called a British soldier'.[7]

While undergoing training in Trinidad, Daaga and his followers seized weapons, set buildings ablaze and riddled the officers' quarters with musket fire. The officers and a handful of loyal black soldiers held off the mutineers until reinforcements from a white regiment reached the barracks. Some of the mutineers made for the nearest town, where the mostly black local militia fought them off. About forty of the mutineers were killed before the revolt was suppressed.

Daaga and two lieutenants were sentenced to death. On the morning of their executions, the three men asked for a large breakfast, saying it was the custom of their nation. Guards were amazed as the trio ate voraciously. They were still wolfing down morsels when they were led out of their cells for the last time. A band played the 'Death March' as the prisoners, showing no fear, were paraded through the barracks with coffins carried

---

7    Charles Kingsley, *At Last, A Christmas in the West Indies*, p.59.

in front of them. Open graves waited beside three stakes at the execution site, where the surviving mutineers stood in ranks. An army chaplain read prayers and shook hands with the condemned men, after which they were tied to the stakes and shot by a firing squad. Apart from this incident, the WIR had a reputation for loyalty and devotion that exceeded that of most white regiments.

★★★

Britain's abolition of slavery in 1834 and the freeing of hundreds of thousands of slaves in the West Indies solved the WIR's recruiting problems forever. Thereafter, the regiment was sustained by a large and willing flow of volunteers. Army service was far easier than the back-breaking poverty faced by the great mass of landless ex-slaves. Men were lured by the WIR's reasonably good pay, clothing, rations and, as one recruiting notice put it, 'a still higher rank in society' and 'a footing of perfect equality' with white soldiers.

# 5

# GUARDIANS OF THE WEST

The enormous wealth of the sugar islands peaked just as British forces triumphed in the long struggle for mastery of the Caribbean. Almost overnight, the plantations that had made the West Indies such prized possessions were beset by a fatal combination of plummeting prices, competition and soil exhaustion. By the 1820s, a spiral of decay set in, ruining the once fabulously wealthy colonies. London came to see the West Indies, for which the lives of tens of thousands of soldiers and sailors had been sacrificed, as a worthless encumbrance, and begrudged every penny spent on them. Local defences were reduced to the flimsiest of fig leaves. Warnings in the 1870s that the largest and most important city in the region, Kingston, Jamaica, could be captured by a single gunboat brought only shrugs from imperial officials.

The guarding of British colonies in the Western Hemisphere during the nineteenth century was increasingly left to the West India Regiment. It had always been intended that the black regulars would be part of the Caribbean garrison, only now the army virtually abandoned the region, slashing the number of white units to a token presence.

Its new role in the West Indies and Africa confirmed the WIR's standing as the army's least prestigious unit – black and fit only for the most forsaken outposts. Predictably, the regiment found itself at the back of the queue for weapons, funds and everything else. It took eleven years for London to approve the modest cost of repairing the WIR's barracks in Trinidad after they were condemned as unfit for human habitation because the drains seeped raw sewerage and bred disease.

A key part of the WIR's duties was policing the slave population, and then helping maintain control over the black masses following the abolition of slavery in 1834. It won praise on many occasions from imperial officials and the white elite for its steely professionalism in these roles. There is no evidence that the black rank and file ever wavered in carrying out such duties. Army training and discipline bred loyalty to officers, the army and the government regardless of race or class and the closed world of the military instilled a sense of apartness from civilians. The pay and social standing, while paltry, were infinitely better than the grinding poverty endured by most black people. It was no different from the situation in Britain where an army made up overwhelmingly of men from the poorest depths of society upheld the power of the ruling elite in these years. If anything, the WIR earned a reputation for being more brutal than white troops in suppressing civil unrest.

Slave revolts roiled the West Indian settlements right up to the final days of slavery. Some 20,000 slaves rebelled in Barbados in 1816, burning scores of plantations, after rumours swept the island that planters were blocking government plans to abolish slavery. Martial law was declared, and the 1st WIR ordered to suppress the uprising.

A WIR column encountered thousands of poorly armed slaves lining the hills east of the capital, Bridgetown. A flag depicting a figure of a white king giving a crown to a black man fluttered over the slave ranks. To limit any bloodshed, Major James Cassidy ordered his men to disperse the insurgents at bayonet point rather than shoot them. This only enraged the slaves, whose leaders had promised that the black soldiers would never attack them, and they mobbed the troops, trying to grab their muskets. Cassidy gave the order to fire after one of his men was killed and seventeen wounded in the melee. Many of the slaves were shot down before the rest broke and fled. How many people were killed or wounded in the clash was never established. Once the black regulars had broken the main resistance, it was left to the white militia to inflict brutal and often indiscriminate reprisals on the slave population.

Even worse excesses were committed when some 30,000 slaves revolted in British Guiana in 1823. Here, too, rumours swept the slave quarters that planters were blocking government plans to end slavery. Thousands of insurgents who tried to march to the capital of Georgetown were dispersed by troops of the 1st WIR and the white 21st Regiment. Two additional companies of the 1st WIR were rushed from Barbados to help put down the insurgency. It was again left to the militia to carry out barbaric reprisals after the rising had been quelled. A visitor to the colony at the time dryly reported:

> The first sight I saw on coming in to the River, was the Fort set round with twenty or thirty Negroes' heads on poles, interspersed here and there with dead bodies hung in chains, and this was continued at intervals on most of the Estates up the Coast. Appropriate garniture to a Slave Colony.[1]

Officials in London and the local administration applauded the 1st WIR for its zeal in dealing with the slaves. A gift of 200 guineas was approved by the colony's planter-controlled legislature to purchase silver dishes to adorn the officers' mess.

One of the last slave uprisings in the British colonies took place in Jamaica in 1832. Some of the hapless insurgents believed that the WIR would liberate them; instead, the regiment unflinchingly helped suppress the revolt, earning the thanks of the island's white assembly. Benjamin M'Mahon, a planter who served with the white militia during the uprising, was appalled by the indiscriminate atrocities he witnessed being inflicted by his unit on helpless black men, women and children, many of whom had refused to take part in the revolt.

The militiamen were terrified, even though they were heavily armed while most of the insurgents had only machetes, clubs and sticks. Officers and men drank themselves senseless out of fear much of the time. Many black men and women were shot on sight, including those who had protected their white owners and their property from the insurgents. Militia men tortured them, looted their homes and took their livestock. 'On the very first night I had an opportunity of witnessing the courage of the valiant heroes of the militia who were as bold as lions when torturing the poor slaves with whips,' M'Mahon wrote.[2]

---

1   *Durbar*, Vol. 32, No. 2, Summer 2015, p.3.
2   M'Mahon, *Jamaica Plantership*, p.89.

In quieter times, WIR troops helped to police the slave populations in some colonies, manning guard posts and controlling the movement of slaves in rural areas. It was a system that worked well except for the soldiers' habit of forming relationships with local slave women, leading to friction with white owners and male slaves. Army officials suggested solving the problem by purchasing female slaves to marry to the best soldiers. It was argued that the troops would be inspired to excel in hopes of winning a wife, with the added bonus that any resulting children would be government property, the boys joining the regiment and the girls becoming military wives. However, cost rather than moral qualms prevented the scheme from being implemented.

On 31 July 1834 some 750,000 men, women and children were liberated in the British West Indies with the abolition of slavery. Little else changed in the settlements with the small white elite continuing to dominate almost every aspect of life. Bereft of rights and land, most black people faced a new form of bondage as desperately poor labourers and peasant farmers. Many whites still feared that the black majority might rebel at any moment. The WIR and local militias, increasingly made up of black and mixed-race men as poorer whites left the islands to find a better life, were the first line of defence against potential disorder. This change in the militia reflected the emergence of a small class of better-off black and mixed-race people who saw maintaining law and order as vital to their interests.

For all the whites' apprehension, the black population was remarkably peaceful following the end of slavery, with just occasional unrest. Dominica was shaken by riots in 1844 after rumours that black people were to be re-enslaved; Jamaica saw a number of violent protests in the 1840s and 1850s against tolls and other taxes; and several colonies were shaken by riots over poverty, lack of work, and demands from the black locals for land to farm. Civilian officials and military commanders across the West Indies lauded the WIR for its vigour and toughness in dealing with the unrest.

In 1867, a parliamentary committee in London examining the use of colonial troops asked if the WIR could be relied upon to put down black disorder. Colonial Office officials said the troops were absolutely loyal. Their only qualm was that the men were, if anything, more brutal than white soldiers in such situations. A Governor of Jamaica told the committee he had used the WIR to deal with unrest three times, and his only concern also had been its propensity for excessive force despite the fact most of the men were from the island and had close ties to the black population. He asserted:

My belief [is] that it would be difficult to find troops who not only display a more thorough and even ardent desire to execute their duty upon occasions in which they are brought in contact with the population of their own colour, but whom it is on such occasions more necessary to control and restrain in order to prevent unnecessary violence and bloodshed.[3]

Black West Indians feared the WIR far more than any white regiment, he added.

If the West Indies were largely peaceful in the decades after slavery, what started as a local altercation at Morant Bay in Jamaica became one of the most notorious incidents in the history of the British Empire. By the 1860s, the largest of the British islands was wracked by poverty, discontent and racial tension. Food prices were high and work scarce as the sugar industry continued to decline. Governor John Eyre dismissed pleas for government aid for the poor, accusing the black population of laziness and failing to help themselves.

In October 1865, a crowd of some 400 black locals clashed with white officials and militia in Morant Bay, an isolated town in the east of the island. They had marched to the town to protest after police had tried to arrest one of their leaders. Most of the white militiamen were bookkeepers and overseers from the local plantations with little military experience. Some barely knew how to load a musket, and they were easily overwhelmed by the poorly armed crowd. About twenty officials and militiamen were slaughtered with just a few survivors escaping into the bush.

Unrest spread rapidly through the area. Local radical black leaders saw it as the start of a race war and urged black soldiers and police to join what they proclaimed as a rebellion to end white domination. Insurgents drilled and paraded with fervent chants of 'cleave to the black' and 'colour for colour'.

Eyre's first response to reports of the incident was to dispatch 100 men of the 1st WIR to retake control of Morant Bay: whatever the insurgents thought, the governor had no doubts about the loyalty of the black regulars. Detachments of the 1st WIR and the white 6th Regiment launched a campaign of wholesale repression at Morant Bay, indiscriminately killing and beating any black people they came across, including many innocent ones who had not played any role in the unrest. One black WIR drummer

---

3   TNA/PRO CO 137/353/18.

was said to have executed six prisoners. Lieutenant Colonel Thomas Hobbs of the 6th boasted, 'I … adopted a plan which struck immense terror into these wretched men, far more than death, which is I caused them to hang each other. They entreat to be shot to avoid this.'[4]

Eyre said the insurgents must have had outside help, insisting that the black population were ignorant savages incapable of thinking, let alone acting on their own. He ordered the arrest of George Gordon, a wealthy mixed-race member of the legislature, and a persistent critic of the governor's harsh treatment of the poor. Gordon was seized in Kingston, taken to Morant Bay, tried by a military tribunal and hanged beside some of the insurgent leaders despite a total lack of evidence that he had anything to do with the uprising.

His execution and the killing of some 430 black men and women by the military and the flogging of another 600 caused outrage in Britain. The controversy split mid-Victorian society, with many of the most prominent figures of the age lining up to denounce or defend Eyre. Subsequent efforts to charge the governor with murder were unsuccessful, and he disappeared into a quiet retirement in England.

Several army officers, including two from the WIR, faced court martials on various charges of wantonly shooting and hanging black people. However, all of the accused men were acquitted, and the Jamaica legislature showed its appreciation of the WIR's steadfastness with the customary gift of silver plate for the officers' mess.

The regiment took immense pride in its unflinching loyalty and ruthlessness. A regimental historian wrote soon after:

> The fidelity of the black soldiers of the 1st West India Regiment could hardly have been put to a more crucial test. Nine-tenths of those men were Jamaicans, born and bred, and in the work of suppressing the rebellion they were required to hang, capture and destroy the habitations of not only their own countrymen and friends, but, in many instances, of their near relatives. Yet in no single case did any man hesitate to obey orders, nor was the loyalty of any one soldier ever a matter for doubt.[5]

---

4  Dyde, *The Empty Sleeve*, p.179.
5  Ellis, *The History of the First West India Regiment*, p.194.

Although the WIR was increasingly seen as indispensable by white legislators and officials, many white West Indians still could not bear the idea of a black man in a British Army uniform.

A series of incidents in the Cayman Islands vividly illustrated this mordant antipathy. A detachment of the 2nd WIR arrived in 1834 to garrison the islands and support the civil authorities. White residents responded by persecuting the black soldiers and demanding their replacement with white troops. False charges of theft and rape, punishable by death, were levied against some of the soldiers, and others were insulted and attacked in the streets as they tried to carry out their duties.

In a typical incident, a magistrate called Evan Parsons was riding down the road on a horse when he encountered a WIR detachment marching in single file. He demanded the soldiers clear the way for him. The corporal in charge replied politely that there was plenty of room for Parsons to ride past. Parsons angrily asked why the corporal had not saluted him, to which the man said army rules stipulated only officers should be saluted. Cursing, Parsons rode his horse at the troops, lashing at the men with a whip when they seized the animal's bridle to avoid being trampled. Parsons tried to have the soldiers charged with assault, demanding that the 'African barbarians [be] withdrawn from this Island, and a hundred white men sent in their place'.[6]

Cayman officials were emphatic that the blame for everything that had happened lay entirely with the white residents, and the troops had shown extraordinary forbearance despite constant provocations. Nonetheless, it was decided to withdraw the WIR detachment to avoid further trouble.

★★★

While Britain did not fight any wars in the Caribbean after 1815, the WIR was involved in a number of confrontations in Latin America. Some of the incidents were mere sabre rattling, such as the Pirara Expedition in 1842 when a detachment of the 1st WIR was sent to the remote southwestern border of British Guiana after reports of Brazilian incursions. Brazilian troops were occupying the settlement of Pirara when the West Indians arrived, and rejected demands to leave. An officer was sent back to

---

6  Quoted in Kieran, *The Lawless Caymanas*, p.51.

Georgetown to seek instructions as the WIR dug in facing the Brazilians. Weeks passed during which the West Indians' supplies ran out, and the soldiers were close to starving when reinforcements arrived with orders to assert British sovereignty. War was averted when the now outnumbered Brazilians pulled back across the frontier.

The WIR was involved in a more serious conflict in British Honduras. Fighting in neighbouring Mexico between settlers and the indigenous native peoples periodically spilled across the frontier. The West Indians were sent to guard the border and preserve British neutrality. Things were fairly quiet until bands of native fighters began raiding British Honduras in the late 1860s, leading to occasional clashes with British forces.

The defence of the town of Orange Walk by a small detachment of the 1st WIR on 1 September 1872 won a modest place in British military history. The settlement, with a population of 1,200 residents, was the main administrative and commercial centre in northern British Honduras. A band of some 200 indigenous raiders from Mexico, under their chief, the renowned leader Marcus Canul, staged a surprise attack on the town. Most of the raiders surrounded the barracks and its small West Indian garrison of two white officers and thirty-eight black soldiers.

The first the troops knew of the attack was when volleys of rifle fire tore into the main building, a crude wooden structure with a thatch roof. Lieutenant Joseph Smith and Assistant Surgeon John Edge were bathing outside when the shooting began and had to run virtually naked across bullet-swept ground to the main building. Smith then realised he had left the key for the magazine in his quarters. He and Sergeant Edward Belizario dashed through intense fire to retrieve the key. With extraordinary bravery, Belizario rushed to the magazine and retrieved the ammunition as dozens of bullets narrowly missed him.

Several attempts by the raiders to burn the barracks and flush out the garrison failed, although Smith was badly wounded. Two American ranchers, who heard the gunfire and rode to the scene, attacked the raiders from the rear, and used the ensuing confusion to reach the main building. Fighting went on for almost six hours until the attackers suddenly retreated.

Reinforcements did not reach the area until three days later, by which time the raiders had re-crossed the border. At least fifty of the attackers were killed and an unknown number wounded; Canul was among the injured, dying a few days later. Two of the West Indian soldiers were killed and fourteen wounded. Hundreds of bullet holes were counted in the flimsy barrack walls.

Belizario and two other men were awarded the Distinguished Conduct Medal (DCM) and the officers received promotions. In a letter to *The Times* of London, a white colonist praised the black soldiers' valour, and asked why the military was much quicker to reward white troops:

> I have nothing to say but what redounds to their credit and high character as British soldiers: and if medals and crosses were distributed among the dusky warriors of Her Majesty's land forces in this part of her dominions as freely as among other branches of the service, all I can say is that every one of the brave fellows, who held with such determined valour and tenacity the barracks at Orange Walk on that memorable Sunday morning against such fearful odds, would be entitled to a medal at least.[7]

---

7    Quoted in Ellis, p.205.

## 6

# BLACK AND NOT BLACK ENOUGH

Major General Garnet Wolseley was the rising star of the British Army in 1873. This prophet of progress and all things modern also had a deep contempt for black West Indian soldiers, branding them as weak, lazy, cowardly 'mongrels'. It was the West India Regiment's misfortune that Wolseley commanded the British Army's most famous campaign in West Africa in the nineteenth century. The Victorian public, which had never cared much about West Africa or the West Indian troops who defended their interests there, was spellbound when their favourite general made a lightning appearance in the region. His triumph with a handful of white regiments lent credence to the fashionable racial theories of the time that degraded the West Indians for being both black and not black enough.

Wolseley was handed the task of subduing the Ashanti kingdom, the dominant African power in the Gold Coast, which had inflicted several humiliating reverses on the British over the years. The aggressive and restless Ashanti power emerged in the early eighteenth century, conquering and subsuming dozens of weaker states and tribes. Its formidable might rested on a military machine that was capable of fielding tens of thousands of warriors supported by an excellent logistics system and a medical arm to care for the wounded and retrieve the dead. Ashanti rulers regarded the British and other European settlers on the coast as mere tenants who they tolerated for the sake of trade. Their disdain was not always unjustified.

In 1823, Sir Charles MacCarthy, then Governor of the British Coastal Outposts, resolved to humble the Ashanti. Sir Charles was a tall and dashing figure whose towering faith in British superiority was matched only by the depths of his own silliness. He was convinced that he could crush the Ashanti almost single-handed and set out to invade their kingdom with just 500 white troops and African tribal auxiliaries.

Things began to go awry as soon as the forlorn force blundered into the interior. Blinding rain buffeted the little army, turning the narrow jungle tracks into ribbons of mud in which the men sank up to their thighs. The column's porters, who had a much better idea of Ashanti prowess than their white chief, began to desert, leaving the column short of food and other supplies. Sir Charles' spirits only rose as his men's morale plummeted.

On 22 January 1824, the soldiers encountered the entire Ashanti army advancing with drums beating and horns blaring, its generals striding along under huge ceremonial umbrellas denoting their rank. Scouts put the Ashanti strength at 10,000 warriors. Sir Charles was not in the least dismayed, despite the terror of his troops. He had convinced himself somehow that the Ashanti would be cowed into submission by a mere demonstration of British moral superiority.

Serenely confident, the governor commanded the military band he had brought along to play 'God Save the King', insisting that it would bring the Ashanti to their knees. As the terrified musicians raggedly bleated out the first notes of the anthem, the Ashanti fired a thunderous musket volley and charged. Only a handful of British officers and soldiers survived the ensuing massacre. Sir Charles was decapitated, and his skull taken back to the Ashanti capital at Kumasi as a trophy to be paraded annually with other national treasures.

A larger force of 2,000 men, which Sir Charles had unwisely detailed to approach the Ashanti domains by another route, fled back to the coast. Despite this stunning affront to British prestige, London uncharacteristically decided against striking back, eventually signing a peace treaty with the Ashanti that settled nothing.

A second clash with the Ashanti in 1863 did not go much better. An Ashanti army attacked the British coastal settlements after officials refused to surrender some fugitives from the royal court. British reinforcements were summoned, including 1,600 men from all of the five West India Regiments then in service; it was one of those rare moments when the regiment fielded a large force. Two companies of the 1st WIR were sent deep into the jungle to guard supply dumps being readied for an attack on the Ashanti kingdom once the rainy season was over. For three months, the West Indians endured torrential rain with little or no shelter, unable to stay dry or cook food. Half of the 200 men went down with fever and thirty died, before the detachment was forced to return to the coast, abandoning large stocks of weapons, ammunition and supplies. Again, London decided to quietly drop the matter, and the Ashanti claimed another triumph.

A far more serious confrontation erupted in the early 1870s when the Dutch sold their coastal outposts in the Gold Coast to Britain. This brought protests from the Ashanti, who said the Dutch, as their tenants, had no right to transfer ownership without permission. An Ashanti army attacked the coast in 1872, inflicting defeats on pro-British tribes and abducting some Christian missionaries. West Indian troops were instrumental in holding off the far larger Ashanti forces, which finally withdrew after being decimated by small pox and dysentery. British Government ministers were left in a quandary as to how to respond. West Africa was a fever-ridden backwater and a drain on the imperial exchequer; the last thing London wanted was to possess more of it by conquering the Ashanti kingdom. 'It is to be hoped that no Government will be mad enough to embark on so extravagant a policy,' the colonial secretary wrote.[1] And yet, it would be a terrible loss of face if the Ashanti were allowed to continue besting the British Empire whenever they felt like it.

After a fair amount of hand wringing, the government decided that prestige outweighed pragmatism, and the Ashanti must pay in blood for challenging British supremacy. It had to be done as cheaply as possible, with ministers insisting that white troops were to be used only as a very last resort: the government was haunted by memories of the armies wiped out by disease in the West Indies in the previous century. A minor miracle was needed, so Garnet Wolseley was summoned in August 1873 as the man who would undoubtedly deliver one.

Wolseley was an unlikely general in an army dominated by the landed elite and imbued with a deep distrust of anything that smacked of 'braininess' such as reading books. The son of an Irish shop owner, he became the youngest general in the army by sheer force of intelligence, determination

---

1   Quoted in Bond, *Victorian Military Campaigns*, p.177.

and relentless energy, along with a great deal of bravery on the battlefield. He was sent to the Gold Coast with thirty officers and instructions to crush the Ashanti threat with local forces, including the West Indian soldiers who had been fighting them for longer than any other British unit.

Wolseley had no intention of staking his reputation on leading black soldiers. Like most Victorians, the general possessed an iron faith that whites were inherently superior to blacks in every way, and white soldiers would always defeat black adversaries no matter how numerous or warlike. And he had a particular contempt for West Indians, asserting they were useless as soldiers. He told the War Office:

> In the first place, the moral effect of their presence upon the Ashantis is not to be compared with that which a similar number of Europeans would exert; and, in the next place, they are not physically by any means as capable of withstanding the climate, still less exertion and fatigue.[2]

It was one of the most ridiculous statements ever made by a British general. Wolseley's assertion that troops fresh from Europe could outdo seasoned West Indian soldiers with years of experience in African conditions contradicted all the painful lessons that the British military had learned in the tropics.

Britain's best general wanted only the best to burnish his reputation, however, and that meant elite white regiments rather than a motley force of black soldiers. White soldiers were indispensable, Wolseley kept telling London and in the end, he was given three of the army's finest units: the 2nd Battalion Rifle Brigade, the Royal Welch Fusiliers and the Black Watch. Wolseley begrudgingly accepted the 1st and 2nd WIRs and some local African units, intending to use them only as labourers.

Despite his racial bigotry, Wolseley was an excellent strategist and administrator. He and his coterie of handpicked staff officers swiftly devised a plan to defeat the Ashanti, despite arriving in Africa with virtually no knowledge of the region and its people. Minutely detailed plans covered everything from building a road and bridges to take the army straight to Kumasi, down to designing loose tropical clothing and the loads each man would carry. Everything was to be ready so that when the white battalions landed, they

---

2   Dyde, *The Empty Sleeve*, p.200.

could march straight to the Ashanti heartlands, thrash the enemy and get back to the coast in three months before the onset of the rainy season and the deadly fevers that accompanied it. Wolseley assigned the two West Indian regiments to guard his supply lines.

After weeks of hectic preparation the force set off into the bush in late January 1874. Clashes erupted almost as soon as British units started moving up the newly cleared route into the interior. Ashanti forces moving unseen through the bush harassed the columns and supplies soon became a critical problem. Virtually everything the force needed had to be carried by thousands of porters, who deserted at the first sign of the Ashanti. Wolseley, facing the collapse of his supply chain, asked the 2nd WIR to act as porters. Some saw this as a racist slight because only a black battalion was employed in this way. However, the regiment's historian disagreed, seeing it as a vital task. 'This duty the men volunteered for, and did it cheerfully and well,' he wrote.[3]

West Indian soldiers slogged through the jungle under loads of 50lb or more, as well as their rifles and equipment. Food became so scarce that the West Indians were put on half-rations, despite the gruelling labour. British officers, meanwhile, rounded up men from the local tribes and forced them to work as porters; villages that refused to provide men were burned. Soon the army had enough bearers, and the 2nd WIR returned to guarding the lines of communication.

Ashanti resistance was far greater than Wolseley had anticipated. White soldiers did not seem to frighten the Africans in the least, despite the fond Victorian belief that black Africans were cowed by the mere sight of an Englishman – the so-called 'moral effect'. Ashanti bands repeatedly attacked the British with their usual fearlessness, lunging out of the bush again and again to strike at the lumbering columns.

After a few days, Wolseley received a report that the Ashanti were falling back across the Prah River. He asked for volunteers to see if this was true. To venture deep into Ashanti territory on such a mission carried a high risk of being captured and tortured to death. Two men of the 2nd WIR, remembered only as Privates Fagan and Lewis, volunteered for the mission. For 25 miles they trekked through the jungle, coming across signs of large

---

3   Caulfield, *100 Years' History of the 2nd West Indian Regiment 1795 to 1898*, p.169.

Ashanti war bands everywhere. It was a nerve-wracking trek; every tree or bush could conceal warriors who would seize and kill them in an instant.

Finally, the two soldiers reached the river and saw definite signs that the main Ashanti force had pulled back over it. Fearing that the word of two black men would not be accepted, Fagan and Lewis wrote their names on a piece of paper and tacked it to a tree to prove they had reached the river, before returning to the army to report their findings. British patrols later found the note, and the two scouts were given medals for their bravery with many white officers saying their exploit was one of the most courageous acts of the entire campaign.

Such courage and the selfless dedication of the West Indians in carrying out any task they were given did not alter Wolseley's scathing views of black troops. When the army reached the abandoned Ashanti capital on 4 February, he ensured that detachments from all of the white regiments were there to share the honour, purposely excluding the West Indians. It was a terrible affront that was felt deeply by the WIR's officers and men. The regimental historian later wrote:

> Great was the disappointment felt ... when the news arrived that Coomassie [Kumasi] had fallen, and that the regiment which had borne the brunt of the campaign for eight months were not allowed to participate in the honour of entering it; the regiment deserved better treatment than it got on this occasion.[4]

Wolseley and his white regiments were lionised by the British public and press after the campaign. The West Indians, when they were mentioned at all in news reports, were invariably portrayed as part of the exotic African scenery or comic caricatures rather than as British regulars. Wolseley tossed the WIR a few crumbs of half-hearted praise in his final dispatch on the campaign, albeit for their work as porters.

Queen Victoria was more generous, making a point of recognising the WIR as the equals of her white soldiers. The men were told they had earned 'in common with the European troops, Her Majesty's approbation'.[5] And

---

4    Caulfield, p.171.
5    Caulfield, p.178.

while it missed the final battle, the WIR was given the Ashanti battle honour to add to its laurels.

At least they were hailed as heroes in the West Indies. The 2nd WIR was feted when it returned to Barbados. Triumphal arches, streamers, flowers and bunting adorned buildings and shops in Bridgetown to honour a regiment now regarded as the colony's 'own'. Banners proclaimed, 'Welcome home' and 'Hurrah for the Gallant 2nd West India'. Crowds of white and black residents cheered, and church bells rang as the troops marched through the town to be welcomed by the governor before the entire regiment was treated to a banquet.[6]

Wolseley was far from alone in his contempt for West Indian and other black troops. Notions that non-whites were inferior and primitive were blithely accepted, despite their essential role in holding up the empire. Such views were part of contemporary social-Darwinian theories that viewed humanity as a racial pyramid with white Anglo-Saxons perched at the apex above descending strata of increasingly darker, and therefore inferior, races. Colour and race were deemed to determine everything from intelligence to honesty. The darker a race or nation, the less able, worthy or moral it was likely to be judged.

Few groups in Victorian Britain embraced these notions more fervently than the army, despite spending much of its time fighting native peoples on the frontiers of the empire, so it should have known better. Military theorists evolved the concept of 'martial races', which linked fighting ability to race, tribe and clan. Whites were deemed the best soldiers, followed by groups such as Sikhs or Pathans with their lighter, more European features, while the darkest races fell into the lowest, least martial category.

There was a profound prejudice against mixed-race people, who were disparaged as the runts of humanity – physically, mentally and morally degenerate because of the supposedly corrupting mix of blood and race in their veins. It was commonly held that interracial breeding produced offspring with all of the defects and none of the strengths of white and black. Long after the Ashanti campaign, Wolseley claimed in a popular journal that West Indians had been corrupted by interracial breeding. He said the West Indian regiments had been excellent in the early days when their ranks were filled with African slaves. Their 'mental faculties were

---

6   TNA/PRO CO 321/1.

little superior to the apes', he wrote in 1888, but they made good fighters because they retained 'the natural instinct of the savage from the interior of Africa'.[7] All that had changed, he claimed, because extensive interracial breeding in the Caribbean had produced soldiers who lacked the fighting qualities of their African forebears without augmenting it with the superior abilities of whites.

It was a common view, even in the West Indies, despite abundant evidence to the contrary. A government official in Barbados told the Colonial Office in the same year that the WIR's reputation as a fighting unit had declined in recent years, and that many put this down to extensive recruiting of mixed-race men, and 'in consequence the recruits are not of pure negro blood'.[8]

This racial degradation was made worse in the eyes of most military men by the efforts of missionaries and other 'do-gooders' to 'civilise' the empire's non-white subjects. Educating or Westernising any native troops, not just West Indians, was seen by many officers as the surest way to make them worthless as fighting men: they held that black troops could never benefit from book learning because it eroded their savage temperaments and it was absurd to imagine natives could benefit from education. It was rarely, if ever, pointed out that such views made a mockery of the vaunted claim that civilising the 'lesser races' was the prime justification of British imperialism.

While Wolseley dressed his prejudice in pseudo-scientific terms, the crudest forms of racial hatred were pervasive among white officers and soldiers. Some of the WIR's white officers were among the vilest bigots. An 1863 article in the *St James Magazine* penned anonymously by an WIR officer accused the black rank and file of being liars, dishonest, treacherous, promiscuous, immoral, cruel and filthy. 'I do not think it would be easy to find in the whole world a more degraded race, morally, than the West Indian negroes,' he wrote.[9]

All too typical of the racism within the WIR's ranks was E. Craig Brown, an otherwise kind, gregarious and enthusiastic young officer who joined the regiment in Jamaica in 1895. He was popular in the officers' mess for his cheerfulness and skill with the bagpipes at social events. Brown loved

---

7    Garnet Wolseley, 'The Negro as a Soldier', p.689.

8    TNA/PRO CO 28/220.

9    'P.', 'Blacks', *St James Magazine*, vii (1863), p.46.

everything about his new life except the black troops. Of his own platoon, he wrote, 'They really are the rottenest lot of sneaky, lazy brutes I ever came across.'[10] In a torrent of spiteful letters to family and friends in Britain, he complained that black soldiers were barely human, incapable of mastering any task more demanding than digging ditches, and unable to remember or comprehend the smallest thing or march properly. He wrote, in a typical outburst:

> I am mortally sick of the negro and everything connected to him. A nicer lot of officers to live with than the W.I.R. fellows [officers] just now I could not well wish for but the native NCOs and men are little removed from the ape.[11]

Brown transferred to a white unit after a few years, and eventually rose to the rank of brigadier general. Everyone continued to think that he was a tremendously kind and friendly chap.

The WIR had struggled from its earliest days to find white officers because of the stigma of commanding black troops, a problem that only grew as racial prejudice became ever more embedded in the imperial psyche. It was widely seen in the army as degrading work that only the most desperate or least respectable officer would accept. A young man who wrote to the War Office in 1860 enquiring about obtaining a commission was told that because of the huge number of applicants his chances were virtually non-existent unless he opted for the WIR, in which case he was likely to get a position almost immediately.

WIR officers had a reputation for being the worst scoundrels and social misfits in the army. A parliamentary committee studying colonial forces in 1867 was told by Edward B. De Fonblanque, a former WIR officer, that the main problem was alcoholism:

> It is an unfortunate fact that the officers of the West India regiments generally drink harder than any other class of officer. I remember meeting one officer who told me that he was the survivor of a batch of 11, who

---

10  E. Craig Brown, Imperial War Museum Document, 1862.
11  E. Craig Brown, Imperial War Museum Document, 1862.

went out to the West Coast of Africa, and with the exception of two who were transported, the others had all died of delirium tremens.

Asked what was meant by 'transportation', he said the two had been convicted of crimes and sent away.

Such derogatory opinions were shared by most of the army, and yet the WIR had a few ardent and influential supporters. Queen Victoria's husband, Prince Albert, was an admirer of the black infantry. Presenting the 2nd WIR with new colours in 1862, he expressed 'every confidence that wherever it may be called upon to maintain the honour of England they will be borne with that gallantry which is at all times displayed by the British army'.[12] A contingent of the WIR attended Queen Victoria's 1897 Jubilee in London, and the monarch was introduced to William Gordon of the regiment, who had won the VC in Africa.

Lieutenant General Sir Charles Pearson, who was Commander-in-Chief in the West Indies in the 1880s, praised the WIR, saying Britain could not hold West Africa without the regiment. His only qualm was that the men did not have 'well-shaped legs', although he added that this did not impede their marching ability.[13]

Sir Henry Campbell-Bannerman, a future prime minister, hailed the WIR in the House of Commons in 1895, 'Its gallantry and endurance have stood every test: the whole Army may well be proud of their comrades in the West India regiment.'[14]

Few British regiments had a more passionate champion than Colonel A.B. Ellis, who commanded the 1st WIR in the 1890s, led it in battle, and wrote a history of the regiment. In Ellis' eyes, the British Empire had no finer troops:

> The English-speaking negro of the West Indies is most excellent material for a soldier. He is docile, patient, brave and faithful, and for an officer who knows how to gain his affection – an easy matter, requiring only justness, good temper, and an ear ready to listen patiently to any tale or real or imaginary grievance – he will do anything.[15]

---

12  Ellis, *The History of the First West India Regiment*, p.15.
13  *United Services Magazine*, June 1894.
14  TNA/PRO CO 321/1.
15  Ellis, p.15.

Ellis waged a lonely campaign for his beloved West Indians to be used to garrison huge swathes of the British Empire, saying no other troops were better suited to the task. However, he fatally damaged his cause when he assailed the much-admired Indian Army and called for West Indian soldiers to take over the garrisoning of India. He argued:

> In India, the native army consists of men hostile to us by tradition, creed, and race, who consider their food defiled if even the shadow of a British officer should chance to fall across it, and assuredly it would be as safe a proceeding to garrison our colonies with English negroes as to garrison India with such men.[16]

While the champions and critics of native soldiers would go on firing verbal salvos at each other in regimental messes and the press, it was widely accepted by the middle of the nineteenth century that Britain must never field non-white troops against white opponents. In 1855, the 2nd WIR volunteered to serve in the Crimean War at a time when the British Army was desperate for reinforcements. Its colonel proudly told London 'that should they be required, I feel confident this complete regiment to the number of 1,078 bayonets will not be found wanting'.[17] The offer was dismissed with a curt note of thanks without being considered seriously.

This marked a reversal from the days when the WIR had been used against white French and American forces without hesitation. It was now held that British prestige would be severely damaged if it used black troops to wage war on whites. Some commentators claimed using black soldiers would make warfare more savage; others warned that Britain's black troops would turn on her if they got the idea they could fight and defeat whites; and yet others said that Britain had an ethical duty to fight its own wars against white foes, and that using black soldiers would be a sign of moral decay.

The Crimean War touched the WIR, despite not being allowed to fight the Russians. The dashing uniforms of France's North African Zouave troops in the campaign caught the imagination of Queen Victoria and many of her subjects. It was decided that Britain must have its own Zouaves – a feat

---

16  Ellis, p.15.
17  Caulfield, p.108.

the army handily achieved by adopting their uniform of a red fez, scarlet sleeveless jackets and baggy blue trousers for the WIR. Some saw it as a compliment to the WIR, and it was generally agreed that the uniform was better for tropical conditions. Others saw it as yet another slight, reducing the West Indians to comic opera buffoons. It was telling that the WIR's officers continued to wear normal British Army uniforms.

Government ministers gave explicit instructions that black troops were not to be used in the Boer War for fear of damaging British prestige. Arthur Conan-Doyle, the creator of Sherlock Holmes, who penned a history of the conflict, grandiloquently summed up the general view of the government and the public, 'This was to be a white man's war, and if the British could not work out their own salvation then it were well that empire pass from such a race.'[18]

A plan by British commanders in South Africa to employ the WIR to guard Boer prisoners of war was blocked by the War Office, despite the army's pleas that white troops could not be spared for the task. Lord Roberts, the British Commander-in-Chief in South Africa, was told in April 1900, 'It is undesirable on political grounds that the Boer prisoners should be put in custody of black soldiers.'[19] This caused problems in Bermuda, where the 1st WIR was part of the garrison when some 4,000 Boer POWs were sent to the colony. General Sir Digby Barker, the governor, was horrified at the idea of black troops guarding white prisoners, despite the fact the Boers were the avowed enemies of the empire and Britain had no more loyal soldiers than its West Indian regulars. A white unit was assigned to guard the POW camps.

★★★

The debate on race and the military spilled into the West Indies, where black locals were playing an increasingly important role in local militia and volunteer defence units as the number of white colonists dwindled. By the end of the nineteenth century, a few of these forces had the first black officers in the British forces – officers with the same authority and standing

---

18 Quoted in John Mitcham, *Race and Imperial Defence in the British World, 1870–1914,* p.79.

19 TNA/PRO WO 108/399.

as their white counterparts, including authority over white soldiers. These units were under the control of local legislatures and officials, some of whom were sympathetic to black emancipation or accepted that concessions had to be made to the aspirations of a growing black middle class.

Few in the regular army could stomach the idea of black officers, even in local colonial units. A general inspecting the Barbados Volunteer Force in 1909 wrote a damning report on the unit, 'It is essentially a colour corps and handled by coloured men'.[20] He was particularly scathing about the black commanding officer, Captain Reece, a prominent local lawyer and member of the legislature, dismissing him as 'a native'.[21] He recommended the immediate dismissal of all black personnel from any positions of responsibility. It brought an angry response from the white governor, who said Captain Reece was highly respected and the unit's white officers and NCOs admired him and were happy to serve under him. The governor deplored the regular army's 'antipathy to the black race', adding that the black population was the backbone of the island and the British administration could not function without them.[22]

A call from London in 1909 to form exclusively white militia units in the West Indies because of possible threats to public order from the 'excitable negro population' met a similar rebuke from white officials in Jamaica, who said local police and the WIR were as reliable as white troops in any situation. The island administration responded:

Properly trained and paid black policemen or soldiers are as trustworthy in encounters with their own race as white or coloured men, and have not the slightest colour prejudice or compunction. Rather the contrary; they particularly enjoy being set in authority among their fellows [and] … pride themselves, as being the lawful embodiment of the power of the State, against all offenders, irrespective of class, colour or condition.[23]

Relations between the WIR and the army's white regiments progressively deteriorated during the nineteenth century. Like their officers, the white rank and file looked down on non-white troops, whether Indian, African,

---

20 TNA/PRO CO 28/273.
21 TNA/PRO CO 28/273.
22 TNA/PRO CO 28/273.
23 TNA/PRO Cab 9/11.

Chinese or West Indian. Many white rankers had a particular contempt for black troops. Not unnaturally, the WIR's rank and file, who emphatically regarded themselves as British soldiers in every sense, bitterly resented the attitude of their ostensible comrades in arms.

The killing of Private Uriah Pritchard of the 1st WIR in Barbados in 1904 illustrated how poisonous relations sometimes became. A detachment of the 1st WIR was based in the same barracks as the Worcestershire Regiment. On 1 May, Private Luke Bannister of the Worcesters reported he had been stoned by some WIR men as he stood guard. Sergeant George Davis, who was in command of the guard, summoned the duty officer, Lieutenant D'Arcy Kay. Leaving some men outside the WIR's quarters, Kay, Davis and Private George Barnes entered the building. Accounts of what ensued differed greatly between the two regiments. The West Indians said that most of them were in bed when the three whites entered and woke a corporal. They also claimed that Kay instructed Davis to shoot anyone who approached, and that Barnes subsequently shot Pritchard on the veranda outside the sleeping quarters.

Pritchard gave the police a death-bed statement that he heard a noise and went to investigate. He said he saw a white officer talking to the WIR corporal and then glimpsed a white soldier on the veranda with a bayonetted rifle. Pritchard said he walked past the man with the rifle, later identified as Barnes, who challenged him with the words, 'You black bastard'.[24] Pritchard turned and looked silently at him. Barnes then raised his rifle and shot Pritchard, the latter testified, and then shot him a second time.

Kay, Davis and Barnes were arrested and indicted for murder. At their trial, Barnes testified he had seen some WIR men run into a room after Kay and Davis. Looking through the blinds, he saw the men surrounding the two whites and one of the black soldiers seizing the sergeant by the throat. Dashing into the room to help, Barnes said he saw several WIR soldiers pointing rifles at Kay and Davis. Barnes claimed when he told the WIR men to back off, they turned on him and he fired because he was convinced that he and the other whites were in serious danger. The three whites ran to the guard room as a group of about thirty WIR men smashed up a hut.

---

24  TNA/PRO CO 28/263.

An all-white grand jury refused to send the three white soldiers to trial and they were released. The army put the blame for the incident entirely on the WIR. Army commanders discussed charging the WIR men involved in the incident with perjury. However, the colony's governor urged that the matter be dropped because of the risk of inciting racial tension on the island. The incident, nonetheless, was an unsettling insight into the racial animosity between white and black soldiers of the same army.

# 7

# CLASH OF EMPIRES

Even as the British Army became ever less willing to tolerate a black formation in its ranks, the soldiers of the West India Regiment were fighting and
dying in some of the most terrible campaigns in the annals of colonial warfare. Among them was the strangest battle in the regiment's long history – a
clash on Christmas Eve 1893 in the unmapped wilds of West Africa with its
old adversary the French Army.

Samori Toure was a Muslim warlord who carved out an empire in central Africa in the 1870s. Little was known about where Samori came from:
some accounts claimed he was the son of a poor peddler, others that he
was a holy man who simply emerged one day from the desert. Whatever
the truth, Samori was driven by a harsh fundamentalist vision and possessed the iron will to impose it on hundreds of thousands of people. He
was a charismatic leader, brilliant administrator and gifted military commander who assembled an army of 30,000 well-armed and zealous troops
known as 'Sofas'. His domains, reaching from the Sahara to the west coast,
were financed largely by ivory, gold and slaves. Samori's imperial ambitions
led him into a protracted war with France, which was carving out its own
empire in the region.

British authorities in Sierra Leone began receiving reports in the early
1890s of Sofa raids on the colony's remote northern frontier regions. Sierra
Leone's governor, Sir Francis Fleming, was a finicky man who liked to be
photographed sitting in his ceremonial uniform on a carpet of leopard

skins. The fact that he presided over one of the most flyblown backwaters of the empire in no way diminished his sense of self-importance.

Fleming, who had spent his career working in legal departments in other parts of the empire, had little experience of Africa. He dismissed the reports of raids on the border, insisting that the area was peaceful. It was no secret that the British authorities, who were aware of Sofa strength and Sierra Leone's weakness, had made considerable efforts to maintain good relations with Samori. Fleming refused to hear a bad word about Sofa emissaries who visited the colony. Instead, he and some of his senior officials insinuated that the claims of Sofa incursions were fabrications by his own police and military commanders, who wanted to start a war so they could win promotions and medals.

Captain E.A.W. Lendy, the commander of the colony's small frontier police force, and one of the few British officials to have visited the northern border, insisted that the Sofas were raiding British territory, destroying villages and enslaving the inhabitants. Failure to protect the border tribes was turning them against Britain, he warned, and many of the chiefs wanted the French to take over because they were willing to fight the Sofas.

Lendy, an energetic 24-year-old regular army officer, was strong willed and impulsive. When his warnings were doubted, Lendy accused some civilian officials of colluding with the Sofas, hinting that they had accepted illicit gifts. He claimed that some of the Freetown merchants secretly sold guns and ammunition to the raiders. Lendy made things worse by scoffing at Fleming's demand for proof of these claims.

Lieutenant Colonel Alfred Ellis, who was now commander of both the 1st WIR and the army garrison in the colony, backed Lendy. He had no doubt that the Sofas were inflicting immense misery in the border region with impunity and trampling on British imperial prestige in the process. Ellis was also openly contemptuous of the civilian administration and backed some of Lendy's allegations of corruption and illicit trade with the Sofas. Charges and counter-charges were hurled back and forth between the military and their civilian counterparts, creating a poisonous atmosphere in the tiny British community in Freetown. However, senior officials in London scanning reports from Sierra Leone did see a threat, and in the autumn of 1893 authorised Ellis to lead an expedition to the border to 'restore our prestige'.[1]

---

1   TNA/PRO CO 879/39.

Ellis set out from Freetown in early December with eleven officers and 369 NCOs and men of his regiment. His force was accompanied by Lendy and forty-seven men of the Sierra Leone Frontier Police, a black unit under white officers, along with a handful of officers and men of the Royal Engineers, Army Service Corps and Medical Corps. Two small field guns, broken down into parts to be lugged by the troops, provided the column with some modest firepower. Hundreds of African porters carried the force's food, ammunition, tents and other supplies, each man loaded down with up to 70lb. Ellis was contemptuous when Fleming protested that fewer than 300 troops and police would be left to defend Freetown, seeing it as evidence of the governor's timidity.

Ellis and his officers had little idea of what they would face. Only a few white men had ever visited the frontier, there were no maps of the area, and the demarcation with adjoining French territory was undefined and disputed. Relations between Britain and France were severely strained at the time by various territorial disputes in West Africa and elsewhere. Ellis was aware that French forces were operating against the Sofas on their side of the border, although he had no idea of where. Anxious to avoid any misunderstanding, he sent letters by runners to try to find the French outposts.

It took the column twelve days to trek through 140 miles of dense forest and thick grasslands where visibility was often reduced to less than a few feet, fording countless rivers and streams along the way. Every day was an ordeal as the force marched through razor grass, thorn scrub and swamps. The troops were alternately drenched to the skin by rain and their own sweat; they had no spare clothing and were hardly ever dry. They often had to sleep in the open at night without shelter, and never seemed to have enough to eat. Ellis was full of praise for the soldiers' stoicism:

> The men are behaving admirably and marching splendidly. No one can have any conception of the frightful places we have had to get over or through, and the difficulties in carrying the two guns, which are all taken to pieces and carried on men's heads, have been enormous.[2]

As it neared the border, the column came across the first signs of the Sofa raids – charred villages and the rotting corpses of slaughtered inhabitants.

---

2   TNA/PRO CO 879/39.

Horrific scenes assailed the column when it reached the fire-blackened wreckage of what had been a large town called Tekwiama, once home to some 4,000 people. A stomach-churning stench of rotting human flesh greeted the men as they skirted the ruins. Ellis recounted in a report sent back to the coast that a carpet of slaughtered men, women and children littered the ground inside the town walls. He wrote:

> Human remains were lying about on all sides, and the stench was intolerable. In one place were counted 40 headless corpses with the hands and feet tied, thus showing that these men had been made prisoners and then slaughtered.[3]

Ellis surmised that the raiders had divided their captives into those fit enough to make the long march to the slave markets and butchered the rest. 'I saw a great number of bodies of little babies and children too young to walk and who were of no use to the Sofas to sell as slaves,' Ellis wrote.[4] Every house and building had been burned. Lieutenant C.W. Gwynn of the Royal Engineers was overwhelmed by the carnage, 'The place was a veritable city of the dead. Not a house possessed a roof, and the only living creatures were the birds which were hovering over their carrion.'[5]

Further appalling sights greeted the column as it passed through a swathe of devastated villages. Every fighting man in the column, from Ellis to the youngest private, became obsessed with catching the slavers. Few were angrier than some of the Frontier Police, many of whom were liberated slaves or had parents or other family who had been slaves.

Ellis decided to split his force to improve the chances of catching up with the Sofas. Most of the supplies were left with the porters in a hastily constructed base camp, while 270 soldiers and police pressed on with just enough supplies for two weeks. Every man must have known there was a real risk the force could be annihilated – the Sofas were formidable and well-armed fighters who greatly outnumbered them, and there would be little hope of help if things went wrong – and yet, as Ellis noted, not one man hesitated.

---

3   TNA/PRO CO 879/39.
4   TNA/PRO CO 879/39.
5   Quoted in Basil Freestone, *The Horsemen From Beyond*, p.174.

On 21 December, the detachment reached the remote village of Waima on the frontier. To forestall a surprise attack, the force cleared the tall grass around the huts and constructed a low fence with piled timber. It was a routine precaution since Ellis was not expecting trouble. He did not know that a force of French colonial troops under Lieutenant Gaston Maritz was advancing on Waima after local tribesmen had reported that the village was occupied by the Sofas. Maritz, an outstanding young officer, said to have a brilliant future ahead of him, had no idea that a British force was in the region. He marched through the night with thirty regular black infantry and an unruly throng of some 1,200 local tribesmen, intent on catching the Sofas by surprise.

It was misty and rainy just after dawn on Christmas Eve, and the British sentries at Waima could only see a few yards as Maritz's force crept up on the village in the half-light. Suddenly one of the sentries spotted movement in the bush and sounded the alarm. It was never established who fired the first shot, although it was later accepted that the French fired the first volley. Within moments, the West Indians answered with rapid rifle fire, which convinced Maritz that he was facing a strong Sofa force. Ellis was equally certain he was being attacked by the Sofas; no one else would dare attack a large British force, and he could distinguish the bark of French-made rifles of a type he knew the slavers possessed.

Dozens of men were cut down as the two forces blazed away at each other for more than forty minutes. Several British officers were hit as they ran from the huts where they had been sleeping. Ellis later insisted that some of them were shot by Maritz, a noted marksman, after he mistook the officers' white pyjamas for the white robes of the Arabs who sometimes worked with the Sofas.

While the West Indians fought with unflinching discipline, most of the Frontier Police broke and ran. Lendy, who may have been trying to stop the rout, was killed after being hit fourteen times by the fire of his panicking men. After a while, the steady volleys of the West Indian soldiers began to tell. Maritz realised something was wrong because the gunfire raking his men was too disciplined for any native force he had ever faced. He seized a trumpet to try to sound the ceasefire, only to be hit three times by bullets. Moments later, the West Indians advanced, their bayoneted rifles forming a line of steel, and drove off what was left of the attackers.

Only when the West Indians found the first wounded French soldier huddled in the grass, and one of the officers recognised the man's uniform, did the British realise there had been a terrible mistake. A search found Maritz lying unconscious nearby. He was carried to the village where the column's doctor battled without success to save his life. In a statement taken down by the doctor, the young Frenchman said just before he died, 'My father is General Maritz, Seine et Oise, near Paris. I am not married. I did not know I was attacking the English. I was told that it was the Sofas were here.'[6]

Of Maritz's force, ten men had been killed and twenty-seven wounded while the British suffered seventeen dead and seventeen wounded. Later that afternoon, the British buried the dead from both sides in a clearing with full military honours in a sombre ceremony. A firing party fired a salute over the adjoining graves.

Ellis sent a dispatch to the coast with news of the incident he candidly described as a disaster. His West Indian troops' bravery and professionalism had been the only redeeming aspect of the tragic incident, he wrote:

> The only satisfaction to be gleamed from this melancholy affair lies in the wonderful steadiness displayed by the West Indian troops who, especially at the outset, were exposed to a storm of bullets from the magazine rifles. Not a man moved from his place, all remained cool and collected, and delivered their fire under the orders of their officers with great precision.[7]

Ellis tried to mitigate the conduct of Lendy's police, saying they were mostly young, untrained men who had only recently enlisted.

On 26 December, Ellis resumed the hunt for the Sofas. He was more determined than ever to find the raiders after the events at Waima. He fretted over being unable to establish contact with the French, fearing they might unknowingly stage a second attack on his force. The march was torturously slow – the column had to move at a speed the wounded could endure – and the African scouts, the only ones who knew the country, had deserted in terror after the clash at Waima. With just enough food for seven days, the men were put on half-rations despite the gruelling conditions.

---

6   TNA/PRO CO 879/39.
7   TNA/PRO CO 879/39.

It took the force nearly a week to cover some 40 miles. Incessant storms lashed the column, drenching the troops and adding to their misery. Everywhere, they came across signs of the raiders: abandoned and burned villages, butchered bodies and terrified survivors hiding in the bush.

On 31 December, the column found a 'perfect charnel house of ... slaughtered captives, men, women and children' in a devastated village.[8] Further terrible sights were encountered on New Year's Day 1894 when the column reached Ka–Yima, a large settlement that the Sofas had used as a base to sort captives, killing those they deemed useless. Ellis wrote in his official report:

> Here a spectacle met the eyes which exceeded anything yet seen. On the left-hand side entering the gate in the stockade was a pile of corpses from 7 to 8 feet high. The lower ones were probably some weeks old but those on top were quite recent. In an examination, necessarily brief because of the horrible effluvium, I counted, on the surface of the heap, the bodies of 27 women, children and infants; and the heap itself must have contained at least 100 corpses.[9]

Finally, the column caught up with the Sofas later that day at a place called Bagbwema. Some 700 raiders were camped in a fortified settlement with hundreds of captives, mainly women and teenagers destined for the slave markets. It was a strong position, roughly oval in shape and about 150 yards across, ringed by a stockade of felled tree trunks. Thorn bush fences in front of the stockade supplemented the defences.

The outnumbered British attacked at sunrise the next day, catching the Sofas by surprise. Ellis refused to squander the lives of his men with a direct assault on the stockade walls. The two little field guns, which had been carried across hundreds of miles of bush, bombarded the settlement as the troops fired from prone positions in the surrounding high grass. Shells tore into the settlement, setting fire to the thatched roofs of the huts, and causing a stampede. Hundreds of Sofas were killed or wounded as the cannon and the rifle fire raked the camp.

---

8   TNA/PRO CO 267/413.
9   TNA/PRO CO 267/413.

Sofa fighters who tried to flee through the stockade's four gates found lines of West Indian troops with bayonetted rifles who had been waiting for this moment for weeks. Just a tenth of the Sofas, or some seventy men, were taken prisoner; the rest were all killed. British casualties were two wounded – an officer and a private. Ellis said 673 slaves, all women and children, were rescued. His reports said nothing about casualties among the slaves, even though some must have been caught in the bombardment.

A final, exhausting journey now faced the column. Supplies were almost gone, and little or no food could be spared for the freed slaves or the Sofa prisoners; there might be more fighting, and the soldiers had to be given what little food there was to keep up their strength. The tired troops found the going more arduous than anything they had faced so far. A path had to be cleared with machetes and back-breaking toil as the column forced its way through vast expanses of dense bush. In just one day, the winding procession had to wade through ninety-six streams and twenty-five swamps where the slippery black mud rose up to their knees and every step was a battle with the thick, syrupy sludge.

By now, the West Indians barely looked like soldiers. The men's boots, rotted by damp and fungus, had disintegrated, while their uniforms, torn by thorns and razor vines, hung over their emaciated ribcages in ragged strips. And yet the men were ready for action, their weapons clean and their discipline and pride intact. Ellis was sure of one thing. 'No European troops could have withstood the fatigue and exposure of such an expedition in such a climate,' he later told the army authorities.[10]

The column marched through a landscape devastated by Sofa ravages. Ellis reported that virtually every town, village and hamlet in an area measuring 75 miles from west to east and 55 miles from north to south, had been destroyed. Human habitation had virtually vanished. Ellis wrote:

> The part of this region traversed by the expedition was a complete desert, without a single human inhabitant, except at Yardu and Fasardu. The entire population had been killed or sold into slavery, and it will take many years to repair the mischief done.[11]

---

10  TNA/PRO CO 879/39.

11  *Ibid.*

It took a week to reach a Frontier Police post where supplies were waiting for the column. Ellis turned over the Sofa prisoners to the local chief to inflict whatever punishment he and his people wished. No word survives on what befell the prisoners. It is unlikely they found any mercy at the hands of people they had terrorised, which is perhaps why Ellis chose not to take them back to the coast to face a trial and possibly easier fates. There is no indication in the official correspondence that Ellis' decision was questioned or caused any concern.

Finally, the column reached the coast in late January. It had covered an estimated 541 miles in fifty-one days. Most of the troops were barefoot and clothed only in tattered greatcoats. The health of many of the officers and soldiers had been shattered; some would never recover.

News of the Waima incident caused consternation when it reached Europe in early January. It was the first battle between Britain and France since 1815, and the news sparked outrage and recrimination in both countries. It led to a decade-long dispute over responsibility and reparations. Much of the subsequent wrangling centred on who had fired first. Even though it was clear that Maritz had ordered the attack, some French officials and officers claimed the British started the fighting. Efforts to apportion blame were bedevilled by the lack of a clear demarcation between British and French territory; both sides complained that they could not find Waima on any map.

Some French Army officers tried to put the blame for the clash on the black West Indian troops, accusing them of being little more than brigands, bereft of discipline, who abandoned their officers if there was trouble. French black troops, they insisted, were models of discipline and loyalty. Such views were played up by some French newspapers, adding to the friction over the incident. For once, the British Government stood up for its West Indian regulars – to do otherwise would lend credence to the French claims. Henry Campbell-Bannerman, the Secretary of State for War, expressed complete confidence in the WIR. 'The perfect discipline, bravery and cheerful endurance of unusual hardships by the soldiers of the West India Regiment have my warmest admiration,' he said. [12]

A few weeks after reaching the coast, Ellis was to die at the age of 42, worn out by the exertions of hard campaigning. He had spent nineteen years in

---

12 *Ibid.*

West Africa, an extraordinary length of time in an age when most whites could barely endure a year or two. His men mourned him as a courageous leader, one of the few officers who had always cared for the black soldier.

The deaths of Ellis and Lendy did not end the spat with the governor and his officials. Fleming, who could hardly deny the seriousness of the Sofa raids, instead accused Ellis of failing to inform him about his proposals for a frontier campaign, and of going behind his back to London. The governor's shrill protests about violations of protocol went on for months. Although he was removed halfway through his term, in what looked like a tacit rebuke, Fleming spent the rest of his career as Governor of the Leeward Islands in the West Indies, which he probably considered a blessed escape from Freetown.

More serious were accusations against the expedition from a chief named Nyaqwa. Embarrassed British officials were sparing with details, but it appears that the West Indian troops were accused of molesting women in some of the villages where they had camped. Ellis died before the claims surfaced and surviving officers from the expedition stated that they had seen nothing untoward. For once, civilian and military officials in Sierra Leone acted in perfect harmony and rebutted the charges. London hurriedly declared the matter closed.

Campaigners in Britain waged a long fight for compensation for the families of the three white British officers who were killed at Waima. Eventually a Belgian diplomat was appointed to adjudicate on compensation. It was not until 1902 that a decision was rendered in favour of Britain. The French Government paid a paltry £9,000 in compensation. Of this, £4,000 went to Lieutenant Robert Liston's widow, who had been left to raise three children on a beggarly pension, while £2,000 each went to the mothers of Captain Lendy and 2nd Lieutenant C. Wroughton. The remaining £1,000, or about £70 each, was divided among the families of the white sergeant major, the nine black WIR privates and four policemen who had been killed.

No one had campaigned for them. Instead, the British Government tried to void some of the payments by asserting that several of the West Indians were illegitimate, and thus their relatives had no legal right to compensation.

A monument was constructed by the British at Waima six years after the clash to honour the soldiers who died on both sides. For once, the West Indian rankers were named along with the white officers. Maritz was also named and the fact that he was leading black soldiers was mentioned, but not how many were killed or their names. An epitaph of a different kind was left by Lieutenant F.B. Morley, one of the WIR officers who served in the expedition. He said:

> The hinterland of Sierra Leone is very poor and the country can hardly produce the food required for the natives. The peninsula of Sierra Leone is valuable as a coaling station [for ships] but apart from that the country is not worth fighting for.[13]

No impartial observer could deny that the West India Regiment performed heroically throughout these years in West Africa, one of the most taxing terrains on the planet. A handful of West Indian troops guarded vast swathes of British territory and fought innumerable little wars and police actions with the slenderest resources. However, gratitude was not the general habit of the British Government or the army when it came to black troops. Critics continued to carp about the military and racial inferiority of the WIR, and the few officials and officers who argued that the empire needed more West Indian troops were increasingly drowned out by the din of the detractors.

It was decided in 1888 to merge the 1st and 2nd WIR into a single, two-battalion regiment. This was in line with reforms at the time to merge British Army regiments for greater efficiency. The amalgamation was not popular within the WIR, given the historic disdain the two regiments held for each other; the 1st was still largely Jamaican while the 2nd drew most of its men from Barbados. A third battalion was formed in 1897, partly to garrison St Helena, but the local people resented the presence of a black unit, and it was disbanded after just six years despite performing well in West Africa.

More ominous for the WIR's future was the raising of black West African military units. Local forces were first formed in the 1860s, and these evolved into the Royal West African Frontier Force, which would earn an excellent reputation. African troops had some advantages over the WIR: they spoke local languages and possessed better knowledge of local conditions; as colonial units they fell under the local administrations, whereas the WIR as regulars were under London's control; and it did not help that the West Indians looked down on African soldiers as savages. Above all, the African

---

13  Quoted in Freestone, p.205.

troops were cheaper. They were paid less than the West Indians and their benefits were far less generous. African troops, aware of the discrepancy, agitated to be paid the same as the West Indians. Colonial Secretary Joseph Chamberlain told Parliament in 1898 that while the WIR was an excellent unit it was expensive because of higher pay and the cost of the rotations of battalions between the West Indies and West Africa.

While officials and politicians in Freetown, London and elsewhere debated whether they were worth their pay, the West Indians went on fighting and dying in West African outposts. These now almost forgotten campaigns became increasingly difficult as the British sought to impose total control, and the local people fought back with growing ferocity and skill.

Typical of these conflicts was the 1898 Hut Tax War in Sierra Leone. To raise funds to help run the colony and its administration, British officials imposed a tax on African dwellings. Not surprisingly, many of the Africans bitterly resented this intrusion into their centuries-old way of life and resisted.

Tribal forces built formidable log stockades and trenches from which marksmen cut down government forces. These fortifications were well camouflaged and almost invisible from a few yards away. Even the light artillery used by the West Indians had little effect on the rugged structures. African marksmen concentrated on picking off the white officers, knowing it would disrupt the attackers. Each position had to be taken in gruelling and often costly attacks. All too often the British took a stockade only to see the defenders escaping unharmed into the bush. West Indian patrols reported having to clear up to twenty stockades a day.

African forces showed remarkable defiance. When the British offered a £100 reward for one of the leading rebel chiefs, he responded with a £500 reward for the territory's British governor. In the end, the military said the only way to break the Africans' resistance was to burn their towns and villages. It made a mockery of the war if the army was going to destroy the dwellings the government was fighting to tax, but the British now believed their vaunted prestige was threatened by the half-naked tribesmen. Soon the sky was dotted with spiralling pillars of smoke as one village after another was torched. British commanders praised the courage and fortitude of the young West Indian soldiers who bore the brunt of the campaign. One of their officers wrote:

The men were constantly soaked to the skin on the marches, and as they had no change of clothes, they were obliged to remain in their wet garments; nearly every night the bivouacs were deluged with rain; it was comparatively seldom that the troops were sufficiently fortunate to sleep in towns, for if the last town attacked during the day was not set on fire by the shellfire of the attacking party, it was frequently burnt by the enemy on being driven out, so as to leave no shelter for the troops. These discomforts were not only borne uncomplainingly by the men, but even cheerfully.[14]

Superior British military might and the systematic destruction of homes and villages eventually broke the Africans, and they submitted to the new colonial order. By the dawn of the twentieth century, it seemed that war and revolt were receding into the past in Britain's West African colonies.

Hard campaigning in West Africa brought few rewards for the West Indian soldiers, who survived years of arduous and dangerous service. Many of the men were broken physically and mentally by their experiences, while those in reasonably good health frequently faced misery and poverty after leaving the army. Few old soldiers were able to find work in the West Indies, where good jobs were scarce and the veterans were too old, ill or proud to work as labourers or field hands. More than a few of the ex-WIR men had acquired a fair amount of education and other skills in the army so most of them looked, often in vain, for government posts such as clerkships where their abilities could be put to use. Having served the empire and the queen, they now hoped for some small position that would allow them some modest dignity and to feed their families. Government files are littered with appeals from veterans for employment.

Typical was George Hinkson of Barbados, who rose to the rank of sergeant major after fifteen years of hard service, including three campaigns in Africa. He was well educated and handled administrative work in the army before being discharged in 1898 because his health had broken down. In 1909, aged 47, he petitioned the Barbados Government for help because he could not support his wife and two children on a miserly military pension of 5½d a day. In exquisite handwriting, he told of not being able to find work, despite going out every day to look for employment and now faced

---

14  Quoted in Ian Hernon, *Britain's Forgotten Wars*, p.723.

losing his house because he was unable to pay the tax on it. He pleaded for an increase in his pension to avoid having to live on public assistance, 'which I shall very much regret and be ashamed of, after serving my late Queen, present King and Country'.

Joseph Jasper, a native of Jamaica, who joined the WIR in 1864 and served in the Ashanti War under Wolseley, petitioned in 1916 for help. African service had wrecked his health, and he begged for money for food. Colonial officials in the West Indies and their counterparts in London invariably responded to such pleas by saying they could do nothing. In a final indignity, a plea for WIR veterans to be buried in the military cemetery in Barbados alongside other men of the regiment was denied because the graveyard had been sold to a private developer.

# PART II

# THE FIRST WORLD WAR

# 8

# PATRIOTIC BRITONS ALL

Great Britain's declaration of war on Germany in August 1914 was greeted in her West Indian colonies with exuberant shows of patriotism and a flood of black volunteers eager to fight for the mother country in her hour of need. Rather than welcoming these eager young men, however, the British Army would do everything it could to prevent them fighting in a 'white man's war'.

Many black West Indians possessed a deep sense of loyalty to the British Empire and believed that they were as British as the white denizens of England or Scotland. A black Jamaican politician spoke for many when he said, 'We desire to be English in spite of some faults which we see [in her] … there is much that is good and sound in the great hearts of England and we have confidence in Her good intentions.'[1]

If their loyalty was unconditional, many black West Indians still hoped that Britain would reward them with greater rights and better lives if their young men fought and died for the empire. The region's economic decline had continued over the decades, many of the settlements were racked by poverty and decay, and a tiny white elite still dominated life. Just one in 100 black Jamaicans possessed the vote on the eve of the First World War.

Some educated and better-off black men saw war service as an opportunity to prove that they were equal to whites. Some argued that black men had a right to fight just as much as they were entitled to the vote or other

---

1    Quoted in Glenford Howe, *West Indians and World War One*, p.33.

rights their race had been historically denied. Others said that it was the duty of black men to fight for Britain because she had ended slavery and speakers at public rallies warned that a German victory would lead to a new kind of bondage. Black churches, like their white counterparts, said it was the Christian duty of their followers to fight.

Some influential voices saw the war as an outright struggle for black rights. An editorial in the *Federalist* newspaper of Grenada proclaimed:

> As coloured people ... We will be fighting to prove that the distinction between God-made creatures of one empire because of skin, colour or complexion differences should no longer exist ... We shall be fighting to prove that we are no longer merely subjects, but citizens – citizens of a world empire whose watch-word should be Liberty, Equality and Brotherhood.[2]

A few in the black community opposed the conflict, arguing that they should not fight for the state that oppressed them. Such views were denounced by most black leaders, newspapers and the larger community.

Eager offers from the West Indies to send men to fight for Britain poured in to London within days of the outbreak of war. There was no chance of the conflict reaching the Caribbean, and the men clamouring to fight expected to go to the battlefields in Europe. Every colony wanted to raise its own unit or send men to serve in the British forces.

Bowing to pressure from the West Indies, the Colonial Office in late August approached the army with the offer of raising black West Indian units. 'The West Indian is of African origin, and should make a good soldier, though it will probably take longer to train him than to train a European,' a senior official wrote.[3] The War Office in September expressed perfunctory gratitude, but said the army did want not black West Indian volunteers; instead, the Caribbean colonies should raise local units to guard against raids by enemy warships and maintain law and order among the black population.[4]

---

2   *Federalist*, 27 October 1915.
3   TNA/PRO CO 537/604.
4   TNA/PRO CO 318/333.

Official and popular reaction in Britain to the West Indies' offers to send black troops ranged from scorn to hilarity. Government officials fretted about hordes of black men descending on London, expecting to be hailed as saviours and treated as equals. 'The West Indian negro is in general proud of his British nationality (even to the point of being obnoxious about it when abroad),' a Colonial Office official grumbled.[5]

It was tacit British policy not to use black soldiers in conflicts with European opponents. Many scientists, writers, church men, politicians and the great weight of public opinion still held that black people were racially inferior and lacked the intelligence and moral stamina to fight white opponents in a modern war. Besides, it would be – as *The Times*, the voice of the empire, put it – 'unsporting':

> We British are constitutionally the last people in the world to take unfair advantage in sport, war or commerce of our opponents. The instinct which made us such sticklers for propriety in all our dealings made us more reluctant than other nations would feel to employ coloured troops against a white enemy.[6]

Army officers and colonial officials who pointed out that the empire depended on the skill and courage of Asian and African soldiers were brushed aside. Lieutenant General G.M. Bullock, the Commander of British Forces in Bermuda, pleaded in vain with the War Office to accept black West Indian volunteers. 'It is most important to welcome colour,' he wrote.[7] The army High Command said black troops should stay in the tropics and fight men of their own race. There was broad contempt in Britain for the French use of African troops on the Western Front, regardless of their excellent fighting record.

Notwithstanding these entrenched attitudes, the army was forced to rush Indian troops to the Western Front after the British Army suffered serious setbacks in the first weeks of the war. It was presented as a purely temporary measure until white reinforcements could be recruited and trained, although Indian cavalry served on the Western Front for much

---

5   TNA/PRO CO 318/348.
6   *The Times History of the War*, Vol. 1 p.155.
7   TNA/PRO CO 37/258.

of the war. None of this changed the vehement opposition to using black West Indian or African troops. A senior Colonial Office mandarin wrote in an internal memo:

> It's all very well to have Indian troops fighting in Europe, but to have negroes seems to me to be quite a different matter. Moreover, the Indian troops are part of a trained and efficient military machine whereas W. Indian troops would not be. Is it likely that public opinion here would welcome a raw W. Indian negro troop being sent over here to be trained alongside of the regiments in Lord Kitchener's army?[8]

The same attitudes influenced the army's refusal to use the West India Regiment in Europe, even though it was part of the regular army with an excellent fighting record. The 1st Battalion was in Sierra Leone and the 2nd Battalion in Jamaica at the start of the war. Calls to send the entire WIR to Europe in 1914 were ignored even as virtually every other regular regiment was being hurled into the desperate battles to halt the Germans. The WIR had more experience of African bush fighting than any other unit in the British Army, and yet it played almost no part in the protracted 1914–16 campaign to take German Cameroon. British commanders preferred to use African and Indian troops. Finally, the 2nd Battalion was sent in April 1916 to fight in East Africa.

While it shared the general disdain for black West Indians, the Colonial Office worried that refusing to accept the offer of volunteers for the British forces would weaken the region's loyalty to the empire. Officials were already concerned about growing US influence in the Caribbean, and there were fears that the British settlements would seek American rule – some white West Indians were said to favour switching allegiances to benefit their business interests.

Lord Dundonald, a peer who had business interests in the Caribbean, warned the Colonial Office that the loyalty of black West Indians was the main bulwark to exchanging 'the Stars and Stripes for the Union Jack'.[9] Colonial Office bureaucrats debated how to tell the West Indian colonies that their offer of black troops had been rejected without alienating them.

---

8   TNA/PRO CO 152/342.
9   TNA/PRO CO 318/333.

One wrote helpfully, 'Their probably low military value could not of course be referred (to).'[10]

Various excuses were offered in the end, including the supposed inability of black people to withstand European weather and the claim that it would be too dangerous for them to serve in white units because 'their colour would render them conspicuous' and more vulnerable to enemy marksmen.[11]

The army's rejection of black volunteers caused dismay, shame and anger in the West Indies. Indignant black and white leaders cited the WIR's long and illustrious record as proof of the fighting prowess of their men. They also pointed to the success of black French troops in the trenches, and made allusions to the defeats that white British troops had suffered in Africa at the hands of the Zulus and other black opponents. *The Clarion* newspaper of British Honduras stated:

> ... the Empire cannot dispense, unless she is obsessed with the spirit of self-destruction, with the services of her blackest and humblest citizens ... The killing of a German is an imperial duty ... and God forbid that the complexion of the man who does the killing should stand in the way of the victory.[12]

Official rebuffs only hardened the desire of many black West Indians to fight for the country that did not want them. Government suggestions that the West Indies could best aid the war effort by growing food or serving in local defence units were rejected. West Indians wanted to fight the Germans. 'We have put up sugar and money for the various subscriptions, but that won't win our battles. It's lives we desire to give,' a black patriot in Barbados said.[13] Pleas to send men to fight continued to flow into London. 'If only the W.I. [West Indies] would stop telegraphing for a bit,' an exasperated Colonial Office official wrote.[14]

A few determined men tried to find their own way to Britain in hopes of enlisting in the military. It is difficult to comprehend, in the modern age of

---

10  TNA/PRO CO 28/284.
11  TNA/PRO CO 28/284.
12  Quoted in Howe, p.80.
13  Quoted in Richard Smith, *Jamaican Volunteers in the First World War*, p.70.
14  TNA/PRO CO 28/284.

mass air travel, how extraordinarily and potentially perilous it was for young black men with very little money or knowledge of the world, many of them teenagers who had never left home, to try to find their way over thousands of miles to the imperial capital. Most stowed away on cargo ships, which invariably led to their discovery at sea, rough treatment by ship captains and prosecution by the British authorities who, far from welcoming them as volunteers eager to fight, hurled them into jail.

Nine men from Barbados who stowed away on the *SS Danube* were arraigned in court in May 1915 after the ship docked in London. White court officials and police officers mocked the men's colour and ridiculed their hope of joining the British Army. When told that the men had been found hiding in the cargo hold, Magistrate Gillespie quipped, to general laughter from the white spectators, 'In a dark corner, I suppose'.

Prosecutor J.W. Richards replied that the men wanted to join the army.

'What, do they want to enlist in the Black Guards?' interjected Gillespie.

When the court officials and spectators had finished laughing, a police officer said that the local army recruiting office had told him the men would not be accepted because of their colour. Still chuckling at his own humour, Gillespie sentenced the men to a week in jail.[15]

A handful of black West Indians already living or studying in Britain managed to join the British Army despite numerous barriers. Pre-war army regulations classified black men as aliens, including those born in the United Kingdom, but allowed them to enlist. Black soldiers could not be officers nor make up more than 2 per cent of a unit.

In reality, the army discouraged and frequently excluded black recruits. Whether or not a black recruit was accepted was left largely to the whims of individual recruiting officers, and lighter-skinned men had a much better chance of being taken. Colonial Office officials were alarmed when they learned in 1914 that some British units were accepting black recruits, and tried to stop it. 'We must discourage coloured volunteers,' wrote Gilbert Grindle, head of the West India section.[16]

Few men were better candidates to be soldiers than Norman Manley, the future Prime Minister of Jamaica. Manley, who was studying at Oxford University as a Rhodes Scholar in 1914, possessed outstanding intelligence

---

15  *Stratford Express*, 19 May 1915.
16  TNA/PRO CO 318/333.

and character, natural authority and athletic prowess. The army would have made him an officer in a heartbeat – except for the fact that he was of mixed race. It was an insurmountable barrier, although Manley was, as he said, 'near-white'.

Manley volunteered as a gunner or private in the horse artillery, and after a time was accepted by the working-class whites in the unit: the men stopped referring to Manley as 'darkie' when they realised he did not like it. Manley excelled in the army, as he did in most things, and soon was promoted to corporal and sent to the front in France.

> Here I came up against violent colour prejudice. The rank and file disliked taking orders from a coloured N.C.O. and their attitude was mild by comparison with that of my fellow N.C.O.s. Corporals and Sergeants resented my sharing status with them. It was only the Officer class that I could expect to behave with ordinary decency and both aspects of this phenomenon I fully understood. To be frank I had the greatest contempt for my fellow N.C.O.s and I was later to discover that a sense of superiority was a good protection from the obsessions that colour-feelings can create.[17]

British imperialism was often justified as a selfless mission to 'raise up' lesser races to resemble their rulers, and yet nothing frightened or outraged many whites more than a Westernised, educated black man who was as much at home in their offices, homes and clubs as they were. Manley gave up his rank and transferred to another unit, where he was accepted as long as there was no question of his being put over whites. He fought on the Western Front for the rest of the war, won the Military Medal for bravery, and lost his brother, Roy, who was killed at Ypres in 1917 serving with the same battery.

White men from the West Indies who wanted to fight for Britain had a very different experience than black men from the same colonies. Colonial officials, local politicians and businesses in the region quietly arranged for white volunteers to travel to Britain and Canada, where the military warmly welcomed them. Local firms organised and funded 'merchants' contingents' of young men.

---

17  Norman Manley, 'The Autobiography of Norman Washington Manley', p.7.

Typical was a group of twenty-four men that Barbados sent to London in 1915 with the enthusiastic assistance of the Colonial Office.[18] The British military regarded many of these men as officer candidates because of their social class and privileged upbringings. It was not a view accepted by all, however. Robert Graves, the famed soldier-poet, complained that some white West Indians were given commissions despite being completely unsuitable. He singled out a white officer from Jamaica, claiming he was commissioned only because his father was a rich planter. 'He was good-hearted enough, but of little use as an officer, having never been out of the island in his life or, except for a short service with the West India militia, seen any soldiering.'[19] The army's claim that black soldiers could not serve in Europe because they could not endure cold weather was never seen as a problem for white volunteers from families who had been born and bred in the Caribbean for generations.

A few young black men tried to join the contingents of white volunteers. C.L.R. James, the writer and historian, was eager to enlist when he heard that merchants in his native Trinidad were raising groups of young men for the British Army. Like Manley, James appeared to be an ideal candidate – he was the son of a teacher, a member of the island's black middle class, a gifted athlete and a scholar who had imbibed the patriotic ideals of the empire from his white British school teachers. 'Everything began from the basis that Britain was the source of all light,' he remembered.[20]

James skipped school one day and went to the office where candidates were being interviewed for the next contingent for the front. He sat happily chatting with white school friends until he was summoned to be interviewed by the local magnate handling the affair. 'He took one look at me, saw my dark skin and, shaking his head vigorously, motioned me violently away.'[21]

For once privilege had a heavy price, with white West Indians in the British forces suffering very high casualty rates. The all-white Bermuda Volunteer Rifle Corps detachment of 126 men, which served with a British infantry regiment on the Western Front, suffered a 30 per cent death rate

---

18  TNA/PRO CO 28/287.
19  Robert Graves, *Goodbye to all That*, p.136.
20  C.L.R. James, *Beyond a Boundary*, p.41.
21  C.L.R. James, *Beyond a Boundary*, p.41.

and 29 per cent wounded.[22] And yet many young black men, who knew about the terrible losses of their white compatriots, insisted on their right to fight whatever the price they might have to pay.

★★★

By the end of 1914, the West Indian colonies could only watch as every other part of the empire sent men to the battlefields in Europe, the Middle East and Africa. Lord Dundonald suggested to the colonial secretary, Lewis Harcourt, that a West Indian unit might be raised to fight in the Middle East against the Ottoman Empire. This would get around the unspoken prohibition on using black troops against white opponents, and salve West Indian pride. The Colonial Office, which was also worried about the political consequences of the repeated rejections of a West Indian force, presented the proposal to the War Office in December 1914. It was promptly rebuffed by the Army Council on the grounds that black troops would not be suitable for service against the Turks; and while the possibility had not even been suggested, it also ruled out their serving in East Africa, where British troops were being thrashed by a much smaller German force composed mainly of black troops.

And then the army, which had finally started to comprehend that something had to be done to appease patriotic sentiment in the West Indies, suggested raising a black battalion for garrison duty in captured German colonies in West Africa. It was now the turn of the Colonial Office to object, bizarrely claiming that West Indians could not endure the West African climate despite the WIR's long and outstanding service in the region. British officials in West Africa also opposed the plan due to their bias in favour of their own African troops, and because a West Indian unit would have to be paid, fed and housed like white soldiers. Harcourt rejected the proposal, telling the army it was unlikely to appease the West Indians, who would see it as an empty gesture.

Even the most ardent supporters of a black West Indian unit seemed to have given up hope by the spring of 1915, when the one person who could resolve the impasse intervened unexpectedly. On 17 April, Harcourt received a letter from Lord Stamfordham, private secretary of King George V. A lady

---

22  TNA/PRO CO 537/672.

engaged in charitable work in the West Indies had written to the monarch urging him to support the ardent desire of black West Indians to fight for the empire. 'His Majesty cannot help thinking that it would be very politic to gratify this wish of the West Indies to send a Regiment to the Front,' Stamfordham wrote.[23] Anticipating possible objections on racial grounds, the secretary added that if a contingent was raised it could be sent to the Middle East to fight the Turks.

The king did not control government policy, and yet he had considerable influence behind the scenes. A horrified Harcourt penned a long and defensive reply detailing his department's efforts and the obstructions put up by the army. The War Office, he wrote, had refused to accept a black unit:

> ... owing to the colour question; that I was well aware that it is not possible to enlist black or coloured men in British regiments; and that the formation of a West Indian contingent for service at the Front in Europe is impracticable for various reasons, of which the difficulty of colour is only one. I went on to say, however, that I had begun to feel anxiety as to the possible effect of continued rejection of offers of service on the loyalty of the black population of the West Indies and on their existing attachment to the Empire ... and that I should, therefore, be glad if, consistently with military considerations, which I recognised to be paramount, some means could be found of drawing on the black population of the West Indies for the purposes of the war.[24]

George V responded by raising the matter with Lord Kitchener, the war minister. Kitchener blithely told the king that he could not recall the War Office rejecting any offer of troops from the West Indies. Stamfordham informed an incredulous Harcourt that Kitchener had assured the monarch he would be 'very glad' to accept 'a complete unit' from the West Indies as long as there were no restrictions on where it could be posted.[25] It was hoped, the king's secretary concluded, that this would settle the matter.

Harcourt read the letter as a suggestion that his department was blocking the patriotic aspirations of the king's loyal West Indian subjects. He sent

---

23  TNA/PRO CO 318/333.
24  TNA/PRO CO 318/333.
25  TNA/PRO CO 318/333.

Buckingham Palace copies of all the Colonial Office's correspondence with the military on the matter, and a whining cover letter saying the War Office's 'refusal was so absolute that I informed all of the West Indian governors … that coloured Contingents from the West Indies could not be accepted'.[26]

Whatever the cost to Harcourt's pride, the king's quiet intervention saw the military establishment's resistance to a black unit evaporate overnight. A War Office directive announced on 19 May that a black infantry formation, to be called the British West Indies Regiment, would be raised for front-line service. Its badge featured the sailing ship of Christopher Columbus – perhaps the designers thought it symbolised how the New World was coming to the rescue of the old.

---

26  TNA/PRO CO 318/333.

# 9

# RAISING THE BRITISH WEST INDIES REGIMENT

Many black West Indians saw sending their men to fight as the prelude to assuming their rightful place as equal citizens of the empire. A newspaper in Grenada gave voice to such hopes when it proclaimed the war as a new beginning, 'This is history. We have before us today a blank page on which to write our glorious record. This is an hour that will not sound again for centuries.'[1]

It was implicitly understood that this equality would be earned with the lives of young black men on the battlefield, a sacrifice that would form a blood bond with the other peoples and nations of the empire. W. Peter, a member of Saint Lucia's Legislative Council, told his fellow lawmakers in July 1915:

> We in Saint Lucia claim to be second to none in our loyalty and devotion to the British Crown, and we experience a thrill of genuine satisfaction in being given this opportunity of proving that loyalty and devotion by giving our manhood.[2]

Some of the young men who would do the dying spoke of their eagerness to prove themselves alongside white youths on the battlefield. Seaford John wrote:

---

1   *The West Indian*, Grenada, 24 July 1915, quoted in *Howe Social History*, 38.
2   TNA/PRO CO 321/282.

We all have a fixed determination that we unite under the same old flag to fight for one King and one Empire, with one hope and one desire and with gallantry we'll march along, until we conquer, win or die.[3]

If the hopes and aspirations of black West Indians were going to be realised, many thought it was essential they send their very best sons to fight. White colonial officials and black leaders, who might not agree on many things, were united in wanting to pick only the finest men to represent the West Indies. They knew that there would be many in Britain and elsewhere looking for any excuse to criticise the new regiment. Recruiters were instructed to enlist the fittest, best-educated men from good backgrounds who could hold their own in the classroom and middle-class living rooms as well as on the battlefield. Jamaican recruiters rejected every other applicant: some colonies had even higher rejection rates. More than a few of the rejected men had already quit their jobs in expectation of going into the army and struggled to go back to their old lives or find new work.

It proved fairly easy to attract superior recruits, at least initially, because many young men from the black middle classes with strong notions of patriotism and self-advancement were among the first to volunteer. The men of the first contingents were widely judged to be excellent troops. A white chaplain who served with the 1st British West Indies Regiment (BWIR) for much of the war, Major the Reverend W.J. Bensley, never forgot his first experience of black West Indian soldiers. He was thrilled by:

… the keenness of the men to learn, the very high standard of intellect and education among the N.C.O.s, the splendid loyalty of all to the Empire, and their impatient desire to show it as soon as possible by active work in the field.[4]

Recruiting for the BWIR was not entirely free of problems. Integrating men from different colonies was difficult because of traditional rivalries. Men from Jamaica or Barbados had little in common beyond strong mutual aversion. There was also friction with some mixed-race men, who had not

---

3   Quoted in Santanu Das (ed.), *Race, Empire and First World War Writing*, p.268.
4   *The Belize Independent*, 16 July 1919.

been able to get into white units, and resented serving with black soldiers in the BWIR.

No matter how promising many of the early black volunteers were, the army mandated that all of the regiment's officers had to be white. While it could not prevent the BWIR's formation, the army adamantly refused to accept black officers. Many of the BWIR's senior officers were regulars of the West India Regiment and most of the junior officers came from the various West Indian militia and volunteer forces. Black and white men served as NCOs, reflecting the well-established practice in the local defence forces, except that whites tended to hold most of the senior positions, such as sergeant major.

Hopes for the new regiment were boosted by talks between officials in London and the West Indies on its status. The West Indian authorities insisted the BWIR was a British Army unit while the War Office wanted to classify it as a 'native' colonial formation with lower standards of pay and allowances. The government ruled the BWIR would be a regular army formation like white British units, with the same pay and almost identical allowances. As one of the BWIR's commanders exultantly noted, the regiment 'is paid entirely from British funds'.[5]

Furthermore, the High Command was reconsidering its opposition to black West Indian troops as the army suffered staggering losses on the Western Front. Initially, the army had agreed to accept just a single West Indian battalion of about 1,000 men. It then asked in September 1915 for a second battalion, before quickly raising the request to four battalions. Soon there was talk of a West Indian infantry brigade with additional battalions.

There had never been any doubt that the BWIR would be trained in Britain. The West Indian colonies lacked both military facilities and funds to provide clothing or any equipment for the volunteers. Some settlements could only send their men off with good wishes and cheers at the dockside as they sailed away. George Haddon-Smith, Governor of the Windward Islands, said the colony could not provide uniforms for its contingent.[6] A group of 220 volunteers from British Guiana not only had to wear their civilian clothing on the Atlantic crossing, they never got the

---

5   TNA/PRO CO 318/341.
6   TNA/PRO CO 321/282.

garments back after the war or compensation for their loss, despite army promises to the contrary.[7]

The first volunteers to arrive in England in October 1915 were overwhelmed at the warmth of the welcome they received in a country where many people had never seen a black person. Troops wrote home of being cheered as the trains conveying them to training camps passed through towns and villages, and of white girls blowing them kisses. Civilians spontaneously gave the men snacks, cigarettes and other gifts. Such kindness was both welcome and disconcerting; even the most privileged black men were accustomed to being treated as less than equal by whites at home. 'One thing that really strikes me is the manner in which we are appreciated and respected by the English people. You can just imagine how it makes us darkies feel at ease in our minds,' L. Malabre wrote home.[8]

Many whites lionised the West Indians as loyal imperial subjects who had come to fight for Britain and as exotic curiosities. Black men in the khaki uniforms of British soldiers were indeed a remarkable sight in a country where black people had invariably been depicted as savages or comic simpletons. And yet, most whites laughed at the West Indians' insistence that they were British. Private Peter Lambert of Jamaica wrote, after marching in a military parade, 'The people in the streets cheered us black boys more than the white boys. "That's because you're black," said somebody to me. But we are English really; it's only the climate we've lived in that makes us black.'[9]

Not all of the West Indian volunteers were made so welcome. Army bureaucrats were outraged when they found out that the 1st BWIR had arrived with some forty so-called 'East Indians', members of the West Indies' large migrant community from the Indian subcontinent. Even though Indian Army troops had excelled in the fighting in Europe and the Middle East, army officials said the East Indians would not make good soldiers, claiming, with no apparent evidence, that they could not speak English or eat British Army food. With mind-bending illogic, the War Office said the men must be rejected because many Indian soldiers were already serving in the British colonial forces. The bewildered East Indians were sent back to

---

7  TNA/PRO CO 950/707.
8  *Jamaica Times*, 8 January 1916.
9  Quoted in Howe, *West Indians and World War One*, p.255.

the Caribbean with other men who had been rejected as 'medically unfit, and undesirables'.[10] Army officials then bizarrely decided that 'Red Indians' or indigenous people from the West Indies could serve in the BWIR if they were willing to eat British Army rations.

The 1st and 2nd Battalions of the BWIR were sent to a training camp at Seaford in East Sussex and the 3rd and 4th Battalions went to a camp at Withnoe near Plymouth. Seaford was a vast complex of hastily built huts, classrooms and parade grounds. It was one of dozens of camps erected to turn hundreds of thousands of civilians into soldiers overnight. Hasty and often shoddy construction work meant the camps were plagued by bad accommodation, inadequate sanitary facilities and abysmal feeding arrangements.

The West Indians were shocked by the conditions at the camp. Colonel C. Woodhill of the BWIR complained the huts were 'death traps' that provided little protection against the cold. Men were soon going sick in droves, he wrote, and conditions were 'so terrible that hospitals in the locality were filled to overflowing and the entire life and training of these two battalions paralysed thereby'.[11] Things were worse at Withnoe, where men of the 3rd and 4th Battalions, as well as not having sufficient warm clothing, had to sleep in tents during the winter because of a shortage of huts.

It was not long before the BWIR suffered its first death in Britain with the demise at Seaford from pneumonia of Private T.D. Primo of British Guiana on 20 October 1915.[12] Colonial Office bureaucrats dithered over how to communicate news of the death to his family. The BWIR was an infantry regiment destined for the front, and yet no thought had been given to how to report casualties. Eventually, it was decided to telegraph the information to the governor to pass on to Primo's family. Other deaths soon followed, and nineteen BWIR men would be buried in the Seaford military cemetery by the end of the war.[13]

Morale plummeted as men shivered in the barely heated sleeping quarters or went sick with the onset of winter. There were also complaints about the quantity and quality of the food. Men who had been accustomed to a diet with plenty of fresh vegetables, spices and fruit likely found the stodge served by army cooks harder to stomach than most. Mail from home was

---

10  TNA/PRO CO 318/336.
11  TNA/PRO CO 318/341.
12  TNA/PRO CO 318/336.
13  TNA/PRO CO 318/341.

also erratic or did not arrive at all because of intermittent shipping from the West Indies made worse by the German submarine threat.

Discontent reached a peak when Henry Somerset, a former policeman from British Guiana, and several men from Trinidad refused to turn out for parades because the contingent had not been paid due to bureaucratic snarls. There was talk of a strike and graffiti denouncing the authorities appeared on some of the BWIR's huts. It was not clear how many men were involved in the protest, and officers soon smoothed things over by promising the men would be paid. Somerset and the other ringleaders were treated fairly lightly, given how the army usually handled men who refused to obey orders in wartime: they were booted out of the army and sent home in civilian clothes as a mark of disgrace. Somerset claimed in a newspaper interview on his return that the troops had been treated badly, although his complaint that the men were fed mutton most days may not have seemed so terrible to many poor West Indians.

Difficulties in adjusting to army life and grumbling in the ranks were hardly unique to the BWIR. Welsh troops had been threatened with the firing squad after going on strike at Seaford the year before. It was not easy even for the most idealistic or committed volunteer to adjust to the Spartan realities of the armed forces. Algernon Aspinall, who was sent to investigate the grievances of the BWIR rank and file at Seaford, recognised this when he reported back to the Colonial Office, 'Experience has told that we must not attach too much importance to these complaints.'[14]

The troops received modest help in adapting from the West India Committee, a private group that promoted the region's interests. Like the many British civic groups that supported their local units, it raised funds to provide warm clothing, sporting gear and musical instruments, organised recreation activities and served as a conduit between the regiment and the authorities in Britain and the West Indies.

Military life soon showed that not every BWIR recruit was an ideal representative of the West Indies, despite the efforts of recruiters to pick only the best men for the regiment. At least a few delinquents got through the selection process, while some enlistees rebelled against the pressures of army life. Few were as egregious as Private Randolph Pond, who was sent back to St Kitts in 1916 after serving several months in jail in England for

---

14 TNA/PRO CO 318/341.

bad behaviour. His superiors only discovered in England that Pond had a long criminal record for theft, disorderly conduct and begging in several West Indian islands. Pond's commanding officer said he was a 'most undesirable character to have in the Regiment, and I consider him totally unfit to be a soldier'.[15]

A report to the War Office said the presence of a few rogues was troubling for the 'better class of West Indian ... [who] are already beginning to resent having to serve with such men as these'.[16] A trickle of malefactors was returned to the West Indies, where they were discharged from the army and kicked out on to the street. A few gave nonchalant interviews to local newspapers, insisting they had done nothing wrong.

Some men may have been sent home for protesting conditions in the BWIR rather than bad conduct. Colonel A.L. Barchard hinted as much when a group of five men was discharged in late 1915:

> These men are a most undesirable type to have in the West India contingent and should never have been enlisted. They are agitators who are already trying to cause discontent, and they are very insubordinate. If men of this description are not got rid of at once the West Indian contingent can never be a success.[17]

One man who was sent back to the West Indies turned disgrace into triumph of a kind by escaping from his police escorts at St Pancras Station and disappearing into the crowded streets of London: army records do not show if he was ever caught.

Despite such cases, it is clear that the BWIR was a well-behaved unit by the general standards of the British Army and the colonial forces. Most of the men adapted to army life and worked hard as they underwent basic training comprising a great deal of marching, practice sessions in mock trenches and target practice.

Off duty, the West Indians revelled at being in the land they regarded as their 'mother country'. Men who had known only small islands with clapboard colonial capitals marvelled at London and other great cities with

---

15  TNA/PRO CO 318/339.
16  TNA/PRO CO 318/336.
17  TNA/PRO CO 318/336.

their imposing architecture and bustling throngs. It reinforced the soldiers' proud sense of being part of a great empire and of helping to defend it in its hour of need. On the other hand, some BWIR soldiers were shocked and angered by the prosperity and modern conditions they encountered in Britain; it made them realise that the empire, far from being the beneficent guardian they had imagined, allowed the West Indies to languish in poverty and backwardness.

Many whites continued to treat the men with kindness and interest, and the sight of a black soldier strolling down the street frequently caused heads to turn. Some of the men enjoyed the attention, others found it uncomfortable, particularly the misguided or ludicrous notions more than a few white people held about black people. Soldiers wrote home that white people were astonished that they could speak English. 'We perforce, have to smile at the simple, benighted folks at Seaford who know so little of the Negro race. How they could not comprehend our dark skin and were astonished because you spoke such good English,' one wrote to his local newspaper.[18]

A BWIR sergeant remarked:

> I spent a couple of days in the county of Durham and the miners as they expressed themselves were awestricken to hear a coloured man speak English as good, and in the majority of cases, more correct than they, and they seemed more puzzled to know that you were conversant with the history of their own country more than they themselves.[19]

Not everyone was so welcoming. White troops, in particular, sometimes mocked BWIR men, and black soldiers were denied access to military and public recreational facilities by their ostensible comrades in arms. White soldiers and civilians fretted about romantic or sexual relations between the West Indians and white women, especially with so many local men away in the armed forces. Government and army officials, who shared the disquiet, looked at ways to discourage relations between black soldiers and white women, but failed to come up with practical measures, and some BWIR men clearly had local girlfriends.

---

18  *The Belize Independent*, 16 July 1919.
19  Quoted in Howe, p.257.

Private G.J. Dadd of Jamaica wrote home, 'Plenty of girls. They love the boys in khaki. They detest walking with civilians. They love the darkies.'[20] The Colonial Office worried about the impact on white racial prestige if word got back to the West Indies that BWIR troops had slept with white women in Britain. Some observers said the problem was the unbridled appetites of white women rather than the black troops. Riots in the East End of London in 1917 over relations between black troops and white women were blamed by *The Times* newspaper on 'the infatuation of the white girls for the black men'.[21] Whatever the lurid delusions of many whites, most of the BWIR men were fairly demure young men with as little experience of sex and women as their young white counterparts.

★★★

Nothing the first BWIR trainees endured in Britain compared with the ordeal of the regiment's 3rd Battalion, which left hundreds of men stricken with frostbite in the middle of the Canadian winter. The 3rd, with twenty-five officers and 1,115 men, left Jamaica in early March 1916 on the SS *Verdala*, an old transport ship totally unsuited for long voyages. Major G.V. Hart, commanding the contingent, said the men were excited and in fine health when the ship sailed. Hart did not know that the Admiralty had ordered the *Verdala* to sail to Britain via Canada because of the German submarine threat. Nothing had been done to ready the ship or the men for cold weather, perhaps because of efforts to keep the voyage secret.

It was the *Verdala*'s misfortune to sail into Halifax in the middle of a bit-terly cold snap with temperatures as low as −14°C (7°F). Warm clothing was handed out to the men, but it turned out that bales of warm socks had been left in Jamaica due to 'some unlucky mishap', and the volunteers had only light cotton ones that were useless in the cold.[22] The ship had virtually no heating except for a stove in the first-class saloon and radiators in a few of the officers' cabins. Within hours of the ship's arrival on 23 March, some of the men were suffering from swollen feet, the first sign of frostbite. Hart contacted the local military authorities for help, only to be told they had

---

20  Howe, p.260.
21  *The Times*, 3 July 1917.
22  Account of the *Verdala* incident based on the extensive reports contained in TNA/
PRO CO 318/339.

not been informed about the contingent. He was told it would be impossible to provide accommodation ashore for the men even though the ship was scheduled to remain in the port for a week.

Scores of men went down with severe frostbite that night. By 24 March, the contingent's medical officer reported 537 cases of frostbite and swollen feet, with thirty-seven men requiring hospitalisation. It was impossible to give the men hot food or drinks after all of the ship's water pipes froze; a little tea was made by melting snow gathered from the deck. That morning the Red Cross delivered 700 pairs of socks and more arrived from the military along with some stoves. It all came too late, as another sixty-eight cases of severe frostbite were sent to local hospitals.

Finally, the *Vardala* was given permission to sail on 26 March to the warmer climate of Bermuda. 'We had on board 377 men unable to do more than crawl about' on hands and knees, Hart subsequently reported.

The military authorities in Bermuda were appalled by conditions on the *Verdala* when the ship arrived on 29 March; more than 100 men were hospitalised, including twenty-seven suffering from gangrene. Scores of men with milder cases of frostbite required treatment in clinics. Medical officers judged that just a third of the contingent was fit for duty. A damning report by the Bermuda military authorities said the ship was not suitable for cold climates or to carry large numbers of troops of any nationality or race.

The Colonial Office attempted to hush up the incident. Nonetheless, reports found their way into the press. There were predictable attempts to blame the incident on the supposed inability of black West Indians to cope with cold weather. Captain F.H. Cooke, the 3rd's medical officer, dismissed such claims, noting it was army policy that white troops be housed in Halifax in wintertime in heated barracks with four blankets per man. The *Verdala* could not be heated, he said, and the BWIR troops were given just two blankets each. Five men died during the incident, and an unknown number perished later. More than 100 men had to have feet or toes amputated, leaving them disfigured or crippled for life.

# 10

# PYRAMIDS AND PREJUDICE

Corporal Samuel Alfred Haynes and his companions were glad to be ashore after four long weeks in a cramped troop ship. They were in Egypt and a step closer to fighting the empire's enemies, even if it would be the Turks rather than the Germans. Arriving at an army camp after a tiring march from the harbour, a group of West Indians headed for the canteen to buy refreshments. Some of the men began to sing 'Rule Britannia'. The words filled all of them with pride, and they straightened their backs and pushed out their chests. At that moment, the door to the canteen was blocked by a line of scowling white soldiers. 'Immediately we were confronted by a number of British soldiers, who asked, "Who gave you n★★★★★s authority to sing that, clear out of this building – only British troops admitted here",' Haynes later recalled the whites yelling, their faces twisted with fury.[1]

The West Indians were stunned momentarily, and then someone threw a punch. A melee erupted as black and white soldiers flailed at each other. Haynes boasted for the rest of his life that the West Indians had held their ground. Although an inquiry into the brawl by the camp authorities ensured the canteen was open to all British soldiers regardless of race, it was an omen of what lay ahead.

The British West Indies Regiment did not spend very long in Britain. Military commanders claimed that the Middle East with its hot climate

---

1   TNA/PRO CO 123/296.

would be better for the West Indians, and it conveniently fitted the army's dogma that black troops must not fight white men. After some basic training, the existing five battalions of the BWIR were shipped one by one in 1916 to Egypt, which had been turned into a vast base for British and colonial forces. While the West Indians may have been disappointed at not going to the 'big show' in France and Belgium, they were confident of seeing action soon. Resplendent in their new army uniforms, the men were full of pride at being British soldiers.

British forces in Egypt were on the defensive after an abortive attempt to take Palestine from the Turks. Army commanders welcomed the arrival of the fit and eager BWIR battalions. Australian, New Zealand and Indian formations made up a large part of the British Army in Egypt, and the arrival of the BWIR added to its air of an all-empire force.

Soon after its arrival, it was suggested the BWIR might be deployed against Senussi tribesmen fighting the British in the Western Desert. West Indian commanders objected because their troops had only learned basic skills in Britain and needed advanced combat training before being sent into battle.

While the BWIR battalions underwent further preparation, selected officers and men from the regiment were sent to the Imperial School of Instruction at Zeitoun for training as machine gunners, signallers, bombers and other specialists. Instructors were impressed by the West Indians – hardly surprising considering that many were well educated and highly motivated – and the BWIR achieved one of the school's highest pass rates.

The West Indians worked and lived with white troops at Zeitoun. Camp authorities were delighted by how well the different groups got along. 'One of the most gratifying features of the presence of West Indians in Egypt is the bond of good fellowship which exists between West Indians, Australians, New Zealanders, and men from all parts of the Empire,' an instructor reported.[2] White troops from Australia and New Zealand tended to treat the West Indians more fairly because they were all fighting far from their homes in a common cause.

Away from Zeitoun, imperial fraternity was reinforced by sport and social contacts with white units. Teams from BWIR battalions earned a scorching reputation for their prowess at football and cricket. Increasingly confident in their abilities as soldiers, the West Indians' morale was further buoyed

---

2   TNA/PRO CO 318/344.

by visits to the pyramids and Cairo; many of the men, raised in a strong Christian tradition, were awed by the country's biblical associations.

Not all white troops were welcoming; many white British soldiers were shocked and angered when they encountered black West Indians who insisted not only were they equal, but they were also British. White British soldiers from lower-class backgrounds were particularly shaken by well-educated West Indian black soldiers who spoke like officers. This outraged white soldiers, who had been raised with the inflexible belief that all black people were vastly inferior and had to obey whites.

Typical was the experience of Private David McKoy of the BWIR who was hospitalised with dysentery: after three days, the white medical orderly told him to get up and sweep the floor while white soldiers remained in bed. McKoy protested that he was too weak to eat, let alone do chores. 'He then told me that we black bastards think too much of ourselves,' he recalled.[3]

Far from being intimidated, West Indian troops pushed back when they encountered prejudice, unlike many other troops and local labourers from Africa and the Middle East, and there were occasional violent confrontations with white British troops. News of how the West Indians were being mistreated caused dissension at home. Governor Eyre Hutson of British Honduras warned the Colonial Office that it:

> … has given rise to a strong and dangerous ill feeling among negroes in the West Indies against Europeans. In my opinion this has been caused by the failure on the part of the British European Troops to recognise that the majority of Black West Indians have been accustomed, rightly or wrong, to receive treatment in the West Indies differing from that usually meted out to Egyptians, Arabs and natives of Africa.[4]

Egypt gave many of the young West Indians the first, bitter taste of the racism that would dog the BWIR on and off the battlefield for the rest of the war. It bred disillusionment and resentment in some of the men, and this only increased with time. George Bennett of British Honduras said the West Indians enlisted 'with patriotism and loyalty akin to worship',

---

3   TNA/PRO CO 123/296.
4   TNA/PRO CO 123/296.

but rather than being 'treated with a spirit of comradeship, by British soldiers especially … were discriminated against on account of … colour
and racial characteristics'.[5]

In June 1916, the 1st, 2nd and 3rd BWIRs were moved to the Suez
Canal Zone, where they did more training and constructed trenches, roads
and other installations. While such work was essential, the West Indians
seemed to get far more of it than white units, and the men started to
wonder when they would get a chance to fight. There was widespread
envy when the 3rd BWIR was attacked by a Turkish plane as it was drawn
up to be inspected by a visiting general; a regimental report grumbled
that the unit 'had the luck to have been bombed'.[6] The plane dropped five
bombs, injuring one soldier, and the general commended the way the battalion had coolly taken cover.

Conditions in the desert were as much a shock for the West Indians as
they were for white British troops. Summer temperatures routinely reached
46°C (115°F) and higher in the tents, where men drained by the smother-
ing heat lay prostrate on their bedding for much of the day. Not that the
troops got much sleep: flies and other insects tormented them at all hours.
Many men went down with the fever inflicted by the maddening bites of
sand flies or were stricken with dysentery, cholera and other diseases.

The war seemed to be on permanent hold. Inactivity and boredom took
a heavy toll on the men's minds. Units spent weeks and months holding
isolated positions in the empty desert, the barren landscape and monotony
eroding morale and triggering nervous breakdowns. Soldiers' first impres-
sions of Egypt as a fabled, exotic land gave way to contempt for a country
that seemed to consist of nothing beside dust, heat and flies.

Still smarting at being forced to accept a black West Indian unit, army
commanders in London resisted employing the BWIR as an infantry formation. General Sir Archibald J. Murray, the British Commander in Egypt,
was asked in June 1916 if he thought the West Indians could be employed
as pioneer or labour troops in Mesopotamia, mainly on the railway system.
Murray replied that medical officials had concluded the BWIR was 'not fit',
of 'poor stock'[7] and not up to such work. It seems he was not being racist

---

5   TNA/PRO CO 123/296.
6   TNA/PRO WO 95/4732.
7   TNA/PRO CO 318/339.

because he said his white British troops were no better. Unlike most generals, he championed the West Indians' desire to fight:

> It must also be borne in mind that these battalions look upon themselves as representing the West Indies, and are anxious to fight for the Empire. They were very anxious not to be turned into garrison troops, and it is possible that they and their supporters at home might resent their being turned into labour corps.[8]

It would be in Europe rather than in Egypt that the BWIR would finally see action.

A small black unit on the Western Front in the summer of 1916 was demolishing the army's bigoted belief that race was a barrier to courage or martial prowess. Bermuda's segregated Local Defence Force comprised the all-white Bermuda Volunteer Rifle Corps and the black Bermuda Militia Artillery, which manned the island's coastal batteries under white officers. Both formations had sent detachments to the Western Front, the white infantry forming a company of the Lincolnshire Regiment while three officers and 195 men of the artillery formed an ammunition company attached to the Royal Artillery.

The black artillerymen won praise during the Battle of the Somme in the summer of 1916, hauling heavy shells up to the front-line batteries. It was gruelling and dangerous work with the men frequently under enemy fire. Impressed by the black Bermudans' example, the War Office decided to employ the 3rd and 4th BWIRs in the same role on the Western Front. Both battalions hurriedly left Egypt for France at the end of August. In addition, a draft of 500 officers and men from the 1st, 2nd and 3rd BWIRs was sent to join the campaign against German forces in East Africa, and a smaller detachment went to Mesopotamia to do clerical and transport work. Still nominally infantry units, the 1st and 2nd BWIRs stayed in Egypt along with the 5th BWIR as their depot unit. It would be a long time before they saw any real fighting.

---

8   TNA/PRO CO 318/339.

A slave soldier of the West India Regiment (WIR) in the uniform of the regular British Army at the start of the nineteenth century.

A WIR soldier in the Zouave uniform based on the exotic costume of French North African troops.

Sergeant William Gordon of the 2nd WIR, one of two members of the regiment who were the first black soldiers to win the Victoria Cross for heroism, stands with a private.

An officer and soldiers of the WIR in formation.

Officers of the WIR look serenely masterful as they pose on a veranda, but the rest of the army looked down on them for leading black troops.

General Garnet Wolseley did not want the WIR to be included in the Ashanti War despite romantic depictions of the regiment in the campaign.

A dramatic depiction of WIR troops in action in West Africa in the 1890s. The troops excelled at fighting in the wilderness.

A detachment of the WIR fires a salute over the graves of British and French troops killed in an accidental clash at Waima in West Africa in 1893.

WIR troops at Orange Walk in British Honduras, where in 1872 a detachment of the regiment fought off an attack by hundreds of Native American fighters.

The British public saw black West Indian troops as simpletons and clowns, as typified in these cartoons of the 1880s from the popular press.

White WIR officers dance with African women at a ball in Sierra Leone in a cartoon lampooning such men for their close association with black people.

Officers of the Jamaica militia in the 1890s.

White and black NCOs of the Jamaica militia around 1890.

British officers take a ride in the West Indies. Postings to the region were not popular.

A white trooper of the Trinidad Light Horse.

Black and mixed-race men are sworn into the British West India Regiment (BWIR) in Barbados in 1916.

# YOUNG MEN
## OF THE BAHAMAS

The British Empire is engaged in a Life and Death Struggle. Never in the History of England, never since the Misty Distant Past of 2,000 years ago, has our beloved Country been engaged in such a conflict as she is engaged in to-day.

To bring to nothing this mighty attack by an unscrupulous and well prepared foe, HIS MOST GRACIOUS MAJESTY KING GEORGE has called on the men of his Empire, MEN OF EVERY CLASS, CREED AND COLOUR, to

### COME FORWARD TO FIGHT

that the Empire may be saved and the foe may be well beaten.

This call is to YOU, young man; not your neighbour, not your brother, not your cousin, but just YOU.

SEVERAL HUNDREDS OF YOUR MATES HAVE COME UP, HAVE BEEN MEDICALLY EXAMINED AND HAVE BEEN PASSED AS "FIT."

### What is the matter with YOU?

Put yourself right with your King; put yourself right with your fellowmen; put yourself right with yourself and your conscience.

# ENLIST TO-DAY

THE GLEANER CO. LTD., PRINTERS, KINGSTON JAMAICA.

A recruiting poster for the BWIR tells West Indians of all races that it is their duty to fight for England as the mother country.

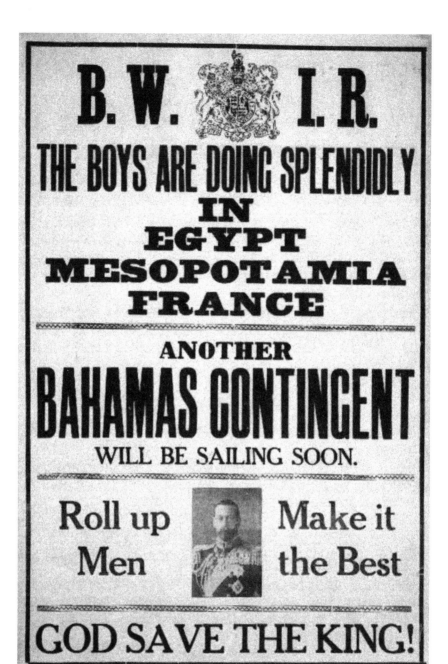

A recruiting poster appeals to the men of the Bahamas to join the BWIR battalions serving in Europe and the Middle East.

Infantrymen of the BWIR in a camp on the Western Front. (Photo: Imperial War Museum)

Black West Indian and white Australian troops pile artillery shells on the Western Front. The BWIR spent much of its time doing this dangerous and gruelling work. (Photo: Imperial War Museum)

A painting depicting black West Indian troops carrying shells up to white artillerymen during the First World War; the men were only allowed to do manual labour because of their race.

Men of the BWIR dig emplacements in the Middle East. Despite the cheerful smiles, the regiment was bitter at not being allowed to fight until the last days of the war. (Photo: Imperial War Museum)

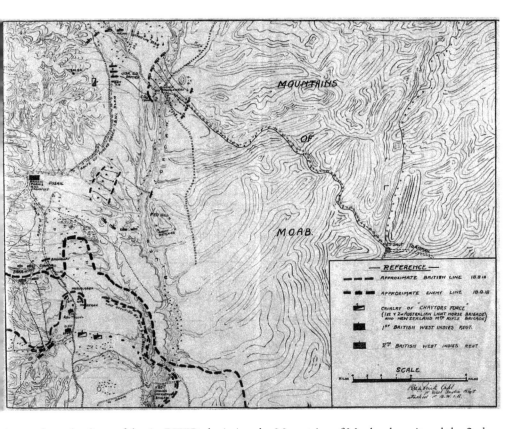

A map from the diary of the 1st BWIR depicting the Mountains of Moab where it and the 2nd BWIR played a key role in defeating Turkish forces.

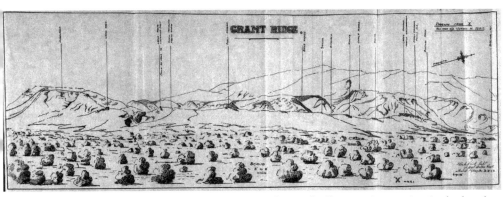

A drawing of Turkish positions faced by the BWIR when it finally went into action in the last days of the First World War.

BWIR soldiers return home. The government feared they might lead revolts and sent warships to shepherd the contingents. (Photo: Imperial War Museum)

Wilbur Simons of Bermuda with a monument to men of the BWIR who died from illness on the island en route to the front.

The Trinidad Volunteers receive a new standard on the eve of the Second World War.
The local West Indian defence forces were far from ready when the conflict came. (Photo:
Imperial War Museum)

A contingent of the 1st Battalion Caribbean Regiment is mobbed by well-wishers and
spectators as it sets out for Europe in 1944.

A member of the British Honduras Forestry Unit, which came to help in Britain but endured discrimination and mistreatment from some whites. (Photo: Imperial War Museum)

A white officer inspects men of the 1st Battalion Caribbean Regiment. (Photo: Imperial War Museum)

Machine gunners of the 1st Battalion Caribbean Regiment take aim during exercises in the Middle East. (Photo: Imperial War Museum)

A mortar crew of the 1st Battalion Caribbean Regiment. (Photo: Imperial War Museum)

A Bren gunner of the 1st Battalion Caribbean Regiment. (Photo: Imperial War Museum)

Troops of the 1st Battalion Caribbean Regiment exercise with a Bren gun carrier. In reality, the army rarely allowed the unit such weapons. (Photo: Imperial War Museum)

Musicians of the Caribbean Regiment rehearse. (Photo: Imperial War Museum)

# II

# BAIT FOR THE GERMANS

The British West Indies Regiment served on the Western Front during some of the bloodiest battles of the war, and yet it was never allowed to fight, despite being acclaimed for unwavering devotion and bravery. White commanders, soldiers and civilians treated the black troops during these years with a mix of contempt, condescension and camaraderie.

The BWIR was used mainly as ammunition units for the British artillery in France and Belgium, transporting shells to batteries in the front lines. It was gruelling and dangerous work. The shells, some weighing hundreds of pounds, had to be hauled or carried through a devastated landscape of mud, craters, tangled barbed wire and the corpses of men and horses. Enemy artillery peppered the routes used by the supply parties, filling the air with jagged white-hot shrapnel.

It was even more perilous at night when the heavily laden soldiers stumbled half-blind through the pitted terrain, in constant danger of falling into the mud and drowning. Ammunition detachments routinely worked for days with little or no sleep, especially during major offensives when batteries consumed thousands of shells in hours. The West Indians also served as stretcher bearers, bringing wounded men back from the front line, and built and repaired gun emplacements and other installations.

The one thing the army would not allow them to do was fight, even though the BWIR, at least on paper, was an infantry regiment. It was a prohibition that rankled the West Indians more than any of the many racist slights they had to endure; they wanted to be counted as men and hit back at the Germans. Corporal Charles Booth said, as he lay dying in hospital after being caught by enemy artillery fire, 'I valintery joine [*sic*] up I am not helpless.'[1]

The West Indians were humiliated whenever they saw the black infantry regiments of the French Army, who earned a ferocious reputation as shock troops.[2] And yet the BWIR's main role as ammunition troops was combat work, even if they could not use their rifles, and most of the men took pride in it, working alongside white ammunition detachments from Britain, Australia, Canada and elsewhere.

Young men from Jamaica or Barbados were no better or worse prepared than young men from Britain or Germany to face the ordeal of life and death on the Western Front. Each man dealt with the conditions as best they could. Pride, personal strength, fear of failure and comradeship helped them to endure the terrors of the trenches and the constant risk of violent death or maiming. Or, as Private G. Milne of the 10th BWIR put it, 'We come out here [and] grew, majarily [majority] did not know what things was like, but Still we have tried our worthless best.'[3]

With time, the men became largely inured to the enemy bombardments and other dangers, acquiring the soldier's knack of knowing when shells could be ignored and when to take cover. Even so, Private C.H. Jenkins from British Guiana never forgot his first experience of being shelled:

> We spent about thirty-five days more or less in the same position. During this period our experiences were innumerable, and very grave, for at any moment anyone of us could have been hurled into eternity. We were face to face with high explosives and wizbangs and shrapnel too, bursting over trenches which could have cut any of us to pieces at any moment. One of the first awful sights I witnessed was seeing one of the high explosives fall in a dugout and blow two of my chums from British Guiana to pieces; another was severely wounded and another driven mad.[4]

Scores of West Indians were crippled, losing limbs, their sight and other vital senses. Corporal A. Giew wrote to a well-wisher:

---

1   Quoted in Matilde Mallet, *Letters from the Trenches During the Great War*, p.47.
2   Richard Fogarty, *Race and War in France*, p.2.
3   Quoted in Mallet, p.5.
4   Quoted in Howe, *West Indians and World War One*, p.281.

I am indeed Glad to tell you that I count myself Be very lucky, that is I only lost one leg, an [*sic*] for what I have past [*sic*] through an only lost one leg, I count myself to Be very lucky. I am sorry to tell you, Lady, I am in bed at present; an [*sic*] I don't know when I will get fitted up with an 'artificial' leg. I believe it will Be a long time Before I get fitted up. But I am still living in hope, until my time come.[5]

There was a strong sense in the ranks of the BWIR that they represented the British West Indies, and if they did not do well it would reflect badly on their homelands and their race. Belief in the righteousness of the Allied cause also helped to sustain the men. Lance Corporal A.E.A. Lewis of the 10th BWIR haltingly summed it up, 'The men of the brave who has sacrificed happiness and pleasures; and has made up their minds to fall victims to the grave for the reservation [preservation] of Freedom and loves and home.'[6]

Another BWIR soldier wrote of how some of those who stayed safely at home mocked the men who enlisted, jeering that they would be slaughtered. 'Wee was goin to make Blait [bait] for the german. But thank God wee have don our bit and We Will not let the old flarg faild [flag fail],' he wrote in broken English.[7]

West Indian casualty rates were relatively low by the horrific standards of the conflict. In the course of the war, the BWIR suffered 185 men (1.22 per cent) killed in action and 697 men (4.58 per cent) were wounded, with 1,071 dying of disease: that compared to an overall British Army rate of 12.9 per cent killed in action and 31 per cent wounded.[8] Such comparisons are misleading since the overall figures include front-line infantry, which suffered by far the greatest losses. BWIR casualties were comparable to the losses suffered by white British and colonial units in the support role. It might be argued that discrimination actually saved the West Indians from the slaughter that shattered so many British, Indian and other formations. The men of the BWIR undoubtedly would have been insulted by such prevarications – they had enlisted to fight as equals, whatever the price.

---

5   Quoted in Mallet, p.3.
6   Quoted in Mallet, p.10.
7   Quoted in Mallet p.13.
8   Sir Charles Lucas, *The Empire at War*, Vol. 2, p.335.

Although they were banned from fighting, the West Indians lived in fear of being taken prisoner. Germany stridently denounced the British and French use of black troops as a betrayal of Western civilisation. German propaganda depicted black troops as savages and vermin who mutilated wounded and captured German soldiers and committed bestial outrages against helpless white civilians. Hans Friedrich Blunck, a German front-line soldier, wrote after fighting black troops, 'The enemy had sent half-animal peoples of Africa … the enemy mobilised Asia and betrayed thousand year old Europe.'[9]

This created an abiding dread among black troops that they would be tortured and killed if captured. Norman Manley, the future Jamaican Prime Minister, always carried a rifle because of the risks of being captured. 'I was half-Negro and the stories of what happened to coloured men taken prisoner of war were very grim and of course believed by all of us implicitly,' he said.[10]

There is no indication that any BWIR soldiers were captured, or that the Germans systematically mistreated black Allied prisoners. Black West Indian seamen serving on cargo ships captured by the Germans during the war were treated reasonably, as were British Indian prisoners of war.

★★★

West Indian families who lost sons, brothers, husbands and fathers during the war often had to endure long and needless delays in learning of their fates. While great pains were taken to notify families in Britain of deaths or injuries as quickly as possible, the army had made little or no effort to compile addresses, next of kin and other vital details for the BWIR, making it difficult to contact relatives of the dead and wounded.

A typical example was Private Alexander Forbes of the 7th BWIR, who died of wounds at No. 2 Canadian Stationary Hospital in France in August 1917.[11] His records indicated only that he was from Jamaica; his birth date, address, marital status and next of kin were unknown. Military authorities and police in the West Indies were given the task of tracking down the

---

9   Quoted in Das, *Race, Empire and First World War Writing*, p.129.
10  Manley, 'The Autobiography of Norman Washington Manley', p.9.
11  Imperial War Museum Doc. 16413, A. Forbes.

relatives of the BWIR's dead and injured, often with nothing more to go on than a surname. Some families may have only found out about the deaths of their men when comrades returned from the war; other families may never have found out what happened.

Lack of records also meant that some relatives never received the pensions they were entitled to. A group of clerks at the Colonial Office in London spent months trying to update BWIR personnel records. A mid-level official observed that the problem was not treated as seriously as it should have been. 'After all they are only n★★★★★s,' he sarcastically wrote.[12] And while the work brought some improvement, the Colonial Office complained subsequently about the resulting increased cost of telegrams to families in the West Indies.

When they could be traced, families of slain BWIR men received a message of sympathy from the king, as was done with white British soldiers. After the first royal condolences arrived in the West Indies, the local military authorities expressed concern because this had never been done for the countless WIR soldiers killed over the decades. Bureaucrats at the War Office in London tried to shrug off the matter, saying condolence messages were not sent to 'native regiments',[13] a claim it knew full well was false because the WIR was a regular regiment. Only after officials in Jamaica warned of a serious public backlash did the army agree to give the WIR equal treatment – more than a century after its founding.

★★★

Like the troops of every nation and race, many of the West Indian soldiers believed war made them better and stronger men. However, not every man could endure the hellish conditions, and a few abandoned their posts and tried to flee. Desertion was punished by the firing squad because of the generals' fear that it would otherwise infect the entire army, and at least one BWIR soldier was executed.

Herbert Morris of the 6th BWIR was arrested at the English Channel port of Boulogne on 21 August 1917 after guards saw him acting suspiciously. He was wearing his uniform and steel helmet, but did not have a

---

12  TNA/PRO CO 318/347.
13  TNA/PRO CO 137/723.

rifle, gas mask and other equipment. It soon became clear that Morris had deserted, and he was sent back to his battalion to face a court martial. The court papers stated that Morris was 'a soldier of the regular forces'.[14]

At the court martial, Lieutenant L.R. Andrews testified that Morris had been part of a work party assigned to a battery of heavy guns some 2 miles behind the front line near Ypres in Belgium. It was only discovered that Morris was absent after the detachment arrived at the battery. Seven members of the work party were injured by enemy artillery fire, the officer told the court. 'We had a very hot time of it while we worked there from the shelling,' he said. Andrews told the court that Morris had deserted once before. He had been returned to the battalion, where he was stripped of privileges, given extra work for two weeks and a second chance. Andrews showed some sympathy for the accused man, saying, 'His intelligence is higher than that of the ordinary men in my platoon.' Captain Russell also spoke for Morris, testifying, 'The accused has never given me any trouble and is a willing worker.'

Morris, who had enlisted in Jamaica in December 1916, gave a brief, rambling defence of his actions. 'I am troubled in my head and cannot stand the sounds of the guns. I reported to the doctor and he gave me no medicine or anything ... He gave me no satisfaction,' he said. His pleas made no difference. After a brief recess, the court martial sentenced Morris to death, a decision confirmed by Field Marshal Douglas Haig, the Supreme British Army Commander on the Western Front.

Morris was executed at Poperinghe on 20 September. A padre said Morris was very calm and had told him that he was ready to die just before he was blindfolded and tied to a stake. He was just 17 when he was shot at dawn.

Morris was executed by a firing squad of seven West Indians and three soldiers from a white unit. It is not clear why white troops were added to the squad: it may have been because of the army's habitual distrust of black troops and fear they could not be trusted to kill one of their own.

★★★

Impressed by the exploits of the BWIR, the War Office in late 1916 asked for another 10,000 black West Indian recruits.[15] Eventually, the BWIR

---

14  TNA/PRO WO 71/594 for all quotes from the court martial.
15  TNA/PRO CO 318/344.

would expand to eleven battalions with some 15,000 men, the great majority of them serving in Europe. British commanders no longer looked down on the regiment as a useless black rabble. Haig, who was never an admirer of black soldiers, praised the West Indians' physique, discipline and high morale in a November 1917 dispatch:

> This work has been very arduous and has been carried out almost continuously under shell fire. In spite of casualties the men have always shown themselves willing and cheerful workers, and the assistance they have rendered has been much appreciated by the units to which they have been attached.[16]

Praise from the High Command did not mean the army, or most whites, were ready to embrace the West Indians as equals. Some BWIR officers and men complained of persistent racism and mistreatment throughout the war, claiming they were always given the worst quarters, clothing and food while white units received far better treatment. Such complaints were often ignored or dismissed as untrue by the military and civilian authorities.

A letter written in December 1917 by Harry M. Brown, the chaplain of the 10th BWIR, however, set off a storm of controversy in London and the West Indies when he charged that white German POWs were better treated than the battalion's black troops. Brown said in a letter to the West India Committee, the private group in London that helped look after the regiment's welfare:

> I visited a barracks today and discovered German prisoners warm and comfortable – their rooms adequately heated by stoves, and in some barracks our own West India boys on the extreme top floor without warming apparatus of any kind, cold and suffering. In every room where I saw West Indians there was at least one sick man, and in one room two men were stretched on a concrete floor both with high temperatures and both huddled up trying to secure as much warmth as possible from a couple of blankets. The Officer who took me around described the rooms as the ghastliest and a perfect abomination. I asked about the

---

16  TNA/PRO CO 318/344.

stoves and was told that they had been promised. I had the same reply some weeks ago.[17]

Brown vented his anger and anguish at what he saw as the wilful waste of the lives of British soldiers:

> Our men are certainly worth better treatment. They do not complain; in fact they are most cheerful, but at the same time it is pitiable to see them dying, as I do see them, when all this waste of life might be averted.[18]

The 10th was a Jamaican battalion, and a copy of Brown's letter found its way to Reverend Ernest Price, head of the Baptist Theological College in Kingston. Price promptly sent it to the governor, expressing concern that 'the thoughtlessness or the foolishness of those who are responsible for the conditions' meant 'our Jamaica men are being treated in a very cruel way'.[19]

Informed of the letter, the Colonial Office in London tried to play it down by saying white troops also often went cold and hungry, and that the BWIR seemed especially prone to complaining. 'I think W.O. [War Office] must be tired of these enquiries about this not very important regt [regiment],' one exasperated official wrote.[20]

Worried about the possible impact on West Indian public opinion, the Colonial Office felt compelled to pass the complaint to the War Office, saying only that it had come from a serving officer. Outraged army officials responded by demanding the officer's name, 'in order that we can begin proceedings against him if we find that he has deliberately circulated an untrue statement'.[21]

Lord Derby, the Secretary of State for War, was sufficiently alarmed by the allegations to order an investigation into the claims about the 10th's treatment. A subsequent report, while insisting the battalion was adequately housed and denying that sick men had been left lying on concrete floors, admitted a section of the battalion did spend several days in unheated huts despite intense cold. This was the fault of their white

---

17  TNA/PRO CO 318/345.
18  TNA/PRO CO 318/345.
19  TNA/PRO CO 137/725.
20  TNA/PRO CO 318/347.
21  TNA/PRO CO 318/347.

commanding officer, who had failed to order stoves, and his 'slackness' was being investigated, it added. There was no admission of any failings on the army's part.

It seems very unlikely that Brown lied or exaggerated about seeing sick black soldiers lying cold and shivering on the concrete floors of unheated rooms while white prisoners enjoyed heated quarters. Officials in London and the West Indies smothered the affair with denials and the old excuse that black troops could not cope with cold weather. And anyway, it was wartime and 'considerable sickness and even mortality would have to be regarded as regrettable and unavoidable', the army said.[22]

There was no doubt that the BWIR endured flagrant discrimination when it came to the vital issue of leave for the troops. W.H. Manning, the Governor of Jamaica, expressed concern in late 1917 after reports reached the island that black West Indian soldiers stationed on the Western Front were not being given leave in the United Kingdom like other British troops. White BWIR officers faced no such restriction. Even the army's most fervent martinets accepted that leave was vital to maintain soldiers' morale. Moreover, many of the West Indians had never been to Britain, the governor added, and were 'most anxious to visit the Mother country' they were fighting for.[23]

And yet Manning did not like the idea of thousands of black West Indian soldiers at liberty in the streets of Britain, especially if it meant they were free to meet white women. At the same time, he worried about the negative impact on black public opinion and recruiting for the new BWIR battalions. Primly, he suggested a solution:

> I recognise the difficulties of allowing West Indians to proceed to England and the dangers and temptations which they would incur, but I think that it might be possible to allow the men to come to England in detachments in charge of a responsible officer, who would take charge of them while in England and would prevent their being brought into contact with loose women and other undesirable characters.[24]

22  TNA/PRO CO 318/347.
23  TNA/PRO CO 318/345.
24  TNA/PRO CO 318/345.

Colonial Office supervisors, who shared the governor's qualms, passed the proposal to the army, which promptly buried it and did nothing.

West Indian troops had prejudices of their own, despite having to endure frequent discrimination. Seeing themselves as Englishmen, the BWIR's rank and file especially resented being lumped with the African, Asian and Arab labour units at the very bottom of the military hierarchy. Rightly or wrongly, the West Indians despised these men as ignorant savages. Just as some white soldiers objected to sharing facilities with the West Indians, so BWIR troops resented being made to share accommodation or hospital wards with Africans and Asians. Manning tried without much success to explain the problem to London. He told the Colonial Office:

> I can quite understand that Medical Officers and ... [hospital] orderlies find difficulty in distinguishing between the [black] South African and the West Indian, but I would suggest that it might be possible to issue instructions that West Indians who are for the most part educated men should be accorded similar treatment in hospital as is given to the fighting ranks of other Corps.[25]

★★★

Race inevitably coloured the BWIR's contact with French and Belgian civilians in the farms and villages where the unit was billeted behind the front line. The civilians had been reared with the usual firm European belief in white supremacy and black inferiority, and many resented or were uncomfortable with the presence of the black troops. A Catholic priest, Father Achiel Van Walleghem, left an account of how people in his Belgian parish reacted to the arrival of a BWIR battalion. He wrote in his diary:

> Negroes [from West India and Jamaica] have arrived to work at the farm of Alouis Adriaen and Drie Groen. They are dressed like English soldiers, are civilised, speak very softly, but they are not much liked because of their sticky fingers, and on the whole the civilians prefer to see the back

---

25  TNA/PRO CO 318/345.

of them, because when they enter a place for a cup of coffee they can stay anything from five minutes to a couple of hours.[26]

And yet the priest's less than charitable view of the soldiers was shaken when he found a letter written by a mother of 'one of these blacks' that had been left behind. 'What sincere, Christian and motherly feelings! None of our mothers could write better,' he wonderingly wrote.[27]

★★★

A BWIR detachment was sent to East Africa, where the closest it came to combat was a murderous rivalry with the regulars of the 2nd WIR serving in the theatre. The German colony of Tanganyika and the surrounding region was the scene of one of the most extraordinary campaigns of the entire war. A small German force of mostly black African infantry outmarched and out-fought an army of British, Indian and African troops, not laying down their arms until after Berlin had surrendered.

The campaign was already two years old in 1916 when the 2nd WIR arrived from West Africa. It took part in the bloodless capture of the German capital at Dar-es-Salaam, providing the honour guard at the raising of the British flag. It then formed part of a column that drove south, occupying the coastline and forcing back the Germans.

A detachment of fifty men from the regiment defeated a much larger German force in a clash at Schaeffer's Farm, inflicting heavy losses on the enemy. Casualties and disease had reduced the 2nd to a shell with just 250 men by this point; all of the officers were dead or sick, and it was commanded by a mere second lieutenant from another regiment. It had to be assigned to garrison duty on the coast. Only its machine gun and mortar sections took part in subsequent operations, winning high praise for their skill and bravery.

West Indian colonial officials said it was impossible to find replacements for the 2nd because the BWIR was sucking up every available recruit in the Caribbean. Military commanders in East Africa hit on the seemingly simple solution of merging the 2nd with the newly arrived BWIR

---

26 Quoted in Das, *Race, Empire and First World War Writing*, p.149.
27 Das, p.149.

detachment to form an integrated battalion. News of the planned merger created consternation and fury in both units. The BWIR, with its high number of men from better social positions, regarded itself as the true representative of the British West Indies, while despising the WIR as a 'second-class colonial unit'.[28] The WIR was equally dismissive of the BWIR, dismissing them as rank amateurs and mere boys.

Alarmed by the real threat of British soldiers killing each other, the army dropped the plan. The East Africa command told London in an April 1918 cable:

> If it is carried out serious trouble will result involving riot and probable murder. Some disorder had already been threatened. Trying to discover ringleaders but think feelings so general that it is impossible to fix responsibility on individuals. The units well behaved in other respects.[29]

A short time later, the remnants of the 2nd were moved to the Middle East. It did not see action again, although it was kept in the region until well after the war, mostly guarding stores, and did not return to the West Indies until July 1919.

The BWIR detachment in East Africa was used in support roles and never saw action. Nothing in their lives had prepared the troops for the hardships of the campaign. Long marches through the bush in searing heat exhausted the men; they often had to sleep in the mud beside the primitive tracks; and insects feasted on them by day and night. Almost every man went down with fever, stomach ailments, malaria and other diseases; some died or endured broken health for the rest of their lives. Hunger was commonplace because food and other necessities were always in short supply. Men wore the same clothes for weeks at a time, and soon resembled scarecrows as their uniforms rotted and fell apart; the garments of the dead were swiftly divided among the living.

Corporal A.H. De Gannes of Trinidad never forgot the horrors of the African wilderness. He wrote:

---

28  TNA/PRO CO 318/339.
29  TNA/PRO CO 318/347.

I have never yet experienced such an unhealthy country as Africa. It is absolutely a place of fever, dysentery, etc., and other diseases caused by the mosquitoes, flies and all sorts of insects that Nature can produce … We are all quite anxious to leave this country as it is nothing compared with England, Egypt and Asia Minor.[30]

★★★

Miseries of a different kind were endured by the small BWIR detachment in Mesopotamia. It was composed largely of educated and skilled clerks and artisans and performed vital work running transport and administrative services. Lieutenant General F.S. Maude, the theatre commander, praised the detachment of some 400 men for their work, saying, 'They have been especially welcome as representatives of such a distant portion of the Empire.'[31]

However, far from being welcome, the men faced some of the worst discrimination endured by the BWIR. It seemed the West Indians always got less food, clothing and other privileges than white troops doing the same or less important work. Some black NCOs were paid less than lower-ranking whites who worked under them. BWIR men complained repeatedly of being banned from concerts, canteens, sports events and other facilities because of their colour. They were often forced to live in dilapidated native accommodation that did not keep out the rain, wind or sun, while white personnel were housed in purpose-built huts with heating and electric light. Attempts to complain, as allowed by army regulations, were ignored or met with threats of retaliation. Discrimination even extended to religion, with the West Indians at times forced to stand outside church services.

All British forces in Mesopotamia suffered terribly from malaria, sand fly fever and other diseases. As a British Army unit, the BWIR was entitled to the same medical treatment as white troops, but the West Indians complained that their sick were often ignored or had to wait days for treatment. Corporal Samuel Alfred Haynes recalled:

---

30 Quoted in Howe, p.208.
31 TNA/PRO CO 318/347.

The medical attention paid to our men in hospitals was exceedingly poor compared with that paid to British soldiers. When admitted to hospitals we were generally set apart from Europeans and put in wards with Africans and Asiatics who were ignorant of the English language and Western customs.[32]

When West Indian patients were treated in the same hospitals as white troops, in accordance with army rules, it was the turn of white officials to be outraged. 'It is monstrous that coloured men should be treated in the same hospital as white men. I only hope white nurses have nothing to do with them,' A. Fiddian, of the Colonial Office in London, fumed.[33]

Nothing angered the West Indians more than the constant refusals to recognise their status as British infantry. They were particularly offended when local commanders put them in the same category as African and Chinese labourers. 'We were the only fighting unit so shown on the return,' said Sergeant Ezekiel Augustus Grant.[34]

Regimental Sergeant Major Frederick McDonald of the BWIR, who oversaw a transport office with mostly white subordinates, believed the main problem was not so much official discrimination as the refusal of the white rank and file to accept black soldiers. White troops frequently prevented the BWIR from using canteens and other facilities that were officially open to both groups. As the white soldiers saw it, black soldiers who 'put on airs' had to be 'put in their place'. The West Indians refused to be silent and resisted as best they could.

Angry West Indian veterans of Mesopotamia complained after the war that their white officers did little or nothing to help them. Captain Granville Hulse of the BWIR intervened when he found seventy BWIR men living in a segregated area of an army base with no washing or other facilities while white troops had kitchens and latrines. Hulse was ignored when he told the base commander that the BWIR was a British unit and entitled to the same treatment as white soldiers. A new commander subsequently made major improvements, but Hulse admitted he could do nothing about the racism of the white troops.[35]

---

32  TNA/PRO CO 123/296.
33  TNA/PRO CO 318/347.
34  TNA/PRO CO 123/296.
35  TNA/PRO CO 123/296.

★★★

Many West Indians returned home from Europe, the Middle East and Africa disillusioned and bitter. They had volunteered to fight for the British Empire in its hour of greatest need, only to be mistreated and abused. Their anger and hurt was captured in a letter that Roland Green, a white civilian in England, forwarded to the Colonial Office in the last weeks of the war. It was written by a BWIR sergeant who Green knew through Christian circles.

Green's evidently educated and cultured correspondent said service in the British military had profoundly shaken his faith in God and the empire because the treatment of the BWIR violated every Christian tenet. The sergeant wrote:

> We are treated neither as Christians nor British Citizens, but as West Indian 'N*****s', without anybody to be interested in or look after us. Instead of being drawn closer to the Church and the Empire we are driven away from it. Today all that I was taught and believe has been shattered.[36]

Even worse, given the British habit of deploring racial relations in the United States to deflect attention from their own bigotry, the sergeant said:

> Our relations with the other [British] troops are just as strained as those between white and black in U.S.A. with the difference that over there wrong can be redressed while with us there is no redress, for we have no rights or privileges.[37]

A reply from the Colonial Office informed Green that nothing could be done unless he provided the sergeant's name, army number and specific instances of mistreatment. Green promised to pass the reply on, but not surprisingly, nothing further was heard.

Most black West Indian soldiers endeavoured to hold on to their patriotic idealism despite the contempt and mockery of some white soldiers

---

36  TNA/PRO CO 318/347.
37  TNA/PRO CO 318/347.

and civilians. Lance Corporal Walters Als of the 11th BWIR spoke for many of his comrades when he wrote to an English woman about why he had enlisted:

> Us boys ... who has so Patriotically Answered the Call, and has joined the Ever flowing Colours of Great Britain for the Good cause of the Universal world. To set free the liberal Sons and Daughters of Great Britain.[38]

---

38 Quoted in Mallet, p.49.

# 12

# 'SLIGHTLY COLOURED' OFFICERS

Few things horrified the British Empire's rulers more than the idea of black military officers. Army commanders had never wanted a new black West Indian regiment, relenting only because of the intervention of King George V. But the generals adamantly refused to admit black men to the ranks of their own professional caste. Whites from all classes found the notion of black officers from the West Indies, or anywhere else, deeply threatening. It would turn the racial and social edifice of the empire upside down; men regarded as intrinsically inferior would be able to give orders to white soldiers and rub shoulders with the elite.

The question of whether black men could be officers in the BWIR arose as soon as the unit was formed in 1915. There was a precedent, since some of the West Indian volunteer defence forces had a few black officers. In reply to a Colonial Office query on whether black men could be given commissions in the new regiment, the Army Council stated, 'that no candidate, not of pure European descent, should be recommended'.[1] If not enough white West Indian officers could be found for the BWIR, the council said white British officers would be provided to make up the shortfall.

A few of the more liberal West Indian governors tried to challenge the ban, warning it would anger the black population, or they championed

---

1   TNA/PRO CO 28/287.

particular candidates. Sir Leslie Probyn, the energetic Governor of Barbados, wrote to the Colonial Secretary, Andrew Bonar Law, to push the case of F.A.C. Clairmonte, a textbook candidate, except for his race. Clairmonte, who had graduated from the island's best schools and a business college in Canada, left his post as a senior civil servant to enlist in the BWIR, where he rose rapidly to sergeant. His former civil service superiors backed his request for a commission with a glowing recommendation. Probyn told Bonar Law, 'if the colour ban may be relaxed for the West India contingent', he was convinced Clairmonte would be a fine officer.[2] His pleas were rebuffed by the army.

A number of black and mixed-race men who excelled in the BWIR were denied commissions. Few soldiers in the British forces were better qualified or more deserving of a commission than Sergeant E. Gresham of the 1st BWIR. He had been invalided home to Grenada after falling seriously ill in Egypt. Rather than returning to the comfort of civilian life, Gresham threw himself into recruiting for the regiment, winning praise from local officials. Gresham applied in May 1917 for a commission.

His application noted that he was a civil servant with eleven years of education and had won a number of scholarships and academic prizes. Major C.W. Smith, staff officer of the local defence force, said Gresham was his right-hand man and praised his work for the war effort, 'He has gone out of his way to stir up the young men of the island to a sense of duty in time of War.'[3] If his personal achievements were not sufficient, it turned out that Gresham's father was a white Englishman, a graduate of Cambridge University who had been Grenada's chief justice.

None of this helped, and the application was rejected. A Colonial Office official despaired that the army was determined to exclude suitable officer candidates if they were even a 'sixteenth and thirty-seconds' black.[4]

The ban on black officers and other discriminatory practices began to harm the war effort in the West Indies. What was the point of fighting for Britain, some black politicians, editors and church leaders asked, if West Indians were not treated as equals? Governor G. Haddon-Smith of the Windward Islands indignantly complained to his superiors in London that

---

2   TNA/PRO CO 28/287.
3   TNA/PRO CO 321/295.
4   TNA/PRO CO 318/336.

he was being denounced in the local press for refusing to give commissions to suitable black candidates.[5]

Black doctors posed a particular headache for the authorities. A number of black West Indian physicians volunteered for the army, which needed medical personnel, especially men willing and able to serve in the front line. Nearly all of the volunteers were graduates of British medical schools, and several were government medical officials, and yet the War Office rejected them because army doctors were also officers. Only doctors of 'pure European descent' could be accepted, it stated.[6] Even the slightest trace of African blood could bar excellent candidates. Dr W.S. Mitchell of Grenada, who was a surgeon, was rejected because he was 'slightly coloured' with 'African woolly hair'.[7]

A number of officials in the West Indies were outraged both by the waste of valuable skills and the banning of men with only a trace of black ancestry. Probyn, the Governor of Barbados, tried to obtain a commission in the Army Medical Corps for Dr Mortimer Johnson, a respected local physician, surgeon and bacteriologist. Johnson was regarded as 'white' in Barbados, even though he was 'not of pure descent, and this fact is noticeable to an acute observer', the governor wrote.[8] 'I doubt whether the defect would lessen the value of Dr Johnson's services,' he wryly added.[9]

It is not clear if it was the protests from black leaders and sympathetic white officials or the army's terrible losses that eventually overcame the ban on black officers. At the end of 1917, a letter from the War Office unexpectedly arrived at the Colonial Office. Startled Colonial Office officials were told:

> There is no objection to temporary commissions in the British West Indies Regiment being granted to 'slightly coloured' gentleman, at the discretion of the Governors of the West Indian Islands where contingents are raised, provided that the candidates for such commissions are British subjects and are considered in every other respect suitable to undertake the leadership of men.[10]

---

5   TNA/PRO CO 321/295.
6   TNA/PRO CO 351/21.
7   TNA/PRO CO 28/287.
8   TNA/PRO CO 28/287.
9   TNA/PRO CO 28/287.
10  TNA/PRO CO 318/344.

It was a grudging concession intended to exclude all but a few light-skinned mixed-race men with high educational and social qualifications. In a show of petty spite, the army ruled that the commissions would be awarded in the name of the local colonial governor, rather than the monarch as was the usual practice. Still, a handful of black and mixed-race men were given commissions. Ivan Shirley of Jamaica, who had attended an English public school, became a lieutenant in the 9th BWIR and Dr Mitchell, who had earlier been rejected, was made a surgeon lieutenant in the same battalion.[11]

★★★

The BWIR's white West Indian officers also complained of facing discrimination, albeit of a different kind. An officer of the 2nd BWIR in Egypt wrote in June 1917 that most of the white West Indian officers in the unit had been demoted and British officers brought in over them. These new British officers, he claimed, were chiefly men who had joined the army during the war and knew nothing about the West Indies or the black rank and file, whereas most of the West Indian officers had served in the local defence forces.[12] It is likely the British officers, who had front-line experience, were brought in after army inspectors found that the West Indian officers were inadequate or needed further training.

White West Indian officers, many of them scions of the colonial elite, also complained of being looked down on by the rest of the army for serving in a black unit. Commanding black troops was still widely regarded as fit only for men who lacked social breeding or with something to hide.

And yet army snobbery sometimes had unintended benefits. William Slim, the future field marshal and outstanding commander of the Second World War, was a temporary officer at the start of the war: he hoped to make a career in the army after the conflict but feared his humble origins and lack of a private income would make it impossible. His dilemma was solved when he obtained a regular commission in the WIR. 'I find there's a thing called the West India Regiment where the chaps go when they're

---

11  TNA/PRO CO 321/2825.
12  TNA/PRO CO 137/725.

broke,' he happily told a friend.[13] However, it was just a stepping stone, and he never served with the regiment.

Some of the BWIR's white West Indian NCOs were also disgruntled at serving in a black regiment. The West India Committee told the War Office in November 1915 that it had helped a number of NCOs to transfer to white units in Britain. Why or how a private body could arrange such matters was not explained – not that the army seemed in the least perturbed.[14] A key reason for the white NCOs' unhappiness was over having to share authority and status, not to mention living and recreational facilities, with the growing number of black NCOs in the regiment. In the face of the white exodus, the army tried to limit the number of black NCOs, and some of the departing white West Indians were replaced with white British NCOs rather than qualified black candidates. Twelve 'European NCOs' were transferred to the 2nd BWIR alone in 1916.[15]

★★★

The rapid expansion of the BWIR after 1916 led to major changes in the make-up of the regiment's rank and file. Many of the early volunteers hailed from the educated and relatively privileged black elite. Drawn from across the British West Indies, the 1st and 2nd Battalions in many ways represented the cream of black youth. Most black West Indians were poor peasants and labourers from the humblest backgrounds with little or no education, and it was such men who increasingly filled the ranks as the number of BWIR battalions mushroomed.

Another major change in the later war years was the preponderance of Jamaicans in the BWIR; the island would contribute 10,280 men of the 15,601 men who enlisted in the regiment.[16] Many of the West Indian colonies were small and could not provide large numbers of men for military service. Only Jamaica had a population capable of providing thousands of recruits. Colonial Office officials estimated the island could have raised at least twenty battalions for the BWIR.[17] Conscription

13  Ronald Lewin, *Slim: The Standardbearer*, p.29.

14  TNA/PRO CO 318/339.

15  TNA/PRO CO 318/339.

16  Lucas, *The Empire at War*, Vol. 2, p.335.

17  TNA/PRO CO 537/592.

regulations were enacted by the Jamaican authorities. However, they never had to be implemented because the number of volunteers was sufficient to meet army needs.

Army recruiters also signed up British West Indians in Panama, where they had worked as labourers on the construction of the canal. A recruiting official said Panama had provided 'a large number of men of an excellent type and of good physique'.[18] Although they were British subjects, BWIR men from Panama and elsewhere in Latin America were distinguished by a sleeve badge with the letters 'BLAV' for British Latin American Volunteers.

While there were always enough volunteers to meet the regiment's needs, enlistment suffered as West Indian troops in Europe and the Middle East wrote home about the grim reality of war and the racism and mistreatment they endured. Magistrates in some settlements started to give offenders a choice between military service or prison. However, none of this was unique to the West Indies; the number of volunteers and the quality of recruits also declined in Britain and other parts of the empire as the war dragged on.

Many of the later BWIR recruits were stunted by lifetimes of poverty, back-breaking labour and disease. Some British officials branded such men as 'human refuse'. 'They are a degenerate lot and not to be compared with West African natives,' Haddon-Smith, the Governor of the Windward Islands, told the Colonial Office.[19] Doctors inspecting these volunteers rejected many of them as sick or too weak for military service, even though enlistment standards had been lowered because of the insatiable demand for more men.

Despite such efforts, the army complained that far too many unfit men were sent to Europe and the Middle East. There was uproar in April 1917 when the 8th BWIR had to be quarantined after arriving in France: doctors reported the unit of 1,000 men was riddled with rose measles, varicella, enteric and venereal disease. Army inspectors said the 8th was a threat to the health of other troops.[20] There were also complaints that many of the later recruits were underage, some of them were clearly mere boys, or could not speak English.

---

18  TNA/PRO WO 106/868.
19  TNA/PRO CO 537/952.
20  TNA/PRO CO 318/344.

High levels of venereal disease, in particular, afflicted BWIR battalions despite the efforts of doctors to weed out infected men at recruiting centres. Officials in Jamaica told London the only way to ensure that recruits were not infected would be to prevent them seeing women before they went overseas, a measure they said could only be imposed by the regular troops of the WIR 'with [rifle] butt and bayonet'.[21]

The influx of poor labourers and peasants into the BWIR led to other problems. Some men from the black middle classes were reluctant to enlist if it meant rubbing shoulders with men they looked down on as coarse, uneducated and immoral. This was particularly true of those mixed-race men who did not want to serve in a black unit and yet were unable to get into white formations.

Local officials worried about the growing number of promising mixed-race men who shunned the BWIR. Barbados, with a large mixed-race population, tried to remedy the situation with a proposal for a regiment of men 'who may be regarded as too dark for British Regiments' and yet were 'unwilling to serve in the ranks of the British West Indies Regiment along men of the artisan and labouring classes'.[22] Nothing came of the proposal.

And yet the large numbers of men from poor and humble backgrounds who increasingly filled the ranks of the BWIR were no less brave or loyal than other West Indian or British troops. Most believed that the war was worth fighting and served at the battle front under the same appalling conditions as other troops, while also enduring prejudice from many whites and even some better-off black West Indians. 'Over ninty [sic] five percent of the men in this part of the world and the British West Indies who have answered the Kings call are from the poorer class, peasants of the British islands,' as one of them, Richard Bennett of Jamaica, put it.[23]

After a year of breakneck expansion, the War Office in August 1917 abruptly stopped recruiting for the BWIR. The reason for the halt is not clear. While it is true that the army request of 1916 for 10,000 men had been met, the Colonial Office had expected more battalions would be raised, and was clearly surprised by the suspension. Intriguingly, the decision came at a time when the British Government was pressing the army to

---

21  TNA/PRO CO 137/725.
22  TNA/PRO CO 137/726.
23  TNA/PRO CO 318/341.

make much greater use of black troops because of the massive casualties that white troops were suffering.

As losses soared, the government proposed recruiting tens of thousands of black troops from across the empire for the army's artillery, engineer, logistics and medical wings. It was suggested the four branches take 223,000 black troops, or up to a third of their respective strengths. The plan met vehement opposition from British generals, even though black units from various parts of the empire were already doing excellent work at the front.

Artillery commanders claimed that black troops were mentally incapable of handling machinery and could not withstand combat conditions. It was a particularly outrageous slur, given the BWIR's outstanding success as artillery ammunition companies. Grudgingly, the artillery said it would accept 15,000 black troops rather than the 100,000 suggested by the government, and only as drivers and labourers. The Royal Engineers were even more resistant, saying it would take 8,000 black soldiers at most. Any more, it claimed, would 'seriously endanger the working of the Royal Engineer services as a whole'.[24]

Most resistant was the Royal Army Medical Corps, which refused to take a single black soldier. 'These units are invariably in close proximity to the Firing Line, where coolness, courage and initiative are at a premium – qualities of which the ordinary Coloured labourer is deficient,' it replied.[25] Only the Army Service Corps was receptive to the idea, saying it could replace about a third of its force of 144,000 men with black troops. In the end the plan went nowhere because of the army's intractable opposition.

It was around this time that the prospect of black West Indians being conscripted into the American military helped to end the British Army's tacit ban on black soldiers in white units. The British military delegation in Washington advised London in the spring of 1918 that there were some 2,000 black men from the British West Indies living in the United States who wanted to fight for Britain. Army officials reacted with well-practised predictability, 'A.C. [Army Council] do not want [underlined] a unit of these people, unless forced to have one as a matter of policy. They agree we should not put them in British units.'[26]

---

24  TNA/PRO WO 32/5094.
25  TNA/PRO WO 32/5094.
26  TNA/PRO WO 32/4765.

Suggestions that the men join the BWIR came to nothing because of the suspension of recruiting for the regiment. A proposal for an American West Indian regiment was dropped because of doubts there would be enough recruits to replace losses and maintain a viable unit.

London was all too happy to let the matter slide until the British Embassy in Washington warned that the men might be conscripted into the American forces. It would damage the empire's prestige if America conscripted men that Britain refused to accept, the embassy warned, and hand anti-colonial groups in the West Indies a powerful propaganda tool. This led to high-level consultations in London between the War Office, the Foreign Office, the Colonial Office and the Ministry of National Service. Finally, the army agreed to let black recruits enlist in white units – with the bizarre stipulation that they eat the same food as British troops. It was announced on 13 June 1918:

> The Army Council have hitherto refused for enlistment into the British Army all British subjects of colour other than those enrolled in special units formed for their reception. I am commanded by the Army Council to inform you that it has now been decided that British subjects of colour may be enlisted into combatant or other units of the British Army ... such recruits will be posted to existing units according to their medical category and that in no case will they be enrolled in separate formations.[27]

Finally, it appeared that the British Army had dropped its race bar. However, none of the West Indians in the United States ever found their way into white units. Army bureaucrats blocked them with the usual deliberate inaction and excuses about a lack of shipping.

---

27 TNA/PRO WO 32/4765.

# 13

# ON THE BANKS OF THE JORDAN

A conference of senior army officers was held in Cairo on 20 November 1916 to discuss the future of the BWIR. British forces faced deadlock on every front of the war, with commanders clamouring for reinforcements to replace the innumerable dead and wounded. And yet the army, blinkered by bigotry, still did not want the West Indians to fight. The key figure at the meeting was one of the lowest-ranking men in the room.

Lieutenant Colonel C. Woodhill, a peppery professional soldier who commanded the 1st BWIR, was a divisive figure. Some saw him as a fierce and energetic leader who drove his men to make them excel; others feared and despised him as a harsh, occasionally irrational disciplinarian. Whatever Woodhill's strengths or failings, no one was more determined to prove that black West Indian soldiers belonged on the battlefield or fought harder for their right to be there.

The meeting was called after the War Office pressed for the three West Indian battalions in Egypt to join the BWIR units serving on the Western Front as ammunition supply and labour troops. Woodhill fiercely resisted the proposal. Using the BWIR as labour troops, he said, was 'doing untold harm'[1] to the morale of both the men and the West Indian colonies. He complained that his battalion was being wasted on digging roads and

---

1    War Diary, 1st Battalion British West Indies Regiment.

guarding supply dumps in Egypt, despite being fully fledged infantry who had won high marks alongside white troops on training courses. Recruiting had plummeted in the Caribbean, he continued, because young black men wanted to be soldiers and not labourers.

It was heady stuff for a mere battalion commander to hurl at a room full of generals, and yet it worked. It was decided to tell London that 'it is absolutely essential for the War Office to drop the idea that the role of these men should be simply to carry ammunition and do the general work of Labour Battalions',[2] and to instead concentrate all of the BWIR battalions in Egypt as fighting troops.

Expectations in the wake of the meeting that the entire BWIR would be concentrated in the Middle East soon faded. Ironically, some of the strongest opposition came from the 3rd and 4th Battalions on the Western Front, who vehemently opposed returning to Egypt. Their officers insisted the units were performing vital and dangerous front-line work. They were backed by the War Office, which also ruled that the new BWIR battalions being formed would serve in Europe. Instead, the 1st and 2nd Battalions were given a vague commitment that they would remain in the Middle East to be employed as infantry when judged ready; the 5th BWIR would continue to serve as their depot unit, handling reinforcements and supplies.

Not that there was much chance of British forces in Egypt seeing significant action any time soon. Britain had, for years, derided the Ottoman Empire as corrupt and backward, and yet the Turks repeatedly bested British forces in the early stages of the war despite their huge deficiencies in weapons, munitions and other vital areas. Turkey dominated the Egyptian front, with British forces doing little more than shelter behind the Suez Canal. It was not until General Edmund Allenby took charge in 1917, and the government provided more support for the theatre, that British military fortunes began to shift. Even then, progress was halting as the Turks put up ferocious resistance.

For almost two years following the Cairo conference, the 1st and 2nd Battalions did little more than dig defences, repair roads, shift supplies and stand guard in rear areas. It didn't help the troops' morale that much of the work was for white units. The West Indians lived for the odd moment of excitement, such as when an enemy aircraft buzzed overhead and they

---

2    War Diary, 1st Battalion British West Indies Regiment.

could blaze away at it with their rifles, and occasional spells of guarding Turkish prisoners meant they could at least write home to say they had seen the enemy.

There were also dangers unconnected to the war. Private W. Smart of the 1st BWIR was murdered by Bedouin marauders in April 1917. Disease and the climate were a much greater threat than the Turks: for every battlefield casualty suffered by British forces, ten men went down with serious, sometimes fatal, illnesses. Hundreds of BWIR soldiers were stricken each month with malaria, dysentery, scabies, sceptic sores, fevers and dozens of other afflictions. More than 200 officers and men of the 1st BWIR were incapacitated by sand fly fever in August 1917 alone; the bites of the flea-like insects left victims prostrate and raving deliriously with dangerously high temperatures.

There were also psychological menaces. Men who could not endure the soul-destroying routine of life in the empty desert suffered mental breakdowns, with the most severe cases having to be sent home.

The commanders of the 1st and 2nd Battalions pleaded with the High Command to give their men a chance to fight. Woodhill complained in the spring of 1917 that his battalion had been in Egypt for more than a year and a half, and by any standard was ready for battle. 'All ranks are most anxious to be given [the] privilege of being allowed to fight and prove their worth,' he wrote.[3] He also complained that his men were being given inferior or worn-out equipment while white units got the best of everything. Again and again, Woodhill warned of the damaging impact on the loyalty of the West Indian colonies if the BWIR continued to be treated as second-rate labour troops.

Despondency dogged the men, meanwhile, their mood rising briefly whenever combat training picked up, only to plummet again when they were sent off to dig more drainage ditches or build billets for white units. W.J. Bensly, the chaplain of the 1st BWIR, tried to make excuses for the High Command's indifference:

> … how disappointed we all were, that for various reasons, the authorities did not realise for a very long time what splendid fighting [potential] the West Indians possessed … There is no doubt whatever in my mind

---

3   TNA/PRO WO 95/4732.

that first-class fighting material was for nearly two years practically wasted simply because no one in sufficient authority in high quarters knew anything about us.[4]

In July 1917, local British commanders finally gave the BWIR a chance to prove itself. The 1st BWIR's machine gun section was attached to the British 162nd Brigade for front-line training. On the night of 20 July, the gunners took part in a raid with white infantry on Umbrella Hill, a formidable Turkish position ringed by belts of barbed wire.

As well as the daunting challenge of facing action for the first time, the West Indians were issued on the eve of the attack with machine guns of a pattern they were not familiar with. Normally a unit would be given time to master new weapons. Nonetheless, the West Indian gunners covered the infantry assault with the skilled precision of veterans and the raid was a complete success, with the Turks losing 110 men killed and another seventeen taken prisoner.

Lance Corporal C.N. Alexander of the 1st BWIR won a Military Medal for bravery by keeping his machine gun in action after it was hit by rifle fire. The divisional commander praised the gunners for showing 'a keen interest in their work, cheerfulness and energy, coolness under shell fire, and an intelligent application of what was required of them, and the ability to carry it out'.[5] Allenby sent a cable to the Governor of Jamaica echoing the praise.

A bigger step came in August when eight platoons of the 1st BWIR were attached to the Highland Light Infantry for front-line training. Attachments to other experienced units followed, with the West Indians coming under Turkish artillery fire and suffering casualties; two men were killed and two wounded in one incident.

That September, the BWIR took over a section of the front line for the first time. It was progress, and yet it seemed begrudging and maddeningly slow to the troops. It was as if they were being constantly tested and yet never being judged good enough, no matter how many times they proved themselves.

---

4   *The Belize Independent*, 16 July 1919.
5   War Diary, 1st Battalion British West Indies Regiment.

Allenby launched a major offensive against the Turks in Gaza in the autumn of 1917. Although the West Indians were used mainly to build roads during the operation, part of the 1st BWIR was unexpectedly caught up in the fighting. British cavalry rounding up enemy stragglers at a position called Two Tree Farm were forced to retreat after running into superior enemy forces. The West Indians covered the horsemen as they fell back, later recovering the body of the slain cavalry commander despite intense enemy artillery fire. Lance Corporal V.E. Johns and Private C.A. Hydman won Military Medals for repeatedly dashing through the shelling with messages, while Private F. Pullar was decorated for scouting enemy positions alone during the night. British commanders praised the West Indians for their bravery, but the two battalions were once again left behind as the offensive swept the Turks back.

Not that life was easy for the West Indians, or any other British troops. The desert treated all men with a harshness that cared nothing about race or nationality. Men collapsed and vomited as the heat pummelled their bodies. Corpses turned black and rotted within an hour or two of death, cloaking the living in a gagging stench that they never forgot. Swarms of flies covered every bit of exposed skin, crawling into men's eyes, noses and ears, and coating their food and drink with throbbing black crusts. Mosquitoes, sand flies and fleas made sleep virtually impossible; exhausted men wrapped themselves in blankets to escape the insects' painful bites only to feel as if they were being stewed alive.

Worst of all was the lack of water and constant raging thirst. Men went weeks without bathing despite being covered in dirt and sweat, their unwashed uniforms turning black on their backs. For months they lived on tinned meat and dry biscuits; steaming jets of rancid meat and fat shot out when the tins were opened. Constant diarrhoea from the heat and monotonous diet added to the stench of the soldiers' bodies and the misery of their souls.

As the British forces advanced into Palestine in the winter, the sweltering desert gave way to rocky hills, storms and plummeting temperatures. Men who had been willing to give everything for a mouthful of water a month or two before were now drenched and battered by torrential rain as they trudged across the muddy landscape.

In November 1917, the 1st BWIR was still in thin summer uniforms when winter swept over the Judean Hills. Weeks passed before warm clothing could be sent up to them. Losses soared as hundreds of men went down with pneumonia and other illnesses: seven men died from exposure and 100 were hospitalised after the battalion was forced to spend a night in the open in January 1918 because the wagons carrying their tents could not get through.

Spring and the coming of better weather only brought problems of a different kind. Malaria flattened entire platoons, and scores of men had to be sent every week to hospitals behind the lines or to Egypt. Attacks by marauding Turkish aircraft were now laughed off as mere gnat bites.

As the landscape changed, the West Indians passed landmarks they knew well from the Bible and Sunday School teachings. Many of the men were awed as they trod the same ground as Christ and his disciples. There were other historical associations as they marched along ancient roads once used by the Roman legions or passed Crusader fortresses on distant hill tops. There was talk in the ranks of a new crusade to drive the Muslim Turks out of the Holy Land.

★★★

It was not until the closing days of the war that the BWIR (albeit just two battalions) was allowed to fight. In the summer of 1918, the two battalions spent more time on combat training and less on menial labour as the army readied for the next offensive. The men did daily cross-country runs and marches and honed their shooting, bayonet and other fighting skills. Several men were killed and wounded as exercises became more intense and realistic, mostly from mishaps with grenades.

In August, both West Indian battalions were attached to a force under Major General E.W.C. Chaytor on the British right flank in Palestine. This entailed a 150-mile march in full kit in extreme heat and choking dust that left the men looking like bleached scarecrows.

On 12 August, the West Indians took over front-line positions from Australian troops near Jericho. Ottoman batteries intermittently shelled the BWIR as it settled into the trenches, inflicting a handful of casualties. West Indian patrols went out to pinpoint and map enemy positions.

Chaytor's force was assigned to drive back the Ottoman 4th Army as part of Allenby's next big offensive. The 4th Army was strongly dug in along a line of hills defended by redoubts, trenches and dense expanses of barbed wire. Thick desert scrub up to 6ft high masked many of the enemy emplacements. Plans for the attack called for the infantry to leave most of their gear behind to enable them to move quickly; each man took a single spare shirt and a pair of socks wrapped in a blanket on his back along with ammunition, water, iron rations and two hand grenades.

Three years and four months after its formation, the BWIR finally went into battle. On 19 September, the 2nd BWIR attacked Ottoman positions on the Bakr and Chalk Ridges. Lines of black infantry advanced over the stony ground as Turkish shells rained down on them. Observers marvelled at the West Indians' steely discipline as they scaled the ridges and drove the enemy from their positions. By the next morning, the BWIR was in control of the former Turkish front line.

Private Hezekiah Scott won a Distinguished Conduct Medal after crossing 700 yards under withering shell fire to carry a message. He braved the bombardment a second time to try to rescue a wounded West Indian sergeant, only to find that the man was dead. Supplies were sent up to the battalions along the old Roman road, although enemy artillery fire made it impossible to get water and ammunition to the most advanced West Indian detachments. Lance Corporal Richard Turpin ran a signal wire across 2½ miles of ground swept by enemy fire to the battalion's most forward positions, later braving the bombardment twice to repair breaks caused by shell explosions.

Urgent orders were issued to the BWIR and the New Zealand Mounted Brigade on the night of 21 September to capture the bridge at Jisr-ed-Damieh and prevent the retreating Ottoman forces from pulling back across the Jordan River. It meant a forced march of 16 miles for the West Indians across rugged terrain in the dark.

Their water bottles empty, the men were desperately thirsty when the column reached Jisr-ed-Damieh around dawn. Hurried searches failed to find any streams or pools in the rocky landscape to slake their parched throats. After a brief rest, the West Indians advanced on the bridge, where the New Zealanders had been checked by the strong Turkish defences. Mounting a joint attack, the West Indians and New Zealanders pushed back the Turks with a bayonet charge and seized the heights overlooking the bridge. Small parties then pushed down to the river under intense Turkish machine gun and rifle fire, knocking out enemy posts one by one, often at bayonet point.

Some of the BWIR men showed exceptional courage. Private George Dick rushed an enemy machine gun alone, bayonetting two of the crew and capturing the position. When the advance was stalled by intense fire from a Turkish machine gun lodged behind piled rocks, Private Albert Marques crawled around the flank of the position and pelted it with grenades, killing six of the enemy gunners, wounding two others and taking the remaining two men prisoner.

West Indian NCOs played key roles in the battle. Lance Corporal McC. Leekam led a machine gun detachment to the heights above the bridge from where it scythed down enemy soldiers on the crossing and provided covering fire for the advancing West Indian infantry. On the approaches to the bridge, Sergeant William Edward Julien took command of one of the leading platoons after it was separated from their officer. He led the men forward, sweeping away the last defenders to break through to the bridge and capture two machine guns. It took a few moments for the West Indians, adrenalin, excitement and fear still surging through them, to realise that the Turks had been defeated and the bridge was theirs. Detachments of the 2nd BWIR and Australian troops, meanwhile, drove back an Ottoman counter-attack further along the river.

The victory was a remarkable feat for largely untested troops in their first major action against veteran opponents. It was estimated that some 200 Turkish soldiers had been killed and 110 captured along with eight machine guns. West Indian losses were seven dead and forty-six wounded, mostly in the 2nd BWIR.

Despite their fairly modest losses, it had been a terrible ordeal for the men. Captain A.A. Cipriani of the BWIR recalled later:

And it would break the heart of the ordinary human to see the wounded youngsters going backward and forward, each with a ghastly look in his eye. Each youngster went out to do his bit, but he was not ready to die hundreds of miles away from his home. The bleeding, suffering, torn, maimed and almost dead.[6]

Chaytor ordered the 1st BWIR and the Australian Light Horse on the night of 23 September to pursue the retreating Ottoman forces across the

---

6    Quoted in Arthur McShine, *Victory at Damieh*, p.60.

Mountains of Moab – a region filled with biblical associations – and capture Amman. It was an extreme challenge for even highly experienced troops, involving a night march on narrow tracks across heights rising up to 4,000ft.

Most of the battalion's equipment and supplies had to be left behind because the paths were too small and rough for wagons. There were no streams or springs in the barren landscape, and the men's water bottles were soon empty as they laboured up the gravel-strewn hillsides. Blankets and greatcoats had also been left in the rear and cold gripped the troops as the temperature plunged.

Turkish stragglers staged several rearguard actions, forcing the West Indians to hunt them through the jumbled maze of boulders and gullies. After 15 gruelling miles, the infantry reached their first goal, the settlement of Es Salt, to find that the Australian horsemen, who had surged ahead, had taken it. Following a short rest, the weary troops pushed on to Amman. They reached the outskirts only to be disappointed once again because the Australians had captured the city with its large Turkish military base. Nonetheless, Chaytor hailed the West Indians' crossing of the mountains as one of the most remarkable marches of the entire war.

Even though the BWIR suffered light battlefield casualties, both units were crippled by disease and the harsh conditions by the end of the offensive. The 1st BWIR had been at its greatest strength of the war with thirty-five officers and 1,152 other ranks on the eve of Damieh. Malaria, dysentery, pneumonia, exposure and exhaustion reduced it by 10 October to eight officers and 311 other ranks – a loss rate of 75 per cent – with more than 700 men hospitalised.[7] Of the roughly 2,300 men in the two battalions who took part in the Jordan Valley operations, an astonishing 90 per cent contracted malaria. What was left of the two units had to be withdrawn from the front. As a final task, the 1st BWIR escorted 1,400 Turkish prisoners to Jericho.

★★★

The war in the Middle East ended abruptly with the capitulation of the Turks on 30 October. Praise was deluged on the 1st and 2nd BWIR as if at least some in the army wanted to make up for the doubts and mistreatment

---

7   TNA/PRO CO 318/350.

that had dogged the regiment throughout the conflict. Chaytor's official report extolled the BWIR's discipline under fire, dash in the attack and endurance under harsh conditions. Allenby visited wounded West Indians in a Jerusalem hospital after Damieh, praising the men for their valour.

Chaytor was effusive with praise when he reviewed both BWIR battalions on 22 November. 'Indeed all the troops of my division report that they like to fight along with you, in fact, could never wish for anybody better,' the general told the lines of men.[8] He then presented medals to the officers and men who had particularly distinguished themselves in the battle. It was as if the army had suddenly become aware of the existence of the West Indian battalions, the 1st BWIR's war diary drily noted.

The deeds of the Australians at Gallipoli or the Canadians at Vimy Ridge during the First World War are celebrated as defining moments when these nations came of age. Damieh and the epic march of the 1st BWIR across the Mountains of Moab, when West Indian troops proved their worth, were barely noticed at the time and soon forgotten. Not that the importance of Damieh should be overstated. It was a sideshow compared to Gallipoli, Vimy Ridge and all too many other battles and campaigns during the war. Still, those few daunting and exhilarating days had shown what the BWIR might have achieved if given the chance.

Many of the men contented themselves with knowing they had played a part, no matter how small, in a great cause. 'I have lived with a Clean record an [*sic*] now I am a brave soldier in the British army,' Private James Hutchinson wrote.[9]

---

8    War Diary, 1st Battalion British West Indies Regiment.
9    Quoted in Mallet, *Letters from the Trenches During the Great War*, p.17.

# 14

# MUTINY

It was never established just what started the trouble. Some said it was the order to clean latrines used by white labourers. Others put it down to the men being classified as 'coloured natives' and banned from canteens and hospitals. And there were those who blamed it on a dispute over a pay increase. Less than a month after the end of the war, the BWIR mutinied.

Whatever the immediate cause may have been, the fundamental reason for the mutiny was the years of broken promises, mistreatment and discrimination the BWIR had endured. While they were soon over, the events in the southern Italian port of Taranto raised fears in London and the West Indies that the troops would unleash a revolution when they returned to their homes. Panicked government and military officials talked of rushing warships and white infantry to the Caribbean before thousands of disgruntled and war-hardened black soldiers descended on the British settlements intent on toppling colonial rule.

When they did return home, wanting only peace and a decent life, the soldiers who had fought for a new world soon found that very little had changed for them. Wartime mistreatment gave way to peacetime neglect, leaving a legacy of bitterness and discontent.

Joy, relief and hope swept the BWIR and every other British unit when the war finally ended on 11 November 1918: joy that the conflict was over, relief that they were still alive and hope that better things would follow.

Sergeant W. Gaskin of the 7th BWIR expressed the regiment's pride at its part in the Allied triumph:

> Now the great war is over and our task is done, crowning us with 'Victory' for the Allies, and your boys will be able to give you a good account of our experiences, when we returns home.[1]

Hopes of a better world were especially compelling for the BWIR men, whose eyes had been opened in Europe to the poverty and backwardness of the West Indies. Private Charles Weeks of the 3rd BWIR spoke for most of the regiment when he wrote, 'And I only hope that there something greater awaiting for us when the time come when we shall pack our trunk and say Good Bye.'[2]

Amid the optimism of better things to come, some urged the BWIR men to forget the injustices and racism they had endured in the military as discredited relics of the past. *The Belize Independent* newspaper declared in a front-page editorial:

> We want you to forget the insults, the prejudices and treachery; we want you to dismiss them as experiences which have made you wiser if sadder men. Then the war has created a new spirit. The masses through-out the length and breadth of the civilized world are determined that Liberty, Equality and Fraternity shall no longer be mere catchwords; that Democracy shall be no empty romance.[3]

And yet there were signs before the war ended that nothing was going to change. In early 1918, the British Army increased the pay of private soldiers from a shilling a day to one and a half shillings. Even though the BWIR was a British Army unit and had been promised equal pay when it was formed, the War Office excluded the West Indians on the grounds they were 'natives' and not British soldiers. It was a mean and petty act that stunned every man in the regiment.

---

1    Quoted in Mallet, *Letters from the Trenches During the Great War*, p.2.
2    Mallet, p.43.
3    *The Belize Independent*, 16 July 1919.

A petition from the NCOs of the 1st and 2nd BWIR in the Middle East protested, 'We feel that this discrimination is not only an insult to us who have volunteered to fight for the Empire but also an insult to the whole of the West Indies.'[4] The petition breached army regulations, but the NCOs were backed by their commanding officers.

The Colonial Office protested the army's action, warning that it was unfair and would shake the loyalty of the black West Indian population. Lord Milner, the Colonial Secretary, said denying the BWIR the increase was not only discriminatory, it was an insult, given the regiment's fine performance in the war. He noted that it had incurred 'heavy losses from climatic disease and considerable casualties from enemy action'.[5]

The army also demeaned the BWIR in other ways. It was relegated to the back of the queue to return home while white units from Australia, Canada and other parts of the empire were given priority. The West India Committee, which was supposed to be overseeing the BWIR's welfare, was concerned only with ensuring that white West Indians who had served in British and Canadian units went home in suitable style. Although the white veterans were sent back to the West Indies as soon as possible on civilian shipping rather than having to wait like the BWIR, the committee expressed concern to the War Office in February 1919 that they were being housed in third-class cabins, despite the fact many had attended public school and were the sons of planters and merchants. It had also heard that some white West Indians might travel on the same vessels as the BWIR, 'which is entirely a coloured unit; but the objections to this, unless the men are given suitable second class accommodation by themselves, are too obvious to require emphasis'.[6] Apologetic War Office bureaucrats replied that every effort would be made to get the young gentlemen home as soon as possible in accommodation befitting their social station.

Black West Indian troops continued to face mistreatment from some white soldiers. Persistent racial tension at the Belmont Road Military Auxiliary Hospital in Liverpool led to a brawl between some fifty BWIR patients and hundreds of white convalescents. Crippled men lashed out at each other with crutches and hurled bedpans. A nurse who was knocked over in the melee later died. A subsequent army inquiry, while critical of the

---

4  TNA/PRO CO 318/348.
5  TNA/PRO CO 318/350.
6  TNA/PRO CO 318/350.

BWIR men, found the violence had been caused, at least in part, by white orderlies mistreating black patients.[7]

As a first step towards disbanding the BWIR, all of the eight battalions serving in Europe were moved to Taranto, where they worked in the port and the adjacent army base. Morale in the units was far from good: some of the men were unhappy that they had never been allowed to fight, and would now never have the chance; many had not been given leave in years despite dangerous and gruelling work on the Western Front; white units were being sent home while they were still being made to work; and there was deep resentment over the army's refusal to give them the pay increase granted to the rest of the army.

Things were made worse by the bigoted senior officers in charge at Taranto. Black troops were banned from canteens and cinemas used by white soldiers, sick BWIR men were put in segregated and inferior hospitals where some of them allegedly died needlessly and black units had to do chores for white units. Some of the white BWIR officers said it was the most appalling discrimination the regiment ever suffered.

On 6 December, a group of men from the 9th BWIR surrounded the tent of their commanding officer, Lieutenant Colonel R.E. Willis, and slashed it with their bayonets. Contemporary accounts offer differing explanations of what sparked the incident. Some versions say that the men were enraged after being ordered to clean latrines used either by white troops or Italian labourers; others suggest the men could no longer endure the abuse of Willis, a harsh disciplinarian notorious for abusing both white officers and black rankers. A number of white officers were said to have been assaulted after the tent incident.

In what was almost certainly an unfortunate coincidence, a petition signed by 180 black BWIR sergeants was issued the same day, demanding black soldiers be given the same pay and promotion opportunities as white troops. It complained:

> We have been serving as Soldiers of the British Army, assisting in a World War for Justice and Freedom, yet we, ourselves have not derived the same benefits as those along with whom we have been doing our bit.[8]

---

7   TNA/PRO CO 318/347.
8   TNA/PRO CO 28/294.

Such an outburst from NCOs, the disciplinary backbone of the military, alarmed the local army command.

On the following day, the 9th and 10th BWIR refused to work. BWIR officers and loyal NCOs disarmed the two battalions, which did not resist, but the trouble spread to other units as more and more men refused to report for duty. A black sergeant shot one of the protest leaders after an altercation.

It seemed, to panicking white commanders, that the 7,500 West Indian troops in the camp were on the verge of armed rebellion. All of the battalions were disarmed, again without the men resisting, and the 9th BWIR, seen as the source of the infection, was broken up, its men divided among the other units. Still fearful, the army rushed in a white infantry battalion with a machine gun detachment, only to find that the unrest was largely over and the BWIR's officers and NCOs had restored order.

About sixty alleged ringleaders were arrested in the wake of the trouble, and forty-nine men were later convicted of mutiny, receiving jail sentences of between three years and five years. One man was sentenced to death, a verdict later reduced to twenty years' imprisonment.

A few days after the unrest, several black BWIR sergeants gathered to discuss what had happened and what it might mean for the future of the West Indies. A second meeting, two or three days later, attended by sixty or so sergeants from all eight battalions decided to form an organisation called the Caribbean League to work for the rights of black West Indians after the war. Various ideas for future political action in the West Indies were discussed, including campaigns for voting rights and strikes for better wages. Some of the men denounced the white elite back home and talked of smashing its stranglehold. A sergeant of the 3rd BWIR was reported to have declared, 'That the black man should have freedom and govern himself in the West Indies and that force must be used, and if necessary bloodshed to attain that object.'[9] Other participants spoke just as strongly against inciting racial tension and violence. Army conditions were also discussed, with many of the men complaining about the number of white NCOs who had been brought in from the British Army instead of promoting black soldiers from within the BWIR's ranks.

---

9   TNA/PRO CO 318/350.

A sergeant of the 8th BWIR told his commanding officer about the meetings. Army commanders, still shaken by the mutiny, demanded the suppression of the Caribbean League, claiming its members were planning a violent revolution. While Colonial Office officials were also concerned about the organisation, they opposed breaking it up, saying such an action would only foment trouble in the West Indies.[10] The army, which wanted to try the NCOs for treason, had to relent after it became clear there was insufficient evidence to back such a charge. Ironically, the league collapsed a short time later after inter-island rivalries left organisers unable to agree on where it should be based in the West Indies or who should run it.

An army investigation into the events at Taranto attempted to play down or reject the men's grievances. It denied there had been any segregation, rather that every unit was given their own canteens, cinemas and other facilities. It said there was no proof the BWIR were referred to as 'coloured natives' in camp orders, but if it had occurred, it 'was probably occasioned by some inexperienced clerk, and never intended to be offensive'. It conceded only that sick BWIR men had been put in hospitals 'separate from that of [white] British troops', despite the fact the West Indians were regular soldiers.

With breathtaking aplomb, the inquiry then blamed the entire affair on the BWIR's officers, who were said to be 'quite ignorant of how to maintain discipline' – a remarkable charge since it included colonels with up to thirty years of experience.[11] The army tacitly admitted it had been wrong in at least one respect, however, when the War Office announced two months after the events at Taranto that the BWIR would retrospectively receive the pay increase given to white troops.

Nonetheless, Captain A.A. Cipriani of the BWIR said the black rank and file continued to be mistreated at Taranto despite official efforts to resolve the problems that led to the mutiny. The 1st, 2nd and 5th BWIRs, which were moved to Taranto from the Middle East after the incident, complained that all cinemas and YMCA canteens were off limits to black troops, and they had to do fatigue duties for white units. The troops, on the other hand, were doubtless happy to find they were welcome in bars and brothels outside the army camp.

---

10  TNA/PRO CO 318/350.
11  TNA/PRO CO 318/359.

High-level talks were held in London on the future of the BWIR after the Taranto incident. Colonial Office officials suggested punishing the entire regiment by keeping it in Europe as a labour unit. The army decided it would be better to break up a regiment it had never wanted and send the troublesome West Indians home as soon as shipping was available.

Much was made of Taranto at the time and in subsequent years. It was certainly a serious affair, and yet it was more a strike than a mutiny. The thousands of armed BWIR troops in the port could have caused chaos if they had been minded to rebel. Instead, the units gave up their weapons without resistance, the trouble was fleeting and largely confined to two battalions, and the regiment's officers and NCOs swiftly restored order. Rather than throwing off its rule, the West Indians wanted equality within an empire that still commanded their overwhelming loyalty.

Colonial administrators in the West Indies could not decide if the BWIR should be hailed as heroes or treated like dangerous revolutionaries when the regiment returned home. There was even greater apprehension among the white population. J.R.H. Homfrey, a retired officer, told the Colonial Office that whites were terrified that the BWIR would revolt, and the handful of white troops in the region would be unable to stop them. 'Suppose as I am led to believe will happen, the contingents return en masse, and imbued with revolutionary ideas, and they run amok, what is going to happen. They have given trouble at Taranto,' he wrote.[12]

Government officials in London were also worried about the paucity of white troops in the West Indies. A Colonial Office administrator lamented that the only large army unit in the area, a battalion of the WIR in Jamaica, was also black. Discussions about rushing a white infantry battalion to the Caribbean came to nothing after the army said it could not get a unit there in time. Officials also discussed providing West Indian police forces with heavy machine guns to put down any unrest – the fact the police were overwhelmingly black did not seem to cause concern. Instead, the Royal Navy agreed to have warships shadow the BWIR detachments as they disembarked, although the Colonial Office said it should be made to look like routine port visits to avoid offending the black population by implying that their returning men were disloyal.

---

12  TNA/PRO CO 318/350.

Ironically, no one saw the need to discuss safeguards against possible unrest in the only colony where there was trouble. Thousands of people cheered British Honduras' BWIR contingent when it returned on 19 July 1919 and marched through the flag-bedecked streets of the capital, Belize. Local dignitaries welcomed the veterans with florid speeches hailing them as victors. The men were treated to a sports day and then dismissed with small sums of cash and vague promises of future rewards.

Two nights later, a group of BWIR men, in uniform and armed with clubs, led a mob that surged through the streets shouting for an end to white rule, attacking and beating white men, breaking shop windows and looting the interiors. Leading white residents, including the chief justice, who tried to calm the crowd were beaten or pelted with stones. The mob, estimated at between 3,000 and 4,000 or about a third of the city's population, seized control of the city centre. The police retreated to their headquarters, and only a few members of the local Volunteer Defence Force answered an emergency call to assemble. Governor Eyre Hutson said later that 'every white man in the streets carried his life in his hands'.[13]

Hutson, who was barricaded in a hall with a few officials and members of the Defence Force, sent a radio appeal for help that was intercepted by a British warship, HMS *Constance*. To buy time, the governor met with representatives of the disaffected BWIR men, who complained about their treatment in the army and demanded government aid to help them adjust to civilian life. Many of the BWIR veterans had not taken part in the riots, and some of these men, under their officers and NCOs, helped the police and the Defence Force maintain order until the warship arrived on 24 July and landed armed sailors and marines.

Martial law was declared, and the ringleaders of the protest rounded up by the navy and loyal BWIR men acting as special constables. One of the returned BWIR men, Sergeant Major F.H.E. McDonald, was appointed chief of police for his role in helping end the riot, replacing the incumbent who had lost his nerve at the start of the trouble.

A subsequent inquiry into the riots heard a great deal of testimony from BWIR veterans on the racist mistreatment they had endured during the war. Most of the British Honduras detachment served in Mesopotamia,

---

13 TNA/PRO CO 123/296.

where some of the worst abuses took place.[14] Hutson, a moderate and prag-
matic man, was shaken by what he heard:

> Accounts of incidents have been reported to me orally, which are alleged
> to have occurred in Egypt and Mesopotamia which, if accurate, are deeply
> to be deplored, because they caused offence to the native men of this
> Colony who were part of His Majesty's Imperial Army.[15]

The inquiry put the blame for the riot on the BWIR men, nonetheless,
and said the racist abuse they had endured in the army could not justify
attacks on white civilians. It concluded that the veterans had misguided and
inflated notions that the colony owed them better lives in return for their
military service, and they did not want to go back to the low-paid menial
labour most had done before the war.

A few returning BWIR men were involved in similar, if much smaller
disturbances in Jamaica and Trinidad, where a number of white sailors and
residents were assaulted. The veterans were angered at the lack of government aid and continuing white privilege. The black troops of the WIR put
down the unrest with their customary efficiency. Whatever the nightmares
of the white elite, there was never any threat of serious unrest, let alone a
revolution with the veterans of the BWIR replicating what the Bolsheviks
were doing at the time in Russia.

★★★

For all their sacrifices, most of the BWIR's rank and file were not
rewarded with better lives for them or their families. Many came back
to the same poverty, squalid housing, menial labour and lack of rights
they had endured before the war. Only now, such hardships were even
more difficult to bear for men who had seen the wealth and modernity
of Europe. Twenty years after the war, a British Government inquiry into
West Indian conditions was told by aging BWIR veterans how they were
still being denied basic rights. One veteran spoke of 'returning with victory on our bayonet', and yet:

---

14  See Chapter 11.
15  TNA/PRO CO 123/296.

… it is a most shameful and wicked act … how they treated us … we did went and did fought to make this world safe for British Democracy and we are treated bad … they did not thank us for our service … Surfdom [*sic*] and dirt are our class Sir.[16]

Most of the West Indian colonies went through the motions of trying to aid the veterans, mostly exhorting private businesses to hire veterans. The war had not arrested the long decline of the regional economy, and there was little work beyond poorly paid plantation or other manual labour.

Some of the colonies tried to resettle veterans as farmers on patches of public land, but most of the land was inaccessible, unhealthy and barren, and the men, most of who had grown up in towns, had little or no idea of how to farm. Hubert Reid, a veteran of the West India Regiment, said of the plots given to ex-soldiers in Jamaica, 'In some cases, not even wild birds would care to inhabit them. Not even an inch is suitable for cultivation, and as far as the roads are concerned, the inaccessibility of the places renders that impossible.'[17] Notions of turning the soldiers into a new class of black yeoman farmers came to nothing. The men, faced with starvation, abandoned the plots. All of the seventy-two ex-BWIR men given land in one Jamaican parish gave up within a few years.[18]

There were limits to what the perennially poor West Indian governments could do for the veterans, and there was little aid from Britain, which was struggling with the enormous costs of the war and resettling millions of British soldiers. Despairing officials in Barbados asked the island's Poor Law Guardians, who normally provided handouts for the indigent and homeless, to help feed the veterans.[19]

Large numbers of veterans ended up emigrating to the United States, Canada and elsewhere to find work and a chance of some kind of life. Many of those who stayed in the West Indies became increasingly disillusioned, shunning the annual church services and marches to honour the war. The optimism that Corporal Charles N. Booth of the 9th BWIR had spelled

---

16  TNA/PRO CO 950/93.
17  Richard Smith, 'Heaven grant you strength to fight for your race', in Das, p.273.
18  TNA/PRO CO 950/93.
19  TNA/PRO CO 28/292.

out in halting verse as he lay in a military hospital at the end of the war was soon forgotten:

Peace and Victory has before us
Bright and Happy days is nigh
Soon shall one and all will be singing
Peace on earth good will to men.[20]

---

20 Mallet, p.12.

# 15

# DEATH OF A REGIMENT

Everything was a bit rushed on that cold, grey February day in 1927. An official ushered a group of officers into a large, impersonal reception room at Buckingham Palace. Most of the men did not know each other, and English reticence and the regal setting discouraged casual discussion. After some time, King George V entered the room to perform the next function on his schedule that day. Reading from a sheet of paper, the monarch made a few remarks. Not a single black face was there that morning to mark the final moment in the history of the regiment that had for so long served Britain and her empire.

Ferocious cuts were imposed on the British armed forces after 1918. The First World War was supposed to be 'the war to end all wars', so politicians and voters saw little need to spend money on the military if there would never be another conflict. This set off a frenzied struggle among the army, navy and air force to grab as much of the greatly reduced defence budget as possible. There were further bitter struggles within each service over which units and bases were to be axed.

It was only a matter of time before the WIR became a target. Through no fault of its own, the WIR had emerged from the war with a poor reputation. A 1919 War Office report claimed that the regiment had 'not proved very useful or reliable',[1] even though it had deliberately been held back from the fighting for most of the war because of army bias. As the only black regiment, the WIR was still the least prestigious unit in the regular

---

1   TNA/PRO CO 137/735.

army. Its traditional role in West Africa had largely been taken over by local units during the war, and the West Indies now barely figured in the empire's defence plans. All in all, the WIR lacked a purpose or friends as the army looked for unloved and unwanted units to sacrifice to the budget cuts.

In 1920, the War Office decided to reduce the WIR to a single battalion based in Jamaica. Colonial garrisons around the globe were being reduced, and officials claimed that it was proving difficult to attract enough recruits to maintain two West Indian battalions. A War Office memo said the reduction was 'necessary from considerations of Imperial economy to reduce all garrisons overseas to the lowest possible limits, and even to take a certain amount of risk in so doing'.[2]

It didn't help its prospects that the WIR chose this moment to stage a highly unorthodox protest to demand greater rights. There was consternation in Kingston and London when the rank and file of the new single battalion presented a petition drawn up by a lawyer. It complained that the unit had not received the pay increase granted to the British Army in 1918, and later extended to the BWIR. It also protested that white soldiers got larger food allowances. It appealed directly to the king, declaring their loyalty to him, 'The West India Regiment composed almost wholly of coloured men stand second to none of His Majesty's troops in loyalty and devotion to His Majesty's Throne and Person.'[3]

A mass protest delivered outside of normal military channels smacked of insubordination, and it alarmed the imperial government and the army. The petition was denounced by the Colonial Officer as an 'egregious infraction of military discipline'.[4] Colonel A.E. Glasgow, the WIR commanding officer, made the improbable claim that the petition could not represent the entire regiment because his white company commanders had not known about it, although he accepted that most of its points about inferior pay and rations were correct.

★★★

2   TNA/PRO CO 318/350.
3   TNA/PRO CO 318/354.
4   TNA/PRO CO 318/354.

The 1920s saw no let-up in the rounds of military cuts, and the army's only black regiment was far too tempting a target for the military hierarchy. An Army Council study in 1926 concluded that Jamaica's garrison was too large, given the lack of any strategic threat in the region. It proposed disbanding the WIR, asserting it could not be employed outside of the West Indies, despite decades of such service, and there would be no threat to internal security if it was abolished. Disbanding the regiment, moreover, would save £90,000 a year. While the loss of a regiment with such a long and distinguished history was regrettable, the memo continued, its retention could not be justified 'purely on account of sentiment or tradition'.[5]

It was all subterfuge. The same study sanctioned the retention of a white infantry battalion in the West Indies at an annual cost of £304,100, and justified it by the strategic importance of the region and the necessity of keeping down the 'large negro population'.[6]

News of the decision to abolish the WIR provoked consternation and anger across the West Indies. Black politicians, newspaper editors, church officials, business leaders and others led a chorus of protests and pleas to try to save the regiment. Public meetings were held to show support for the WIR with speakers lauding its proud history and importance as a symbol of the region's ties to the empire. Startled military officials in Jamaica told the War Office that the protests reflected 'the keen pride felt, in what the coloured classes in the West Indies very particularly regard as their own Regiment'.[7] It did no good, and the West Indian legislatures, while generally deploring the decision to scrap the WIR, did nothing to save it. Army Order 317 of September 1926 decreed the disbanding of the regiment by 31 March the following year.

A crowd of 20,000 civilians watched as the WIR paraded for the last time at Up Park Camp in Kingston on 31 Jan 1927. Colonial officials in crisp uniforms extolled the regiment's history, paying tribute to the thousands of men who had served in its ranks over the decades. The troops marched and wheeled in what many remembered as a flawless display of precision. And then the men stood stiffly at attention as the band played 'Auld Lang Syne' and the regiment's two flags were marched off for the last time. Now jobless

---

5   TNA/PRO T161/1018.
6   TNA/PRO T161/1018.
7   TNA/PRO WO 32/2899.

and largely homeless, the soldiers broke ranks for the last time, turned in their weapons and began searching for work on an island already groaning from poverty and unemployment.

As a final favour, the regiment's last commanding officer, Lieutenant Colonel W.Y. Miller, had asked that the WIR's flags be presented to the king and laid up at Windsor Castle with the standards of other disbanded regiments. Permission was granted on condition that the party escorting the colours to Britain 'not include any personnel required to return to Jamaica' – ensuring no black member of the regiment could attend.[8]

The flags were taken back to Britain by the WIR's officers. When their ship docked, most of the officers opted to go on leave, and it was left to Miller, one other officer and a white NCO to escort the standards to London to be presented to the monarch on 18 February. Miller tried to round out the presentation party with more WIR officers but could only find five men from other regiments who had been temporarily attached to the regiment. It was only at the last moment that he unearthed a regular WIR officer who was now retired.

At the assigned time, Miller and his party arrived at Buckingham Palace. They were dressed in their everyday khaki uniforms, and the colours were wrapped in their leather casings, so it is unlikely that the little group was noticed by passers-by as it entered the palace. The retired WIR officer arrived too late to be admitted.

The king, who had backed the rights of his West Indian subjects to serve in the armed forces during the war, clearly regretted the WIR's passing. 'It is a sad task to me to bid farewell to a regiment whose fine record of gallantry in the most arduous warfare covers a period of 150 years,' he told the little group standing stiffly in front of him.[9] Miller then solemnly presented the colours to the monarch, who passed them to an aide to be taken to Windsor. For a minute or two the king chatted to the officers, and then it was all over – a saga spanning almost a century and a half consigned to history in less than half an hour.

The flag ceremony did not go entirely unnoticed in Britain, even if it was so forgotten. 'The passing of the West India Regiment, for a century and a half a most gallant and valuable unit of the British Army, will be widely

---

8    TNA/PRO WO 32/2899.
9    TNA/PRO WO 32/2899.

deplored. It is a melancholy break with the traditions of the past,' *The Times* noted in a brief article.[10]

Memories of the WIR lingered a little longer in the West Indies. Men who had spent a large part of their lives in its ranks tried to keep alive the regiment's traditions. In 1936, the Association of Ex-West India Regiment, which had been formed in Jamaica by the regiment's black veterans, sent a request to the Colonial Office in London asking for a flag to march behind at the annual war memorial ceremony. It wanted to honour '150 years ... defending His Majesty's British Empire as loyal and faithful subjects of their Gracious Majesty ... [because the veterans] cannot and will not cause to die those beautiful memories of happy days'.[11] The request was passed on to the Army Council, which replied that the matter was nothing to do with it.

★★★

A petition in May 1939, whose signatures included a few grizzled old men who had served in the Ashanti Campaign of 1873–74, pleaded for help from the army: most of the veterans had not received pensions, many suffered from poor health after years of service in Africa, and all said they could barely feed themselves or their families. Affirming their loyalty to the king and the army, they begged for the same benefits as white ex-regulars in Britain. A curt reply from the War Office said it could do nothing to help.[12]

---

10  TNA/PRO WO 32/2899.
11  TNA/PRO CO 137/810/9.
12  TNA/PRO CO 137/836/11.

# PART III

# THE SECOND WORLD WAR

# 16

# LET US FIGHT LIKE MEN

The British West Indies found themselves at war with Nazi Germany on 3 September 1939. Following instructions from London, governors of British colonies across the Caribbean announced the advent of hostilities, the minuscule local defence forces were mobilised, and emergency regulations hurriedly dusted off. No one asked the people for their consent, and yet the war was greeted with patriotic pride. Black West Indians still believed they were as British as any white inhabitant of the British Isles, and many believed it was their duty to fight for Britain and the empire in their hour of crisis. One man later remembered:

> I held England in very great esteem … All our geography in school was based entirely on England. Whilst one knew very little about West Indian history, one's brain was full of knowledge where English history was concerned. We were always told – and we always had this thing at the back of our minds – that England was the Mother Country.[1]

Such reverence was even more striking since virtually no black West Indians had ever seen the country to which they were so devoted. R. W. Thompson, a newly arrived intelligence officer in Jamaica, who toured the isolated

---

1   Quoted in Robert Murray, *Lest We Forget*, p.19.

interior of the island where whites rarely ventured, was astounded at the 'deep sense of being part of the British Empire that is in these people'.[2]

The loyalty and affection of black West Indians were not reciprocated by the empire's rulers. Most people in Britain were barely aware of their Caribbean colonies, while the officials who ran the empire regarded them as an all but worthless burden. The notion that black West Indians saw themselves as British, or imagined they might fight for Britain, was regarded by most whites as comical, impertinent or outrageous.

By 1939, a century of economic decline had turned the once fabulously wealthy sugar islands into what a government commission called 'the slums of the empire'.[3] Those who had hoped that the West Indies' sacrifices in the First World War would be rewarded were bitterly disillusioned. Small white elites continued to monopolise political and economic power. The black population were largely excluded from voting by strict property franchises, and in Barbados, one of the better racially integrated settlements, just one person in forty had the right to vote, most of them white.[4]

Poverty and hopelessness bred anger, and some of the Caribbean colonies were roiled in the 1920s and 1930s by sporadic riots and violent strikes amid demands for government aid and black rights. Some thirty people were killed in the worst unrest in a 1938 dock strike in Jamaica.

Black veterans of the BWIR helped lead the struggle for equality and reform, insisting that their wartime sacrifices entitled all black citizens to better lives. A 1938 petition from BWIR veterans in St Vincent said that many of them did not have jobs, homes or land, and many widows and orphans of comrades who had died on war service had never received pensions or other aid.

When war came in 1939, some in the West Indies spoke against aiding Britain because of the legacy of slavery, racial discrimination and the treatment of their troops in the previous world conflict. And yet most black West Indians remained ardently loyal to Britain. Adrian Neysmith of Jamaica spoke for many when he explained, 'Since Great Britain was in a war I felt like it was my duty to take part in helping to gain victory for Her, for ourselves and for the world.'[5] He and thousands of other black West Indians

---

2  TNA/PROWO 106/2829.
3  T.O. Lloyd, *The British Empire 1558–1903*, p.315.
4  Parry & Sherlock, *A Short History of the West Indies*, p.287.
5  Quoted in Murray, p.20.

were to face even greater disillusionment than the generation that had served in the First World War.

Imperial neglect and local indifference meant that the West Indian settlements were virtually defenceless in 1939. The region was almost the last place in the world that the British Army cared about. During the interwar era, the army High Command believed the only likely threat was internal black unrest.

Following the axing of the WIR in 1927, the imperial garrison was reduced to a single white battalion split between Jamaica and Bermuda. Army leaders tried to withdraw even this token unit in 1937. The plan was only dropped after civilian officials protested that leaving the West Indies without British troops would tarnish the empire's prestige in North and South America and encourage black unrest.

Army planners argued it was safe to withdraw the battalion, improbably suggesting that in an emergency, troops could be flown in on Pan Am, the American airline that serviced the Caribbean in the absence of a British company.[6] Baffled Colonial Office officials could not tell if the army believed its own claims – air travel was the preserve of the rich and famous, with planes carrying a few passengers in luxurious conditions at sky-high prices.

The West Indian settlements made little or no effort to make up for the cuts in imperial defences. Local legislators, keen as ever to keep taxes low, sliced their already miserly spending on defence even further on the grounds there would never be another war. The defence forces in several colonies collapsed from a lack of funds and volunteers in the interwar years: very few men were willing to volunteer if it meant sacrificing their leisure time or being mocked by friends and neighbours for playing at toy soldiers.

Those forces that survived were small, ill-trained and poorly equipped. British Guiana had just 319 men, including the regimental band, to defend a territory almost as large as the United Kingdom. Plans to defend Trinidad and its vital oil fields against invasion consisted of sending six parties, each comprising two horsemen and a cyclist, to different points on the roughly 200-mile coastline while the remainder of the 110-strong defence force guarded the capital and the oil installations.[7] British Intelligence warned

---

6   TNA/PRO CO 318/432/3.
7   TNA/PRO CAB 9/19.

that Jamaica was totally unprepared for war despite being by far the largest colony – the only map of the island's roads was an incomplete guide compiled by the Jamaica Automobile Association for weekend motorists.[8]

The main role of the local defence forces was helping the police put down occasional civil unrest or strikes. In 1938, the British Guiana Militia's annual exercises focused on mastering 'the new type of Mob fighting' to disperse street protests.[9] Critics complained that too many forces wasted their time on ceremonial parades and Sunday band concerts rather than anything vaguely resembling realistic training. When Colonel A. Mudge, the Army Inspector of West Indian Forces, reviewed the Barbados Defence Force in 1928, just eighty-nine men out of a strength of 221 showed up.[10] A report by the War Office concluded, 'Almost without exception, these forces were of no military value and were an object of ridicule by the civilian population.'[11]

Most colonies continued to rely on the local police as their main line of defence. Many police units were equipped with rifles and machine guns and received some military training. Regular army inspectors generally gave the police high marks, rating them as better soldiers than the local militia or defence volunteers, although one officer worried that if they had to fight a foreign invader and were taken prisoner, the constables 'would probably be hanged without trial from the nearest tree as armed civilians'.[12]

★★★

Despite their distance from events in Europe and Asia, the West Indian colonies mobilised for war from the first day: local defence forces guarded harbours, power plants and other vital facilities, lookouts scanned the sea for enemy warships and censorship was imposed. Beach defences were constructed in many colonies, often with mixed success: the white clerks and shop assistants of the Trinidad Defence Force had little experience with spades and picks, and their efforts at digging trenches produced ruts rather

---

8   TNA/PRO WO 106/2829.
9   'Report of the Commandant', British Guiana Militia 1938, Government Printers, Georgetown 1939.
10  TNA/PRO CAB 9/19.
11  TNA/PRO CO 968/102/1.
12  TNA/PRO CAB 9/19.

than sturdy emplacements. Coastal batteries in Kingston, Jamaica, one of the few existing defences in the region, were manned around the clock, although the nearest they came to action was an occasional warning shot when British cargo ships forgot to hoist recognition signals.

While German submarines would attack local shipping, the only land action in the West Indies throughout the entire war was against an ally. This occurred when Anglo-French forces in May 1940 seized the oil fields on the Dutch islands of Aruba and Curacao, ostensibly to keep them out of German hands.

The colonies put much of their efforts into recruiting troops to send overseas to fight. Thousands of men of all races and classes enlisted in the local defence units and new formations were set up to help absorb the flow of volunteers. One volunteer was amazed by the scenes at the recruiting centre, 'The response was terrific … overwhelming. In fact, recruitment was oversubscribed. Hundreds were turned away.'[13]

Trinidad promised to send 25,000 men wherever they were needed for the war effort. Jamaica started a Volunteer Training Corps that within a few weeks had fifty officers, 1,270 men and virtually nothing in the way of weapons or uniforms. 'Keenness of the members has overcome difficulties such as lack of money, lack of stores and in many cases of any previous military knowledge,' the unit proudly claimed.[14] Reverend E. Elliot Durant, a prominent black church leader, urged Prime Minister Winston Churchill to help raise black West Indian combat units to 'give these loyal subjects of His Majesty an opportunity to help in defending democracy'.[15]

Black recruits knew they would have to serve in segregated units, but they had no doubt that they would be called to fight for the empire. As in the past, West Indian units serving overseas would, of course, be part of the regular British forces.

At the start of the conflict, the War Office briefly toyed with raising a black West Indian pioneer or labour unit to serve with the British Army in France. This was soon dropped on the grounds that Greeks and Arabs were 'the most effective coloured labour' for service in Europe.[16] Following this, and despite a chronic shortage of men and the long and impressive record

13  Quoted in Murray, p.27.
14  PRO/TNA WO 216/149.
15  PRO/TNA CO 323/1801.
16  PRO/TNA CO 323/1801.

of West Indian troops, the British Army would employ every prevarication, racist stereotype and deceit it could conjure up to bar black West Indians from its ranks.

The army hierarchy resisted accepting a black West Indian unit as ferociously as any foreign invader – which is precisely how many senior officers saw it. A May 1941 War Office letter to the Colonial Office said there could be no role for black West Indians in defending the British Isles. 'Experience in the last war showed conclusively that it was undesirable to make use of [black] West Indian personnel for combatant units,' it claimed.[17]

Even in some of the most perilous days of the war, with Britain facing defeat and short of troops on every front, the British General Staff found time to argue that black West Indians were too backward to be soldiers. The High Command evinced a level of prejudice far worse than anything subjected on black West Indian troops in earlier decades. Even the army's West India Command, which knew better, claimed that black West Indians were useless as fighting troops. 'The Jamaican negro has little or no sense of responsibility and definitely dislikes discipline … and they would be more of a liability than anything else,' it opined.[18]

Rather than accept the flood of offers from the West Indian settlements to send thousands of men to fight, the army dispatched white Canadian troops to Jamaica, the Bahamas and Bermuda to guard against black unrest despite the lack of any threat. Officially, the army said that the role of the West Indies was to produce food and other commodities for the war effort, and every man was needed for this vital task. In a region suffering from some of the highest unemployment in the empire, the excuse fooled nobody. War Office officials even told West Indian governors not to recruit local whites for the British forces because it would only encourage black demands to enlist. If white men should find their way to the United Kingdom on their own, 'there would be no difficulty about their acceptance', the army added.[19]

Civilian officials in Britain who were struggling to find men to meet the voracious demands of the war effort were baffled by the army's attitude. In addition to squandering valuable manpower, the Colonial Office said

---

17  PRO/TNA CAB 120/729.
18  TNA/PRO WO 216/149.
19  TNA/PRO CO 323/1801.

the army's stance risked undermining the loyalty of black West Indians, and with it, British control of the region. Churchill intervened by calling for the revival of the WIR. He was well aware of the past feats of black West Indian troops, and suggested the regiment be reformed with three battalions.

Army chiefs batted away all of these proposals and pleas with a series of empty excuses: black West Indians could not be expected to serve in a modern army; reviving the regiment would be too expensive; black troops could not be used outside the West Indies or trusted to suppress black civil unrest.[20]

Army opposition hardened when it was forced to accept the basing of black American Army units on British soil later in the war. An October 1942 War Office letter to Brigadier General T.D. Daly in Jamaica said accepting black West Indian troops 'in Great Britain would add to the already formidable racial problems which we have on our hands here, with the presence of U.S. negro troops'.[21]

When even Churchill's call for re-raising the WIR went nowhere, Lord Moyne, the Colonial Secretary, revived the possibility in January 1941 of raising a black West Indian pioneer unit for the army. 'It is difficult to believe that no use can be found for our West Indian British subjects, many of whom are so eager to serve,' he pleaded.[22] War Secretary David Margesson replied that black West Indians were not an 'industrious race' and he did not like the idea of large numbers of black men arriving in Britain.[23]

Every attempt to enlist black West Indians was met by the army with a seemingly endless stream of objections: black West Indians could not cope with the British climate; there was a lack of housing; and white officers were not willing to lead black troops. In May 1941, Moyne told the West Indian governors that a proposal to form a black West Indian unit of any kind had been rejected by the army. He wrote feebly:

I am sure that West Indians will appreciate that in modern warfare, with all its complexities, it is not given to all individuals or communities even

---

20  TNA/PRP CO 986/17/5.
21  TNA/PRO WO 106/2830.
22  TNA/PRO CO 323/1801/3.
23  TNA/PRO CO 968/37.

in Great Britain itself to serve our common cause in the way in which their most generous instincts dictate.[24]

Later that summer, Churchill again pushed for a black West Indian unit, suggesting it could be sent to Asia where Britain faced a growing threat from Japan. 'I am much in favour of it, and wish the scheme to be pressed forward. They could go to Singapore,' he wrote.[25] Moyne, desperate to appease growing West Indian indignation, told the War Office that even a single battalion would be acceptable. Taking a new tack, Margesson replied that the Indian, Malay and Chinese troops in the Singapore garrison would reject black West Indians as an 'inferior element'[26] and their arrival would create racial tension. 'The cold fact of the matter is that from the Army point of view it would be an inconvenience to raise West Indian units,' he stated.[27]

A few months later, the army's Middle East Command, apparently oblivious of the wrangling, asked for a West Indian pioneer unit to help ease an acute lack of skilled labour in the theatre. Colonial Office officials eagerly accepted the call. Peeved at this unwelcome initiative from its own ranks, the army High Command stressed that West Indian workers created endless problems and said the request would only be approved if the Middle East Command accepted personnel cuts in other areas. Military officials in Cairo quickly got the message and dropped the proposal.

Black West Indians were bewildered and angry at their rejection by the mother country. Trinidad's colonial administration said that after two years of war it was proving difficult to maintain the morale of the local defence forces and the loyalty of the general population. An April 1941 petition from the Leeward Islands Legislative Council pleaded with London to accept the 'fervent wish of people of this colony' to be allowed to fight alongside other British colonies.[28] A white West Indian serving in the British Army said it was unjust that his fellow black West Indians could not serve. 'Surely there is a place for us all in this battle for civilization,' he wrote.[29]

---

24  TNA/PRO CO 968/37.
25  TNA/PRO CAB 120/727.
26  TNA/PRO CAB 120/729.
27  TNA/PRO CAB 120/729.
28  TNA/PRO CAB 120/729.
29  Quoted in Healy, 'Colour, Climate and Combat', p.72.

With the army rebuffing all calls for a black West Indian unit, a few men made their own way to Britain in the hope of enlisting in white units. It was a difficult and hazardous journey because of the dire shortage of shipping, the threat from German submarines and the lack of any official financial or other support.

The Colonial Office urged the army to at least accept black West Indian mechanics and craftsmen at a time when the military was desperately short of technicians. It challenged the army's assertions that black people could not fit into British society, although its own views were hardly enlightened. 'The negro is naturally self-seeking, has few morals and is ill-disciplined – with training, however, many of them can be found who appreciate the British way of life,' it stated.[30]

Army officials eventually agreed to accept qualified technicians on a one-by-one basis, although they were generally sent to the Middle East rather than being allowed to work in Britain. Several hundred black West Indians also found civilian work in munitions factories and other vital war industries in Britain.

The Royal Air Force was the first of the armed services to welcome black West Indians. Hugh Trenchard, the force's founding father, had banned black recruits to reinforce imperial notions of white racial supremacy. He also used aerial bombing during the interwar years to subdue the empire's unruly non-white subjects in a strategy euphemistically dubbed 'air policing'.[31] However, the RAF ban on non-whites was dropped with the coming of the Second World War, and by 1945 some 6,000 black West Indians were serving in the air force, including some 400 officers and air crew in combat squadrons. About 1,100 black West Indians had managed to find places in the British Army by the end of the war, while the Royal Navy, the most resistant to black enrolment, had just some 200.[32]

Black and mixed-race West Indian women were among the first to breach the army's race barrier, thanks to a clerical error. The force enlisted white West Indian women for uniformed administrative duties in Britain and Washington from the start of the war while rejecting non-white volunteers. This ban was only dropped in 1943 when a well-qualified Bermuda woman

---

30  TNA/PRO CO 968/102/1.
31  Barry Renfrew, *Wings of Empire*, pp.171–72.
32  TNA/PRO CO 968/74/14.

was accepted before officials learned that she was black. Army officials feared reversing the decision would incur unfavourable publicity, particularly in the United States, and dropped the ban on non-white women.

Some 600 West Indian women were serving in the army by the end of the war, half of them black and mixed race. Nearly all of these women were well educated and from prosperous middle-class backgrounds.

Rejected by the British Army, many black West Indians joined the Canadian armed forces. A 1941 report by the British High Commission in Ottawa said that the Canadian forces accepted West Indians of all races. Some of the Caribbean colonies paid the travel costs for both black and white volunteers to go to Canada, with Barbados raising $40,000 in the autumn of 1941 to send men. An ensuing flood of volunteers from the West Indies caused concern in Canada about the armed forces' ability to cope with the influx, and officials rejected several requests from Jamaica to send large contingents of men.[33] While willing to accept black West Indian volunteers, the Canadian forces would not allow them to be officers.

★★★

While the British Army refused to accept black West Indian troops, the government did raise a unit of black forestry workers from British Honduras for service in Britain in 1941. Timber was a major part of the British Honduran economy, and the colony boasted some of the most skilled lumberjacks in the world. Similar units were recruited from Newfoundland, Australia and New Zealand. However, only the Hondurans endured prejudice from officials, local whites and even one of the country's leading noblemen.

A unit of 500 Honduran loggers arrived in Britain in the summer of 1941, after an appeal for volunteers had attracted a huge response in the colony, and hundreds of men had to be turned away. Although it was a civilian formation, the British Honduras Forestry Unit was organised like an army unit with the men wearing uniforms and subject to military style discipline.

Sent to work in the Scottish highlands that autumn, men who had never been outside the tropics were left to cope with the increasingly harsh weather without adequate clothing or accommodation by white managers

---

33  TNA/PRO WO 216/150.

who made no secret of their disdain for black people. For months, the men had to handle frozen logs without gloves. Morale plummeted and scores of the loggers fell ill.

Rather than taking elementary steps to improve conditions, managers refused to pay men who were too ill to work, and some of the sick were charged and fined by a local court for absenteeism. Managers tried to blame all of the problems on the Hondurans, accusing them of being bad workers and troublemakers. Eventually, some of the managers were removed and efforts made to improve conditions in the camps after shocked Colonial Office inspectors reported a litany of abuse and neglect.

One of the few bright spots for the Hondurans was the warm welcome they received from some of the local people, who befriended these men who had come to aid the war effort, inviting them into their communities and homes. Theo Lambey, one of the loggers, recalled fondly years later, 'The people were grand; the village was like our own. The people friendly and accommodating. In the public houses, we were treated like special guests. They were really good to us.'[34] Some of the men became especially close with local women and there were romances, a number of pregnancies and marriages. All of this led to a spiteful rift with less-tolerant villagers, who denounced neighbours who mixed with the Hondurans as 'darkie lovers', and women who went out with the loggers as 'prostitutes'.

Matters deteriorated further when the Duke of Buccleuch, one of Scotland's biggest land owners, complained to the government that local women were having sexual relations with the black workers. 'Personally, I dislike this mixture of colour and regret that it should be allowed with no discouragement ... unsophisticated country girls should be discouraged from marrying these Black men from Equatorial America,' he wrote.[35]

While there is no evidence that the duke's intervention was instrumental, the government decided in 1943 to disband the unit, despite the acute need for skilled loggers. In fact, a second detachment of some 330 Hondurans had been brought over at the end of 1942. It had travelled via the United States, where the men were confined to a US Army camp in New Orleans and made to work in demeaning conditions under white guards. When some of the men complained, the British Consul threatened that they would be

---

34  Quoted in Amos Ford, *Telling the Truth*, p.58.
35  TNA/PRO CO 876/41.

punished if they did not behave. 'We felt more like prisoners of war than as volunteers travelling to the United Kingdom to do war work,' one disillusioned veteran remembered.[36]

Officials gave the loggers the choice of returning home or finding work in Britain. About half opted to stay, only to often struggle in finding work because of racial prejudice. A group of ninety-three of the volunteers who went home via the United States were arrested and incarcerated as illegal aliens because officials had not given them the British passports they were entitled to.[37]

A badge featuring two loggers and the arms of British Honduras had been issued to the men to wear on their caps. In a final petty snub, the government rejected the request for a crown – the traditional sign of loyalty to the monarch – to be included in the design.

36 Quoted in Ford, p.50.
37 *The Daily Telegraph*, 19 May 2015.

# 17

# AN AMERICAN LAKE

British military commanders often derided their American allies as bumptious amateurs, and yet they were all too happy to dump the defence of the British West Indies on the 'Yanks' during the Second World War. The generals in London saw the Caribbean colonies as little more than an irritant barely worth defending.

Even before entering the war in December 1941, American forces had set up bases on some of the British islands as part of the Lend-Lease programme. British officers and officials were awed by the scale of the US military's resources. A general who inspected American bases in Jamaica reported that the accommodation for ordinary soldiers was far more lavish than anything enjoyed by British troops, and warned of a 'violent contrast' if they ever found out how the Americans lived.[1]

London fretted that some white West Indians were shirking local military service, happy to hide behind the American troops guarding their colonies as they got on with making money or enjoying themselves. A Colonial Office official complained that such whites had gone 'native', saying they 'were decadent … like other white men who have lived for several generations in tropical climates they are certainly losing their energy and ability'.[2] Thousands of black West Indians found jobs on the sprawling American bases, meanwhile, and far larger numbers were recruited for agricultural

1   TNA/PRO WO 106/28229.
2   TNA/PRO CO 968/122/5.

labour in the US. It seemed that the British West Indies were part of the American war effort rather than that of the mother country.

While the US presence was largely welcomed, many inhabitants of the British colonies were less than happy when black American troops began to arrive in the region. Whites objected to these assertive soldiers who refused to be subservient; some in the local black elite saw them as poorly educated and crass, and poorer black locals resented their money and interest in local women.[3]

A farcical flap over some bauxite mines in British Guiana typified British consternation. The mines were vital to the British aircraft industry. British commanders said that the local militia was too poorly trained and equipped to guard the mines and asked the Americans to supply troops for the task. An offer of a black infantry company was hysterically rejected by the colony's governor, Sir Gordon Lethem, who insisted that the Americans must send white troops even though the colony's militia was mostly black. When American officials rebuffed a formal request from the Colonial Office for a white unit, Lethem fumed that he would rather leave the mines unguarded than accept black Americans.

Efforts to persuade Canada to provide white troops were also rebuffed. This travesty rumbled on for almost a year, embroiling three governments and eight ministries, ending only when the British Army reported that the black British Guiana militia had received sufficient training and equipment to guard the mines.[4]

It was far from an isolated incident. When a black American anti-aircraft unit was withdrawn from Trinidad, the local British commander formally thanked his US colleagues, despite the fact the move had nothing to do with easing the host nation's racial unease. Colonial Office officials echoed the army's satisfaction, saying that black American troops 'were a great nuisance'.[5]

There was more bureaucratic handwringing when the US Army decided to send Hispanic troops from Puerto Rico to guard American bases. Local colonial governors complained that the Puerto Ricans would be a greater headache than the black American troops because they saw themselves as

---

3   TNA/PRO WO 106/2836.
4   TNA/PRO WO 106/2838.
5   TNA/PRO CO 968/102/3.

white, and would expect to use segregated hotels, bars and other facilities reserved for local whites. Trinidad's Governor, Sir B. Clifford, said the Puerto Ricans' presence was 'likely to provoke much quarrelling and riotousness',[6] and Jamaican officials said their segregated resorts 'would certainly not admit Puerto Ricans'.[7] Clifford tried to besmirch the loyalty of the Puerto Ricans by suggesting they might somehow collude with fellow Spanish speakers on the mainland.

Colonial officials also fretted that the presence of black and Hispanic American troops would make the local black population realise that the US treated non-whites better, despite repeated claims to the contrary.[8] British officials in London and Washington implored the Americans not to send the Puerto Rican units, only to be turned down by General George C. Marshall, the head of the US Army. Chastened by Marshall's blunt refusal, the War Office withdrew its objections for fear they were 'savouring of racial discrimination against U.S. nationals'.[9]

By 1943, the British Army's continuing refusal to accept black West Indians was stretching to breaking point the spirits of the thousands of young men who had been training and preparing to fight for up to four years. Volunteers had been transformed from awkward civilians into 'a tough seasoned lot', as one remembered, more than ready for active service.[10] And yet it seemed they would never be given a chance to prove themselves.

Unit diaries of the local defence forces during these years recount an unending cycle of mind-numbing guard duty, digging fortifications, drilling and, above all, waiting. The troops had enlisted because they wanted to fight for Britain and the empire, and the army's rejection was profoundly humiliating. George Rowe spoke for many, 'The only conception I had about the War was that I would be a good fighter and nothing else.'[11]

The lack of realism or urgency was epitomised by October 1942 war games in Barbados to rehearse repelling an invasion. The military were told by the local authorities to select a time and date that would cause the least

---

6   TNA/PRO WO 106/2836.

7   TNA/PRO WO 106/2842.

8   TNA/PRO WO 106/5749.

9   TNA/PRO WO 106/5749.

10  Quoted in Murray, *Lest We Forget*, p.35.

11  Murray, p.29.

inconvenience to traffic, businesses and the public, and to let the troops go home no later than 6.30 p.m.

It became increasingly difficult to maintain standards in some units, as it seemed less and less likely that they would ever see action. The head of the Barbados Defence Force complained that 'some officers preferred to sleep on afternoons rather than devote their spare time to the welfare and enter-tainment of their men'.[12]

It seemed the nearest the Barbados force would get to danger was a series of accidents caused by men who had been distracted by saluting officers while driving trucks or bicycles. An order banning drivers from saluting had to be issued after several mishaps.

Troops were further demoralised by the old West Indian affliction of scrimping on defence spending, even in war time. Those soldiers in Trinidad assigned to coastguard duty had to travel third class on government ferries 'sharing journeys on equal terms with livestock'.[13]

Education courses, film shows and other activities were arranged by some West Indian forces to boost morale, although the screening of US Army films on venereal disease had the opposite effect on troops in Trinidad. 'VD films in glorious Technicolor. Troops visibly shaken,' the unit diary drily recorded.[14] To help battle boredom, the Trinidad force started a library, but the adjutant said that it was little used except for a 'high demand for books of imposing title and appearance, for carrying under the arm' when off duty to impress the local female population. Still, there was no lack of recruits wanting to fight in every colony. Some 800 volunteers answered a call in Barbados in January 1943 for sixty openings in the island's defence force.

It did not help that black soldiers were bombarded with regular press accounts of local white soldiers fighting overseas in the British and Canadian forces. Envy was mingled with sorrow, however, since all too often the reports were of men they knew, who had been killed or injured.

While some white West Indians dodged military service, hundreds of others gave up mostly good jobs and comfortable lifestyles to fight in Europe, Africa and Asia. Major Anthony Smith of Bermuda was a member of the local Volunteer Defence Corps who enlisted in the British Army

---

12 TNA/PRO WO 176/8.
13 TNA/PRO WO 176/43.
14 TNA/PRO WO 176/43.

in 1940 when he was 33, an age at which he could have quite reasonably stayed at home.[15] Smith hated the years of separation from his wife and five children, and the financial hardship it caused, and yet in his letters home insisted that he had to fight because Nazi Germany threatened the entire world. After years of training and waiting, Smith landed in France on 19 September 1944 only to be killed the following month in Holland as his unit cleared a forest of German troops.

White prejudice and racial stereotypes, meanwhile, remained as strong as ever. Sir A. Richards, the Governor of Jamaica, was furious when the army in July 1942 announced plans to billet a unit of local black troops next to facilities housing white civilians who had been evacuated from Gibraltar. 'They contain a large proportion of adolescent girls and the reactions in Gibraltar to quartering a battalion of coloured troops in such close proximity would be likely to be considerable,' Richards told the Colonial Office.[16]

Lieutenant General Mason Macfarlane, the Governor of Gibraltar, was equally aghast, writing, 'Most strongly opposed to the suggested proximity of coloured troops to my evacuees. Effect on morale here would almost certainly be deplorable.'[17] Colonial Office bureaucrats claimed that the plan could cause unrest in Gibraltar that would 'jeopardise the safety of the fortress and the operational value of the Naval Base'.[18] Army officials offered to erect an 'unclimeable [*sic*] fence' between the camps, only now the local Catholic diocese had added its voice to the protests and it was decided to quarter the troops elsewhere.

★★★

With the war finally going better for the Allies in 1943, the Colonial Office and others again raised the possibility of forming a black West Indian infantry unit for front-line service with the British Army. Officials in London and the Caribbean were acutely aware of the mounting frustration and anger among black West Indians over the army's refusal to allow their men to fight. It was feared that, if left unchecked, the resentment would erode

---

15  As in the First World War, a white Bermudian detachment served with the Lincolnshire Regiment.
16  TNA/PRO CO 968/19/4.
17  TNA/PRO CO 968/19/4.
18  TNA/PRO CO 968/19/4.

black loyalty to Britain and encourage calls for independence. A senior Colonial Office official, P. Rogers, warned on 19 October 1943 that a black combat unit was vital to retaining the Caribbean colonies:

> It would remove the feeling of West Indians not being wanted, and of discrimination, which has played an important part in fostering that all too easily aroused sense of grievance and I feel myself that it would make a material contribution towards the success of our general West Indies political policy.[19]

Colonial officials in the West Indies warned that the army's obstinacy was undermining claims of British fairness and racial tolerance. Lethem, the crusty Governor of British Guiana, expressed concern over the growing bitterness among the colony's black troops. The fact that white West Indians were accepted by the British forces while black soldiers, who had been training since 1939, were kept at home, 'has already aroused ridicule' against Britain, he warned.[20]

Matters were made worse by the arrival of US Puerto Rican units in Trinidad, British Guiana and St Lucia. Colonial Secretary Oliver Stanley told the War Office:

> These Puerto Ricans however white they may be in their own estimation, will not be accepted as such by the West Indians, and unless a West Indian contingent is sent overseas to a war theatre, they will inevitably feel that, not only are they thought incapable of overseas service, but considered so inferior that coloured troops of a foreign nation must be brought in to garrison their own Islands for them.[21]

Senior army officers in the West Indies insisted the local troops were outstanding and denying them a chance to fight would prove to be a 'political disaster' for continued British rule. Brigadier General T. Denis Daly, head of the North Caribbean Command, told the War Office in May 1943:

---

19  TNA/PRO CAB 120/729.
20  TNA/PRO CO 968/102/1.
21  TNA/PRO CO 986/17/5.

The outstanding feature of the Local Forces in this Area is their keenness and the very clearly expressed desire of all ranks to serve abroad. In this they reflect the attitude of the majority of [the] Civil population in the different Colonies.[22]

A handful of political figures in Britain also championed the West Indian cause. The Earl of Listowel told the House of Lords in 1942 that racial equality was essential to victory:

It is not enough to point out that if the British Commonwealth is defeated they will become enslaved by the strongest Axis Power. They cannot be certain that this is a black as well as a white man's war unless they can be persuaded beyond any shadow of doubt that the peace which follows it will be a black as well as a white man's peace.[23]

And yet it seemed that no amount of measured argument or pleading could shake the army's prejudice against black West Indians. Nor was the generals' resistance mere racism, since there were now millions of African, Indian, Asian and other imperial troops in the army's ranks. Rather, their animus was fuelled by the old falsehoods that black West Indians were weak, cowardly, corrupt and, worst of all, thought themselves as good as white men.

War Secretary P.J. Grigg said in September 1943 that black West Indians could not be effective soldiers. 'In the first place West Indians are not a very robust race, which would detract from their value as combatant troops and might make them something of a commitment from the health point of view,' he wrote.[24] Grigg added that the presence of large numbers of black US troops in Britain was causing civilian anger, and the arrival of black West Indians would be 'asking for trouble'. He asked the Colonial Office to never again raise the matter.

For once, the Colonial Office was not willing to give up. It pointed to the thousands of black West Indians serving in the RAF to rebut army claims that they lacked the moral strength to fight, could not cope with cold weather and were too backward to handle machinery. Most effective, in the

---

22  TNA/PRO WO 106/2854.
23  House of Lords Deb, 20 May 1942, Vol. 122, cc 1083–128, *Hansard*.
24  TNA/PRO CO 986/17/5.

end, though, were the repeated warnings that army intransigence would damage post-war imperial interests. Moyne told Grigg:

> He [the black West Indian] would bitterly resent any implication that he is not good enough. This is a grievance which will be voiced not only during the war but afterwards, particularly if it proves to be the case that the West Indies is the only part of the Colonial Empire which has not sent a unit overseas.[25]

Under concerted pressure from other ministries, the War Office finally buckled and begrudgingly agreed in December 1943 to raise a unit of black West Indians for the British Army with the same pay, conditions and standing as white troops. Not that the army had changed its views, which soon became apparent when the unit's role and where it would serve was discussed. Grigg raised new doubts about what the troops would be capable of. He felt that they were more prone to sea sickness, which made it difficult to send them anywhere; West Indian troops had 'proved quite unsuitable and caused considerable trouble' in Palestine in the 1914–18 conflict; and they lacked the courage or fortitude to serve as anti-aircraft gunners. That left service as an infantry battalion in the Italian theatre, he wrote, since 'a considerable assortment of coloured troops is already deployed there'.[26]

Objections of a different kind were now raised by the intelligence services. An MI5 report on black political activism in the West Indies, entitled 'The Negro Problem', said the troops would be exposed to radical ideas overseas, encouraging them to demand greater rights when they returned home. The fact that many black men had received military training was already a serious concern because after the war they 'may fall under the spell of the local agitator and become inflamed against the white man and the government', it warned.[27] The agency continued to express concern after the new unit was raised, claiming that many of the recruits were 'loafers and scallywags, and even … known criminals'.[28]

---

25 TNA/PRO CAB 120/729.
26 TNA/PRO CO 986/17/5.
27 TNA/PRO CO 968/122/5.
28 TNA/PRO CO 968/122/5.

The War Cabinet, the ultimate authority for the British war effort, brushed aside the concerns of the army and the intelligence services. A request to approve the new unit was submitted on 3 January 1944 and approved three days later. The ministers made it clear that they wanted the West Indians in the Mediterranean by spring. Churchill, who had been absent from the session, wrote on the decision, 'I favour this'.[29]

29  TNA/PRO WO 106/2854.

# 18

# NOT WANTED HERE

Many black West Indians were electrified by the news that their young men were at last going to fight alongside soldiers from across the empire. It would be the flower of the British West Indies, drawn from every territory, and it would prove that their sons were as good as any. However, British generals, having lost the battle to exclude black West Indian troops, would exact a spiteful revenge by ensuring that they never saw action. The forlorn unit would be thrust from one command to another like a leper, the men enduring repeated humiliation and scorn.

No one, least of all the officers and men selected for the new regiment, realised what lay ahead as they assembled in early 1944. People in the West Indies were convinced that the unit would soon cover itself with success on the battlefields of Europe. Brigadier General A.K. Stokes-Roberts, the regular officer commanding the Barbados Volunteer Force, caught the mood of optimism when he told his men in February:

> ... this announcement by the War Office was probably the greatest thing for the West Indies that has occurred since the beginning of the war, because at last the people at home [Britain], the War Office and His Majesty the King had agreed that the West Indies ... should send a force to an active theatre of war.[1]

---

1  TNA/PRO WO 176/8.

The British Army's newest infantry unit was named the 1st Battalion Caribbean Regiment (1st/CR), although there is no evidence that any thought was given to raising additional battalions despite the numerical designation. Indeed, with a strength of fifty-four officers and 1,159 men it was a token force, given that the various West Indian defence forces fielded at least 25,000 troops with many more eager potential recruits. It was yet another indictment of the bigoted myopia of an army that was chronically short of fighting troops for much of the war, and yet spurned the chance of recruiting tens of thousands of black West Indian soldiers.

Still, the regiment represented the pick of the West Indian forces with carefully chosen men from all nineteen colonies: Jamaica contributed the largest contingent with 246 men, followed closely by Barbados with 196 men and Trinidad with 194 men.[2] While most of the officers, and all of the senior commanders, were white, several black officers were selected at the insistence of local military and civilian officials despite misgivings in London.

A lack of British facilities led to a decision to train the 1st/CR in the United States, even though this meant sending it to a segregated southern state. Shipping to transport the battalion also had to be begged from the Americans because of the lack of British vessels.

It was now the turn of whites to complain of discrimination when a request from Bermuda to provide a white contingent for the 1st/CR was rejected on the grounds that it was a black unit. Brigadier General H.D. Maconochie, the Army Commander in Bermuda, told the War Office, 'The whole White population will lose prestige with the Coloured people after the war' if they were not allowed to fight – an improbable claim, since some 200 white Bermudians were already serving with the British and Canadian forces.[3]

There was jubilation and pride in the British settlements as detachments of men set out for America in the spring of 1944. Flags and bunting decorated the Trinidadian capital of Port-of-Spain with thousands of onlookers crowding the streets, rooftops, balconies and every available window to cheer the local contingent as it marched to the harbour. A farewell service for the Barbados contingent featured 'Fight the Good Fight' and other

---

2   Quoted in Healy, 'Colour, Climate and Combat', p.80.
3   TNA/PRO WO 106/2854.

warlike hymns. The departing men sent a farewell message to the governor promising to drive 'one more nail into the coffin of the Führer'.[4]

However, there was despondency among the troops left behind. Convinced that the war was winding down, some soldiers in Barbados tightened their baggy army shorts and grew sideburns to look more like civilians, prompting a sharp crackdown in the unit.

With the cheers of well-wishers still ringing in their ears, the battalion sailed for the United States at the end of April aboard SS *Cub*. Boredom and seasickness dulled the troops' excitement as the ship slowly plodded its way northwards in a convoy.

One of the unit's first official acts was a mass 'short arm' inspection, with the men lining up to have their genitals inspected by a medical officer for signs of VD. Concerts, tug of war and some unarmed combat training were organised to try to keep the troops occupied. The only notable event was an altercation with some black Royal Air Force recruits on the ship that left two of the airmen injured. The incident was put down to traditional inter-service rivalry.

On 13 May, the ship arrived in Chesapeake Bay to be welcomed by a US Army band and Red Cross workers distributing refreshments, after which the troops entrained for Fort Eustis, Virginia to begin training. Official British press releases played up the 1st/CR's arrival as the first time a British Army unit had trained in the United States since the American Revolution. Pictures of the troops, along with gushing descriptions of their warm welcome, were transmitted across the West Indies and other parts of the empire.

Lieutenant Colonel H. Wilkin, the regular officer in command of the 1st/CR, had been worried about the reception his black soldiers would receive in the United States. Wilkin and other senior officers spent a lot of time during the voyage trying to prepare the men for the racial segregation they could expect to encounter in Virginia. The troops were told to always remember that they were 'guests of the Southern States' and chided to be 'most careful not to bring discredit on themselves or the Bn [battalion] by disregarding local customs and usages'.[5] Men who left the base were instructed to make sure they did not use public transport, bars, restaurants,

---

4   TNA/PRO WO 176/8.
5   TNA/PRO WO 176/41.

cinemas and other facilities reserved for whites. 'If they do so by mistake, they must be careful that they cause no disturbances but leave as quietly and quickly as possible.'[6] A memo distributed during the voyage stated that, above all:

> All Ranks must also be careful that they do not speak to any woman white or coloured on the public highway or in any public place. On no account must there be any attempt at friendship with a white woman whether she is willing or not.[7]

Such concerns turned out to be largely unwarranted, with the battalion getting a warmer welcome from the US military than it had ever received from the British Army. Lieutenant Hurlstone St C. Whitehorne said that black officers were not welcome in some restaurants and clubs, but otherwise relations were amicable.[8]

American officials did everything they could to help the visitors. Buses were arranged to take the men to see local historical sights and sporting events. Some of the troops said the fact they were British soldiers enabled them to use facilities that banned black locals. 'In America, the hospitality both socially and militarily, was kind. We kept to our allotment and today we can proudly say we maintained a very high standard of discipline there,' Lance Corporal Vernon Nicholas recalled.[9] Moreover, the men were quite accustomed to navigating colour bars in public facilities at home, and it was the British Army that had ordered segregated living, eating and washing quarters on the *Cub* because white British personnel were also on the vessel.[10]

A far bigger problem than segregation was that the 1st/CR was a unit in name only. Much of the training the troops had received at home proved to be patchy or of little practical use. Wilkin even had to order extra drill to teach the junior officers how to salute. Traditional rivalries between some of the men's home colonies occasionally ruffled the unit's cohesion.

Morale surged with the arrival from Canada of British Army uniforms and weapons. Battle training was said to be going well by 24 May,

---

6   TNA/PRO WO 176/41.
7   TNA/PRO WO 176/41.
8   *Jamaica Gleaner*, 22 April 2003.
9   *The Infantry Star*, 1946.
10  TNA/PRO WO 106/2854.

although it was clear the battalion had only mastered basic skills before heading for the Mediterranean in June. Still, the officers and men were happy and optimistic.

A final parade was held to mark the king's birthday before the battalion's departure – with British Army publicists rehashing the theme that such an event had not happened on American soil since the War of Independence. The black soldiers marched proudly, their bayonets and brass buckles gleaming in the sun, as thousands of American troops watched. British and US generals then inspected the battalion before the national anthems of the two nations were played and the West Indians gave three cheers for their king.[11]

Another long, tedious voyage ensued as the battalion sailed slowly across the Atlantic in a large convoy. There was nothing to distract the men except lectures, mending clothing and equipment, and the inescapable VD inspections.

However, while the crossing was calm, a political storm was breaking as parts of the British Government pushed to get the West Indians into action for political reasons, while the army did everything it could to obstruct them. Immediately following the War Cabinet's approval in January 1944 for the creation of the 1st/CR, the War Office told the British High Command in the Mediterranean that the battalion had to be given a combat role to assuage black West Indian pride. In the same signal, it inexplicably undercut its own proposal by casting doubt on the soldiers' courage. 'Their value as serious fighting troops is dubious,' it said, and it was likely that the men would break and run if they ever came under fire.[12] Nonetheless, it continued, employing the 1st/CR as labour troops was 'out of question on ground[s] much higher standards than any other coloured unit', nor could it be buried in some minor role in a safe area.[13]

The situation took on a surreal note when the Mediterranean command headquarters in Algiers replied that it would employ the 1st/CR as an army commando regiment for raiding enemy territory in Italy or the Balkans. Using a new and inexperienced battalion in one of the military's most dangerous and difficult roles caused consternation. Startled commando officers

---

11  TNA/PRO WO 176/41.
12  TNA/PRO WO 204/1362.
13  TNA/PRO WO 204/1362.

objected that their men were picked individually for the elite formations rather than entire units, while the Colonial Office questioned if black troops were 'mentally alert enough for Commando duty'.[14]

Army commanders in Algiers shrugged, and said the West Indians would instead go to Italy as an infantry battalion. The Allied Armies in Italy, headed by General Harold Alexander, one of the most prominent British generals of the war, promptly refused to accept the 1st/CR despite being desperately short of troops. The Italian command gave no official reason for its refusal, saying only, 'it is not acceptable ... request it is not sent to this theatre'.[15]

Internal memos reveal a visceral contempt for black West Indians. Major General E.A. Sutton, the head of army medical services in Italy, wrote:

I have had considerable personal experience of the West Indian negro as a soldier, both combatant and non-combatant, and I regret to have to say that my opinion, for what you may consider it to be worth, is an extremely low one ... They are very prone to reporting sick for the most trivial reasons, they are very querulous if medical opinion does not coincide with their own, and they are in the main 'bone idle'.[16]

Where and how Sutton acquired such views is a mystery since there is no record of him serving with any West Indian unit, and yet he undoubtedly spoke for much of the professional officer corps. Army commanders in Italy had been particularly incensed at discovering the 1st/CR had black officers. 'Officers are mixed – white, black and half-caste. There are two pure negro officers – one a major,' an internal report exclaimed.[17] It took the direct intervention of General Alan Brooke, Chief of the Imperial General Staff, to overrule the Italian command's refusal to accept the battalion. While admitting that the 1st/CR would be only half-trained and half-equipped, Brooke said it must be given a combat role to avoid a political backlash in the West Indies.[18]

---

14  TNA/PRO WO 106/2854.
15  TNA/PRO WO 204/7377.
16  TNA/PRO WO 204/7377.
17  TNA/PRO WO 204/6672.
18  TNA/PRO WO 106/2854.

Oblivious of the dispute, the West Indians disembarked on 15 July in Naples. Surveying recent signs of fighting, the men were excited, sure that they would soon see action. The battalion was given a camp site at Torre del Greco on the slopes of Mount Vesuvius, the massive volcano that loomed over the surrounding countryside. It soon became apparent that the site was unsuitable for training and little had been done to prepare for their arrival. None of the local army commanders seemed to know what to do with the 1st/CR, so two of the West Indian officers went to army headquarters in Rome and, in the words of the battalion's war diary, 'were able to explain the composition of the Unit about which little was known'.[19]

Reluctantly, the Italian command began preparing the 1st/CR for front-line duty. A report from the British Commander in the Mediterranean, General H. W. Wilson, written two weeks after the battalion's arrival in Italy, said that an inspection had uncovered major problems.

For once, the assessment did not seem to be motivated by the army's usual prejudices because it singled out the mostly white officers. 'From the commanding officer downwards, the officers are all unfit to look after their men and command in battle,' Wilson wrote.[20] Six months of intense training was needed, after which, if things went well, Wilson said he might 'fit them into a very quiet sector of the line before the weather becomes too bad'.[21] Once again, the army was readying the old myth that black West Indians could not endure cold weather as an excuse to limit their role on the battle front.

More encouragingly, an experienced major arrived from Rome to take over the battalion's training, and it was equipped with machine guns and mortars along with vehicles and some anti-tank cannons. It moved to good training facilities on 24 July, and to an even better site at the end of August. Intensive training was under way by early September, and the battalion suffered its first casualties when two privates were killed after a mishap with hand grenades in a practice session.

A detachment of eleven British officers and NCOs arrived in September to prepare the unit for combat, and the men spent long nights in the open, often under constant rain, on exercises that did not blunt their good humour.

19  TNA/PRO WO 170/1370.
20  TNA/PRO WO 106/2854.
21  TNA/PRO WO 106/2854.

A report by the Director of Military Training said the troops might be ready for a quiet sector of the front by October once they had undergone battle training, including being shot over by artillery. 'The men all seemed keen, intelligent and anxious to fight,' the report said.[22] It was highly critical of the officers, however, saying many were still unfit for their roles. The men were enjoying this new life as their military skills and confidence increased.

There were moments of excitement to break up the exhausting training, though. Gunmen opened fire on a 1st/CR patrol on 19 July, and a search of a nearby dwelling discovered two abandoned pistols; the battalion was also praised for helping to extinguish a blaze at an ammunition and supply dump; and armed detachments acted as guards on supply convoys to prevent theft and ambushes.

Reverend Eric Maxwell, the battalion's black padre, said that the time was 'interesting and even enjoyable'.[23] Vesuvius had a minor eruption, he remembered, after which fine ash covered the men, their tents, equipment and food for days. The ash, they were told, 'was beneficial rather than harmful to our health'. Everyone was keen to see as much as possible of the country, and there were outings to Naples and local historical sites where the men witnessed the ravages of earlier upheavals as well as those of the ongoing war. Maxwell said:

> We visited Naples often and also Pompeii where we saw archaeological remains, the physical destructiveness of war in damaged buildings, as well as the emotional and physical toll. In Naples, there were bread lines that stretched for miles.

Most sobering were the fields of white crosses marking the graves of fallen Allied and enemy troops. 'They had been buried where they fell,' the padre said. A major outbreak of VD in the battalion also indicated that many of the men took every chance to indulge in life while they could.[24]

Despite the steady progress of the 1st/CR under new instructors, Alexander still did not want the unit. Amid the demands of commanding more than a million men in the middle of a major campaign, he found

22  TNA/PRO WO 106/2854.
23  *Daily Gleaner*, 22 April 2003.
24  TNA/PRO WO 106/2854.

time to complain about this single battalion of just 1,000 men. He was furious at having to provide heavy weapons and transport for the West Indians, complaining that his command was already struggling to outfit two Polish brigades, a Jewish brigade from Palestine and Italian units that had switched sides. It was the age-old English disdain for anything foreign. He thundered:

> I cannot accept the West Indian troops here – my battle front is already far too rigid because of the number of nationalities I have. Those responsible must be warned that we shall be heading for trouble if the Italian theatre is made the dumping ground for all sorts of people who want to be in on the show for political reasons.[25]

As the months went by with the 1st/CR still stuck far behind the front lines, Wilkin warned of growing pessimism among his men, saying that if they were not allowed to fight, 'the morale of the Battalion will suffer and a state of unrest will ensue'.[26]

It was at this point that the War Office, after years of blocking the West Indies from fighting for the empire, performed a complete turnabout and proposed raising three brigades of black Caribbean troops with 10,000 men for the South Pacific. The Solomon Islands, Gilbert and Ellice Islands and other British colonies captured by Japan had just been liberated by US forces, and London was worried that Britain's imperial prestige would suffer if it could not provide British garrisons to replace the Americans. No existing units could be spared, so it was suggested West Indians be recruited as garrison troops.

West Indian officials said there would be no problem recruiting large numbers of men for such a role, and British and Australian officials in the Pacific blessed the scheme. Sir P. Mitchell, British High Commissioner for the Western Pacific, helpfully observed that since US forces in the region had black units he could 'see no objection to the same race of people from the British West Indies'.[27] His only concern was sexual

---

25  TNA/PRO WO 204/7377.
26  TNA/PRO WO 204/7377.
27  TNA/PRO WO 106/2851.

contact between West Indians and the local people, 'I should naturally prefer no racial mixtures.'

And then the Prime Minister of New Zealand, Peter Fraser, refused to back the plan. British diplomats told London that Fraser 'would strongly deprecate the sending of West Indian troops into Southern Pacific, as he would regard the introduction of another native race as most undesirable on ethnological grounds'.[28] Several British attempts to persuade Fraser to change his mind were fruitless. The diplomats informed London:

> He regarded the introduction of West Indian negroes into Polynesian or Micronesian Islands as morally wrong and contrary to our duty as guardians of the natives ... He had no objection to West Indians as such, but to the racial intermixture that was bound to result. We are up against a question of conscience.[29]

Unwilling to upset an important colonial leader, London dropped the scheme.

Almost five years of war had greatly depleted the manpower of the British Army, especially its infantry formations. Nowhere was this problem more acute than in Italy. In September 1944, Alexander ordered the disbanding of some armoured and anti-aircraft units and reduced all infantry battalions from four rifle companies to three because of the shortage of men.[30] At the same time, he and other senior officers continued to demand the removal of the army's only West Indian unit – a full infantry battalion desperate to fight.

Even though his own training chief had said the 1st/CR might be ready for a quiet sector of the front line by October, Alexander told London in a dispatch dated 6 September that it must be moved because of the supposed inability of black soldiers to cope with European winters. 'I consider, therefore, that we should be relieved now of all completely unnecessary burdens,' he told London.[31] Alexander's assertions were even more astonishing since he had tens of thousands of troops from tropical nations in his command, including Brazilians and Africans.

---

28  TNA/PRO WO 106/2851.
29  TNA/PRO WO 106/2851.
30  Jonathan Fennel, *Fighting the People's War*, p.573.
31  TNA/PRO WO 204/7377.

Army chiefs in London then suggested sending the West Indians to Burma as part of an African division, an idea quickly rejected by the Far East Command. 'What is the next move in this game,' a staff officer in London sardonically jotted in the accumulating correspondence on the 1st/CR's fate.[32]

Bowing to Alexander's insistence, Wilson arranged to move the battalion to the Middle East. A suggestion that the 1st/CR might be used on internal security duties in Palestine, where there was tension between the Jewish and Arab populations, was met with frantic protests from the Colonial Office. 'Such employment of West Indian troops would be objected to by both Jews and Arabs on racial grounds,' it stated.[33] It was decided to send the battalion to a remote, sparsely populated part of Gaza where its presence would not offend the sensibilities of anyone the British cared about.

In a final, bitter irony, the 1st/CR left Italy from the port of Taranto, where the battalions of the BWIR had mutinied in 1919 because of degrading treatment. More than a few of the men were likely thinking of that earlier injustice as they filed aboard the ship bound for Gaza and yet more uncertainty.

After several aimless weeks in Gaza, the 1st/CR was transferred to Egypt to resume training. Following several further moves, the battalion found itself at Adabiya on the outskirts of Suez in late January 1945. It was a large camp with comfortable accommodation, but the men had to march 4 miles each day for training exercises on a stretch of desert considered barely adequate for the purpose – the target range did not have any targets.

Training conditions and the men's morale improved in April as the unit practised with tank and artillery units for the first time. Instructors complained that many of the officers were still not fit to lead the men and proposed replacing them with seasoned officers from other units, only to be told that none were available.

Although the army considered them unfit to fight the Germans, the West Indians came out best in a clash with white British troops in Cairo on Christmas Eve 1944. The incident began with an altercation over a woman between a black West Indian sergeant and a white soldier at a dance hall.

---

32 TNA/PRO WO 106/2854.
33 TNA/PRO WO 106/2854.

Recreational facilities for British forces were racially segregated, however, the West Indians, as regular British Army troops, were entitled to use
whites-only facilities. Military police failed to break up the altercation,
which turned into a riot as white troops attacked the West Indians in the
hall. Eventually, the outnumbered West Indians barricaded themselves in a
hotel, refusing to give up until American military police brokered a truce,
and took the jubilant black soldiers back to their camp.

Lieutenant Colonel C.H. Nicholson, who had taken over command,
gave the entire battalion a verbal lashing the next day, saying the fracas had
damaged its reputation and chances of seeing battle. After a pause, the colonel undoubtedly won the affection of his men by adding that if they had to
fight, they should hit hard.

Outraged army commanders banned the West Indians from Cairo and
Alexandria for several months as a collective punishment. This did not end
the affair, however. Alarmed military censors who checked the unit's post
reported the troops were boasting that 'they had come triumphantly out
of the fray, and cited this as an example of their superiority not only to all
other coloured troops but even to white men'.[34] Far worse, the censors
said, was that 'conquests made over women in Italy were boastfully and
luridly described by some correspondents'.[35]

With the end of the war in Europe in sight by the spring of 1945,
London began to panic about getting the 1st/CR into action before
the last shot was fired. A message from the army's South Caribbean
Command warned that all the West Indian governments and large sections of the public were unhappy over the way the men were being
treated. Another proposal to send the battalion to the Far East was
rejected by the Indian Army, which said it did not have sufficient shipping even to bring home Indian units serving in Italy. It probably did
not help that the War Office, in making the proposal, had warned New
Delhi that the West Indians were 'extremely colour conscious and
expect to be treated as white tps [troops]'.[36]

London next tried to devise a token role to try to soothe West Indian
public opinion. A signal to the Italian command in April implored,

---

34  TNA/PRO WO 106/2854.
35  TNA/PRO WO 106/2854.
36  TNA/PRO WO 106/2854.

'Politically most important that Caribbean Regiment should take part in operations before end of war if possible.'[37] It suggested, in further messages, that 'honour would be satisfied' if the battalion was used in a minor operation in the Aegean or took part in receiving the surrender of the German garrison on Crete.

A clearly irritated Alexander swatted aside every suggestion, pointedly asking that 'this matter is not pressed further'.[38] For reasons that are not clear, but probably as the result of behind-the-scenes pressure, Alexander agreed in early May to accept the return of the 1st/CR while warning that it would need further training, which could not be done before June. A few days later the war in Europe was over.

★★★

London abandoned all efforts to find some meaningful role for the West Indians, and it was decided in June to send the battalion home, although the army could not say when shipping would be available. In a final, mealy mouthed attempt at soothing West Indian sensibilities, a War Office signal to the Egyptian Command said:

> Would be grateful if, before the Regiment leaves Middle East, you make clear to All Ranks that they are returning to their own country with honour and it is regretted that opportunity did not occur to give them chance to show themselves against enemy.[39]

In the end, the nearest the West Indians got to the enemy was a brief spell guarding prisoners of war in Egypt. 'As it turned out this was the only bit of war service the Regiment actually performed,' remembered Maxwell, the regimental chaplain.[40]

Training ceased, and the men spent long idle days with nothing to do except menial chores as they waited to go home. It was kept isolated from other units because of concerns about potential clashes. Finally, in December the men handed in their rifles and other weapons and moved to

---

37  TNA/PRO WO 204/10158.
38  TNA/PRO WO 204/10158.
39  TNA/PRO WO 204/10158.
40  *Daily Gleaner*, 22 April 2003.

Port Said. A total of thirty-three officers and 1,159 other ranks left the port on 22 December on SS *Highland Monarch*.

Christmas Day was marked at sea with the traditional festive lunch and a bottle of beer for each man followed by a concert, while the officers attended a dance in the first-class passengers' lounge. The ship reached Bermuda on 5 January, where the Bermudan troops disembarked, and then wandered across the Caribbean, dropping off men at various settlements. The battalion war diary, which had recorded months of hope and disappointment, concluded with the terse entry, 'Unit finally disbanded'.[41]

There were concerns in the West Indies that the 1st/CR men, who had now been exposed to new ideas and conditions, might have expectations of greater political and economic rights for the black population. Some colonial officials feared the soldiers with their military skills could pose a threat to British control. The Bahamas administration told the Colonial Office in November 1945 that the imminent withdrawal of a Canadian Army unit meant the colony would be defenceless against a possible threat from the veterans and pleaded for white British troops. Trinidad said the United States should be asked to provide white troops to quell possible disturbances by the returning soldiers.[42]

British warships had shadowed the BWIR on its way home at the end of the First World War because of similar fears of trouble. However, this time the British Government ignored the apprehension of the West Indian administrations and took no action.

Many of the returning soldiers were both disappointed about never seeing action and bitter over the discrimination they had endured in the army. Others tried to make the best of things, glad that at least they had been among the few who were given the chance to serve overseas, despite never firing a shot in anger. Vernon Nicholas wrote in 1946 on his return to Trinidad:

> We really regretted not being able to test our ability in actual warfare. Anyway, we have had the pleasure of seeing foreign lands, of meeting strange people, of hearing their languages and learning their customs. It

---

41 TNA/PRO WO 176/41.
42 TNA/PRO WO 106/2837.

has been the kind of education which can be gained only by travelling. In spite of the hazardous and heart-breaking times we encountered, I say without fear of contradiction, that all the boys of the 1st Caribbean Regt. are now better men for the trip overseas and would not have missed this adventure for anything.[43]

---

43 *Infantry Star.*

# 'AND TO ALL THE FORGOTTEN'

Not much remains to mark the black regiments of the British Army. There are a few decaying monuments in the West Indies, the graves of fallen soldiers on five continents, and a handful of dusty regimental histories and memoirs. It is a very meagre legacy, given a history of extraordinary exploits spanning 150 years. Their bravery and endurance under the most dreadful conditions are beyond doubt. All too often, those they protected and fought for repaid them with contempt and abuse.

It was not until 2017 that a monument was dedicated in London to honour the millions of men from Africa and the Caribbean who fought for Britain in the two world wars. The three formations that have been followed in these pages are named on the striking edifice. Since the monument honours those who served in the global conflicts of the twentieth century, no mention is made of the far longer service of the WIR. Perhaps the men of the WIR who served across the decades may be included in the monument's dedication, 'And to all the Forgotten'.

What are we to make of these men who fought and died for an empire that demeaned and oppressed them and their people? Some will damn them as sell-outs; others will laud their deeds while ignoring the failings of the masters they served. Their most important legacy was to help change and advance the status of black people over the years by matching, and at times outdoing, white troops. Their fight to prove themselves and be treated as equals was no different from the battles of black people to rise and succeed in every other area of life where they faced prejudice and discrimination. Looking back, no one can deny that these black soldiers were the equal of any soldiers in their own times or any other age.

# BIBLIOGRAPHY

Anon., *A Short History of Barbados* (London: J. Dodsley, 1768).

Anon., *Marly: Or, a Planter's Life in Jamaica* (Oxford: Macmillan Caribbean, 2005).

Aspinall, Algernon E., *West Indian Tales of Old* (London: Duckworth and Co., 1915).

Baptiste, Fitzroy Andre, *War, Co-operation and Conflict: The European Possessions in the Caribbean, 1939–1945* (New York: Greenwood Press, 1988).

Barkawi, Tarak, *Soldiers of Empire: Indian and British Armies in World War II* (Cambridge: Cambridge University Press, 2017).

Barnett, Correlli, *Britain and Her Army* (London: Allen Lane, 1970).

Beckett, Ian F.W., *Britain's Part-Time Soldiers* (Barnsley: Pen & Sword, 2011).

Black, Jeremy, *The War of 1812 in the Age of Napoleon* (London: Continuum, 2009).

Bond, Brian (ed.), *Victorian Military Campaigns* (London: Hutchinson, 1967).

Bourne, Stephen, *The Motherland Calls: Britain's Black Servicemen & Women 1939–45* (Stroud: The History Press, 2014).

Boynton, Lindsay, *The Elizabethan Militia 1558–1638* (London: Routledge & Kegan Paul, 1967).

Braithwaite, Kamau, *The Development of Creole Society in Jamaica 1770–1820* (Kingston: Ian Randle Publishers, 2005).

Bridges, George Wilson, *The Annals of Jamaica* (London: John Murray, 1828).

Buckley, Roger Norman, *The British Army in the West Indies* (Gainsville: University of Florida Press, 1998).

Buckley, Roger Norman, *Slaves in Red Coats* (New Haven: Yale University Press, 1979).

Caufield, J.E., *100 Years' History of the 2nd West India Regiment 1795 to 1898* (Uckfield: Naval & Military Press, 2006).

Chandler, David (ed.), *The Oxford Illustrated History of the British Army* (Oxford University Press, 1994).

Charlton, L.E.O., *Charlton* (London: Faber and Faber, 1931).

Childs, John, *The Army of Charles II* (London: Routledge & Kegan Paul, 1976).

Clayton, Anthony, *The British Empire as a Superpower 1919–39* (Basingstoke: Palgrave, 2001).

Craton, Michael, *Testing the Chains* (Ithaca: Cornell University Press, 1982).

Crooks, J.J., *Historical Records of the Royal African Corps* (Dublin: Browne and Nolan Limited, 1925).

Das, Santanu (ed.), *Race, Empire and First World War Writing* (Cambridge University Press. 2013).

Dirom, Alex, *Thoughts on the State of the Militia of Jamaica* (Jamaica: Douglas & Aikman, 1783).

Dow, Henry, *The Militia and Volunteers in Trinidad* (Unpublished notes, 1958).

Duffy, Michael, *Soldiers, Sugar and Seapower* (Oxford: Clarendon Press, 1987).

Dunn, Richard S., *Sugar & Slaves* (Chapel Hill: University of North Carolina Press, 1972).

Dyde, Brian, *The Empty Sleeve* (St John's: Hansib, 1997).

Dyde, Brian, *Out of the Crowded Vagueness: A History of the Islands of St Kitts, Nevis & Anguilla* (Oxford: MacMillan Caribbean, 2005).

Ellis, A.B., *The History of the First West India Regiment* (Driffield: Leonaur, 2010).

Fennell, Jonathan, *Fighting the People's War* (Cambridge: Cambridge University Press, 2019).

Firth, C.H., *Cromwell's Army* (London: Greenhill Books, 1992).

Fogarty, Richard S., *Race & War in France* (Baltimore: The John Hopkins University Press, 2008).

Ford, Amos A., *Telling the Truth* (Whitstable, Kent: Karia Press, 1985).

Fortescue, J.W., *A History of the British Army*, Vols 1–13 (London: Macmillan and Co.).

Freestone, Basil, *The Horsemen From Beyond* (London: Dennis Dobson, 1981).

Froude, J.A., *The English in the West Indies* (London: Elibron Classics, 2005).

Gibson, Carrie, *Empire's Crossroads* (Oxford: Macmillan, 2014).

Goodenough, W.H., and H.C. Dalton, *The Army Book for the British Empire* (London: HMSO, 1893).

Graves, Robert, *Goodbye To All That* (London: Guild Publishing, 1979).

Green, William, *British Slave Emancipation* (Oxford: Clarendon Press, 1991).

Handler, Jerome S., 'Freedmen and Slaves in the Barbados Militia' in *Journal of Caribbean History*, Vol. 19: 1–25 (1984).

Healy, Michael S., 'Colour, Climate and Combat: The Caribbean Regiment in the Second World War', *The International History Review*, Vol. 22, No. 1 (March 2000), pp.65–85.

Hernon, Ian, *Britain's Forgotten Wars: Colonial Campaigns of the Nineteenth Century* (Stroud: Sutton Publishing, 2007).

Heuman, Gad, *The Killing Time* (Knoxville: University of Tennessee Press, 2000).

Holmes, Richard, *Redcoat* (London: HarperCollins, 2001).

Hoppit, Julian, *A Land of Liberty? England 1689–1727* (Oxford: Oxford University Press, 2004).

Houlding, J.A., *Fit for Service: The Training of the British Army 1715–1795* (Oxford: Clarendon Press, 1981).

Howe, Glenford Deroy, *Race, War and Nationalism* (Kingston, Jamaica: Ian Randle Publishers, 2002).

Howe, Glenford Deroy, *West Indians and World War One: A Social History of the British West Indies Regiment* (PhD Thesis, University of London, 1994).

Ingham, Jennifer M., *Defence Not Defiance* (Bermuda: Island Press).

Jackson, Ashley, *The British Empire and the Second World War* (London: Hambledon Continuum, 2006).

James, C.L.R., *Beyond A Boundary* (London: Yellow Jersey Press, 2005).

James, C.L.R., *The Life of Captain Cipriani* (Durham: Duke University Press, 2014).

James, Lawrence, *Mutiny in the British and Commonwealth Forces, 1797–1956* (London: Buchan & Enright, 1987).

Joseph, Cedric L., 'The Strategic Importance of the British West Indies 1882–1932' in the *Journal of Caribbean History*, Vol. 7 (November 1973).

Joseph, E.L., *Trinidad* (London: Henry James Mills, 1839).

Kieran, Brian L., *The Lawless Caymanas* (Grand Cayman: Brian L. Kieran, 1992).

Killingray, David, 'All the King's Men? Blacks in the British Army in the First World War, 1914–1918' in *Under the Imperial Carpet: Essays in Black History 1780–1950* by Lotz, Rainer and Ian Pegg (eds) (Crawley, England: Rabbit Press, 1986).

Killingray, David, 'Race and Rank in the British Army in the Twentieth Century' in *Ethnic and Racial Studies*, Vol. 10, No. 3 (1987).

Kingsley, Charles, *At Last: A Christmas in the West Indies* (California: CreateSpace Independent Publishing Platform, 2015).

Kitchen, James E., *The British Imperial Army in the Middle East* (London: Bloomsbury Academic, 2014).

Knibb, William, *Facts and Documents Connected with the Late Insurrection in Jamaica* (London: Holdsworth and Ball, 1832).

Latimer, Jon, *1812 War with America* (Cambridge, Mass.: Belknap Press, 2007).

Lewin, Ronald, *Slim: The Standardbearer* (London: Leo Cooper, 1976).

Lewis, Matthew, *Journal of a West Indian Proprietor* (Oxford University Press, 1999).

Linch, Thomas, *A Description of the Island of Jamaica* (London: E. Milbourn, 1672).

Lloyd, Alan, *The Drums of Kumasi* (London: Longmans, 1964).

Lloyd, T.O., *The British Empire 1558–1903* (Oxford University Press, 1991).

Louis, Wm. Roger (ed.), *The Oxford History of the British Empire*, Vols 1–5 (Oxford University Press, 1998).

Lucas, Sir Charles, *The Empire at War*, Vols 1 & 2 (Oxford University Press, 1923).

Mackey, Piers, *War for America 1775–1783* (London: Longmans, 1964).

McShine, Arthur L., *Victory At Damieh 1918* (Trinidad & Tobago: Kubik.9, 2014).

Mallet, Matilde, *Letters from the Trenches During the Great War* (Shipston on Stour: The King's Stone Press. No date).

Manley, Norman, 'The Autobiography of Norman Washington Manley' in *Jamaica Journal*, Vol. 7, No. 1 (March–June, 1973).

Martin, Robert M., *British Colonial Library* (London: Whittaker & Co., 1837).

Martin, Robert M., *History of the British West Indies* (London: Whittaker & Co., 1836).

Metzgen, Humphrey, & John Graham, *Caribbean Wars Untold* (Jamaica: University of the West Indies, 2007).

Marshall, P.J. (ed.), *The Oxford History of the British Empire*, Vols 1–4 (Oxford University Press, 1998).

Mitcham, John C., *Race and Imperial Defence in the British World, 1870–1914* (Cambridge University Press, 2016).

M'Mahon, Benjamin, *Jamaica Plantership* (London: Effingham Wilson, 1839).

Morgan, Philip D., & Sean Hawkins (eds), *Black Experience and the British Empire* (Oxford University Press, 2006).

Morton-Jack, George, *The Indian Army on the Western Front* (New York: Cambridge University Press, 2014).

Murray, Robert N., *Lest We Forget: The Experiences of World War II Westindian Ex-Service Personnel* (Nottingham Westindian Combined Ex-Services Association, 1996).

Nalty, Bernard C., *Strength for the Fight: A History of Black Americans in the Military* (New York: The Free Press, 1989).

Newton, A.P., *The European Nations in the West Indies 1493–1688* (London: Adam & Charles Black, 1966).

Nicholas, Vernon, 'Overseas with the Carib Regiment' in *The Infantry Star*, Journal of the Trinidad Regiment, Port-of-Spain, Trinidad (1946).

Nugent, Lady Maria, *Lady Nugent's Journal* (London: Adam & Charles Black, 1907).

'P.', 'Blacks' in *St James Magazine*, vii (1863).

Pares, Richard, *War and Trade in the West Indies 1739–1763* (Oxford: Oxford University Press, 1936).

Parker, Matthew, *The Sugar Barons* (London: Windmill Books, 2011).

Parry, J.H. and J.M. Sherlock, *A Short History of the West Indies* (London: Macmillan, 1966).

Pearson, Sir Charles, 'The West Indies and its Command' in *United Services Magazine* (June 1984).

Perry, F.W., *The Commonwealth Armies* (Manchester University Press, 1988).

Pitman, Frank Wesley, *The Development of the British West Indies 1700–1763* (Archon Books, 1967).

Poyer, John, *The History of Barbados* (London: J. Mawman, 1808).

Ragatz, Lowell Joseph, *The Fall of the Planter Class in the British Caribbean 1763–1833* (New York: Octagon Books, 1971).

Renfrew, Barry, *Wings of Empire: The Forgotten Wars of the Royal Air Force, 1919–1939* (Stroud: The History Press, 2015).

Rolph, Thomas, *A Brief Account, Together with Observations Made During a Visit in the West Indies* (Dundas, 1836).

Schomburgk, Robert H., *History of Barbados* (London: Long, Brown, Green and Longman, 1848).

Sherwood, Marika, *Many Struggles: West Indian Service Workers and Service Personnel in Britain (1939–45)* (London: Karia Press, 1985).

Skinner, Robert, *Kitchener's Camps At Seaford* (English Heritage, 2011).

Sinclair, A.C., *The Handbook of Jamaica 1886–87* (Jamaica: Government Printing Establishment, 1886).

Smith, Jonathan D., *In the Hour of Victory* (Hamilton, Bermuda: TenTen Publications, 2011).

Smith, Richard, '"Heaven Grant you Strength to Fight the Battle for your Race": Nationalism, Pan-Africanism and the First World War in Jamaican Memory' in Das, Santanu (ed.), *Race, Empire and First World War Writing* (Cambridge University Press, 2011).

Smith, Richard, *Jamaican Volunteers in the First World War* (Manchester University Press, 2004).

Spurdle, Frederick, *Early West Indian Government* (Palmerston North: Whitcombe and Tombs, no date).

Tatem, Herbert J., *As You Were!* (No publisher).

Taylor, S.A.G., *The Western Design* (Kingston: Institute of Jamaica, 1965).

Thome Jas., & Horace J. Kimball, *The West Indies: A Six Months Tour* (New York: The American Anti-Slavery Society, 1838).

Tyson, George F. Jr., 'The Carolina Black Corps: Legacy of Revolution 1782–1798' in *Revista/Review Interamericana* (Fall–Winter 1975–76).

Walvin, James, *Black Ivory: A History of British Slavery* (London: HarperCollins, 1992).

Western, J.R., *The English Militia in the Eighteenth Century* (London: Routledge & Kegan Paul, 1965).

Williamson, James A., *The Age of Drake* (London: Adam & Charles Black, 1965).

Winegard, Timothy C., *Indigenous Peoples of the British Dominions and the First World War* (Cambridge University Press, 2012).

Wolseley, Garnet, 'The Negro as a Soldier' in *The Fortnightly Review*, No. COLXIV (1 December 1888).

Woodward, David R., *Forgotten Soldiers* (Stroud: Tempus, 2007).

# INDEX